MORE THAN A
PROMISE

Diane Boyette

ISBN 978-1-68570-355-4 (paperback)
ISBN 978-1-68570-356-1 (digital)

Christian Faith Publishing
832 Park Avenue
Meadville, PA 16335
www.christianfaithpublishing.com

Printed in the United States of America

I have set My bow in the clouds, And it will be the sign of the covenant between Me and the earth.

—Genesis 9:13

For God, who said, "Let light shine out of darkness," has shone in our hearts to give the light of the knowledge of the glory of God in the face of Jesus Christ.

—2 Corinthians 4:6

REALITY CHECK

"Hey, Sis. Are you workin'?" his text message read.

"I am. Do you need me?" was my response.

"Can I fax you something?" he continued.

This *ping* of my phone on a Friday afternoon in late August 2018 deflected my attention from the case on which I was working to my brother's extraordinary late afternoon inquiry. I rarely heard from him unless he needed my help or advice. This message, together with the facsimile that followed it, forced a sudden halt to the crazy chaos of my workday. In that instant, the urgency of endless responsibilities on my to-do list and the caseload on my desk were suddenly diminished to menial tasks and mere stacks of paper filled with hollow words that no longer seemed important. *Life just got real!* It was one of those moments in life, which we all have in varying degrees, when everything suddenly stops. The engine is turned off. The world stops turning—or so it seems.

> There is a large paramediastinal mass, likely a neoplastic mass such as a bronchogenic carcinoma. This has a dimension of 6.9 cm and a transverse dimension of 4 cm. This partially compresses the left pulmonary artery. Tumor mass extends into the middle mediastinum and left hilum.

This is how the radiology report began. I continued reading, finding other similar medical notations and terminology foreign to me throughout this two-page report. I could hear the escalating beat of my heart rushing to my ears in a deafening swoosh. The words *mass, carcinoma, compress,* and *tumor* I knew! Even my medically untrained mind recognized the tragedy of what these words revealed. I sat there, staring at the report in disbelief. One of the greatest fears that my mother and I have shared for many years was memorialized on paper.

Barry's next message asked that I read the report and explain to him what it meant. As I read it twice through, I asked myself, "How am I supposed to do this? What can I say to him?"

I reached for my computer mouse and saw my hand move slowly until my computer awoke. Then I tapped the browser and keyed in a few of the terms I saw in the report. If I had to explain any of this, I needed help to understand with more clarity the prognosis, possible treatments, and the magnitude of the challenge that lay before him. The more I read, the more questions emerged. My mind raced. How do you say to a person you love, "I'm sorry, but the prognosis of your condition appears hopeless. The handwriting is on the wall. And except for a rare miracle, you're going to die soon."

In a follow-up message, he explained that a radiologist handed him this report earlier that day with these brief instructions and nothing more: "Take this to your lung doctor for consultation at your appointment next Thursday. He will explain everything and go from there."

Besides being distraught at the reality of what the report revealed, I was appalled at the very thought that any medical professional—even one in small-town America where my brother lived—would hand a patient an unsealed document containing these words. What made it worse was that he had to wait another week before he could get any answers to a million questions this report elicited.

For as long as I can remember, I am the person to whom my brother came when life threw him a curveball that he couldn't quite handle on his own. When he had run out of all resources and options, his tendency was to call me. I always tried to help him the best I knew how; but this time, I had no answers either. There were no good options to offer him, except "I'm here, and I'll support you and do everything within my power to help you through this." I sensed a silent pleading from him to "fix this thing" the way I'd generally been able to help resolve his problems in the past. He was looking for something to hold on to, anything to give him a measure of hope.

Reluctantly, and with no comforting answers to give, I picked up the phone and dialed his number. I didn't know what I would say, but I needed to hear what he had to say. On the second ring, he greeted me with a rather chipper voice. Surprised that he didn't sound like he had lost his last friend, I listened. This wasn't at all what I expected to hear. Not once did he ask me, "What does this mean?" He already knew!

"Sis," he began, "this blows my mind! Six months ago, the Lord started to change my heart. I had no idea that *this* was going on inside my body. But God knew! He also knew that I was not prepared for this news. He knew I couldn't handle it. He used my counselor at the methadone clinic to help open my eyes to the condition of my soul. If he hadn't done that, then there's no way I could face this news today. In fact, I doubt I would've come to him at all—*ever!* I probably would've just looked for another reason to get high. It just blows my mind how God's timing is always just right! I don't know what the lung doctor will say to me next week, but I have peace. Everything's gonna be okay!"

He continued recounting to me the story of what had happened earlier in the year. He told of how God had used the counselor's words, "Barry, you have a *heart* problem," to plant a seed for change inside him.

For years, he had persuaded himself that he was a child of God and that he would go to heaven when he died. As a boy, he walked the aisle at church, professed to be a Christian, and was baptized. Yet his life from his teenage years forward had been lived in a self-centered and destructive way. He had been on a long and winding road, which led him down a very dark and sinister path. He sought to fulfill his own personal cravings of whatever sort they were for instant gratification. He gave little thought as to how his actions might impact others or even how they might impact him in the end.

I recall times when we were very young how he was so focused on his own personal wants and needs—gobbling down his own bag of candy, then begging for my younger brother and I to give him ours as well. I never understood the obvious selfishness contained in his childhood actions. I just recall the frustration and the sibling fights they triggered. This feeble attempt to give an example of selfishness is a bit comical as I consider it now. It does show, however, the way self-centeredness and other bad habits can become deeply rooted within us, even beginning in early childhood. Left unchecked, these habits tend to attach themselves to every part of our lives, and a sense of entitlement sits enthroned where humility should exist.

Having had many counselors and psychologists over the years who often planted ideas in his mind as to the root of his problems, Barry bought into some powerful lies about how his personal experiences and decisiveness were someone else's fault and not the result of his own personal choices. Self-satisfying indulgences entangled and enslaved him for years on end. He was caught up in a web of destructive behaviors that lasted for decades. These damaging behaviors and their consequences left him empty, lonely, and afraid. He found himself at the end of a frayed rope, and he was losing his grip.

In the past, Barry consistently caved at any reminder of a painful memory or disappointment. When events or people in his life disappointed him or reminded him of past hurts or failures, his response was to go looking for his drug dealers. He consistently pursued temporary escapes to dull the pain of his past and the voices inside his head that told him what a failure he was. Only recently had he sought a different kind of help. He knew that if he didn't find another way to deal with these issues, his addictions meant certain death for him.

He explained how he had seen an ad on TV and had jotted down a number. Coincidence? Maybe! But he was convinced that it was an ad strategically placed on the channel he happened to be watching one night. Seeing it, he was compelled by it at just the right time. He called the number and found that a clinic had recently opened near home. He truly believed that finding this clinic and this counselor was his last chance of finding a way to control his anger and addictions. He was often tempted to fall back into his old pattern of blaming anyone or anything other than himself. But he was tired. Something had to change, and he knew it.

With a single seed planted by one wise and very bold counselor, God began a transformation of his heart and mind. Many before had spoken words and provided him good advice, but his ear was dull of hearing. He told me how the counselor's words had angered him at first and how he still told himself that his soul was just fine.

It's just like the enemy of our souls to whisper these words into our ears: "That person has no idea what they're talking about! You're just fine!"

For any who may be reading this and hearing this or a similar whisper, I challenge you to take that thought captive as we are instructed to do in 2 Corinthians 10:5. Whether you are a believer in Christ or not, I dare say you recognize that a spiritual realm exists beyond what your eyes can see. You sense it. You wrestle with right and wrong, good and evil. We all do! This wrestling sometimes seems more like a fierce battle or a relentless war within your spirit. The struggle within us is part of the spiritual realm of existence that remains invisible to the naked eye but is no less real. The outcome of this invisible battle is revealed in visible tangible ways.

You fight with your spouse and you yell at your children for a reason you can't explain. You go to the office and steal hours of time from your employer—gossiping with your coworkers, surfing the internet, or wasting time doing anything other than what you're being paid to do. You justify your actions with the excuse that your boss doesn't pay you nearly what you're worth to him. In an attempt to quiet the war in your mind and to forget hurts from your present and or past, you choose to drink yourself into a stupor or pop a pill or six—anything to help silence the random voices inside your head, if only for a few hours. A million arguments that begin inside your head struggle to take control of your mind, will, and actions. The struggle really is *real!*

So I will be bold here and say, "You cannot fight spiritual battles with physical weapons that you hold in your hand or verbalize with your tongue." We fight and win spiritual battles with spiritual weapons designed by God to help us overcome spiritual attacks. It's the only effective way to truly overcome those things that wreak havoc in your soul and spill out into your physical life and personal relationships! More specifically, it requires a divine power that comes from a place far beyond yourself. You need help. We *all* need *help!*

Barry left his counseling session that day, determined he wouldn't go back. He rehearsed in his own mind how he was the victim of a painful past. Others had abused him, and it was their fault, not his, that he was here. The counselor was wrong! He wanted to be angry, to reject her words, to walk away from this place and never look back. "After all," he said to himself, "I have nothing to prove to anyone. It's my life. Who is she to tell me anything about my heart or its condition? She can't see inside my soul. She knows nothing about my struggles and the demons that relentlessly chase me!"

These were the thoughts that flooded his mind as she spoke. Thankfully, the relationship of openness and trust he had begun to build with this counselor over a period of weeks helped keep the door of communication open between them. While he disagreed with her opinion about the root of his problem, he refused to let it send him back to where he had been a few short weeks earlier—completely out of control with his addiction.

No Turning Back

Barry had reached a point of no return in February 2018. His drug addiction was out of control, and he had very limited resources with which to continue feeding that addiction. He shared with me how the constant contention between himself and our mother, enhanced by his unbridled drug abuse, had brought him to a breaking point. He fully believed that one of them—either himself or Mom—could not survive in this state of contention very much longer. The two of them had had a significant altercation earlier in the year, and it scared him. Neither of them ever shared the exact details of that incident, but both told me of a day when their thoughts and feelings against the other were like nothing they had ever experienced before.

Realizing it was up to him to do something to change the course of events, he determined it was now or never. He'd spent his best years engaged in self-destructive behaviors driven by internal fears and emotions and fueled by external allurements. Such behaviors had ultimately isolated him from normal social interactions. The dramatic mood swings, erratic bouts of anger, his inability to hold down a steady job for more than a few weeks or months (at best) had pretty much left him completely alone. For the most part, only one person remained who could even tolerate the highs and lows of his daily existence—our mother.

With increasing frequency, she, too, isolated herself from him, refusing to discuss with the rest of the family the nightmare she was living. She spent her days away from home, caring for sick people just to create some space between them. And, at night, she often hid herself behind a locked door to gain a sense of safety, praying all the while for God to *do something*.

The two of them had always found a way to get through every ordeal and disagreement, exchanging requests and grants of forgiveness with the repeated promise, "This will *never* happen again!" She was his safe haven, the person he always ran to when he had nowhere else to turn. He was *the need* she felt destined and determined to meet.

His frequent visits to the methadone clinic, which occurred multiple times each week in early 2018, allowed him the freedom to live at home while receiving carefully monitored medication-based therapy and counseling. It included drug-testing to ensure that he followed the restrictions imposed as well. If he failed a drug test, then he was out! He coaxed himself along with the admonition "I can't mess this up!"

He clearly understood the clinic would only provide help to those who were serious about the program and who genuinely wanted to be free from the addiction of opioid-based drugs. He craved the help more than anything he had craved in a very long time. He told me how he believed his counselor understood him and all his crazy ideas. It was her diagnosis—"Barry, you have a heart problem"—that planted a fertile seed in him. This one statement spoken at just the right time made a world of difference. It was the one thing that all the counselors before had either failed to speak aloud or else failed to speak at the right moment.

He explained to me how he had been driving in his car a few days after the counselor had boldly pointed out the *root cause* of his addiction *and* every other problem in his life. He said to me, "The Lord began to walk me through all the years of my life, stage by stage from childhood to adulthood. He showed me people and places and events. He took me back to my grade school days and then high school and revealed how every decision led me down a wrong path.

"As I drove, the thoughts continued to unfold so vividly. He showed me how much I've hurt my daddy and my family with all the things I've done and said over all these years. Then I realized that all the things I've been through are no one's fault but my own. My own choices led me to this point. But then God showed me that he loves me and he has forgiven me. I am so humbled by it all."

Humility is the first response of a person who, in recognition of their broken and helpless condition, has experienced the unimaginable grace of God. When a person fully embraces what *grace* really means for them, a whale of gratitude swallows up pride and a spirit of blame. Such a response occurs without effort or conscious exertion. The human spirit of a man melts in that moment when he sees himself in the perfect order of God's design. The sudden realization of the imperfect nature of humanity and the sinfulness that has created a vast divide between God and man ignites a flow of humility that can't be faked. Once a person comes face-to-face with the filthy disgusting ugliness of their human condition, exposed and illuminated by the light of Jesus Christ's righteousness in its purest form, the only possible human response is an outward expression of humility. It's spontaneous, genuine, and visible. You know it when you see it and when you hear it. It's written in the joy-filled expressions of one's face.

I could hear it in his voice that day—the humility and the brokenness. As I heard the sound of it, the tears flowed from my eyes. This was the one thing I'd longed to hear for so long. This was the one critical missing element from each of his "I've changed!" declarations in the past. Prior to this August phone conversation with him, I don't recall ever hearing him use the word *humbled*, and most certainly, no evidence of humility had ever exhibited itself in his outward behavior, not for many years—and maybe not ever.

Real change doesn't come by simply declaring it to be so. It comes from a deeper place, not from the head but from the heart. In fact, no words ever need to be spoken where humility exists. It's visible to the naked eye. I've watched, waited, and listened for this genuine expression of humility in him because I knew it to be unequivocal evidence of a changed heart.

For years, my mother tried to convince us, "He's changed! He's really different this time!"

My thought was always, *Save your breath, Mom! I don't buy it.* I wasn't convinced that she even believed her own words. It was the hope of change she held in her heart that poured from her own soul, I'm sure. I remember telling her time and time again, "When he's different, we will be able to see it. Neither you nor he will need to tell us he's changed. When or if it happens, his actions will show it."

I always *hoped* but never fully believed that he could or would change. I feared he had gone way too far to turn back. This happens when promises are broken repeatedly. Trust and faith begin to wear thin. Resentment and doubt creep in.

Barry tried many times to convince everyone around him that he had changed. He said all the right things, quoting from memory Bible verses like no one I had ever heard. He went to church for brief amounts of time over the years. He listened to television evangelists and condemned others for acting hypocritically. Over and over, I and my family members watched his failed attempts at change unfold. We heard his empty promises, declaring he would never return to his old ways. Each time we heard them, and with any measure of hope embraced them, we were always disappointed (*but never surprised*) as he slowly slipped back into his old habits.

TRAPPED INSIDE A SPIDER'S WEB

I believe Barry wanted to live free and happy. Every promise he ever made to change, I believe, came from a place of longing in his heart. I recall a prolonged stay in prison when he wrote several poems. This was a dark time for him and one that we had hoped would be a turning point in his life. I came across this poem among his writings during that two-year period:

Free at Last

Free at last from a prison of drugs,
But I am here, now, without my little girls' hugs.
I am not the person I used to be,
Because Jesus, the Son of God, has set me free.
It took so much destruction and so much pain,
To realize, with drugs, I had nothing to gain.
I grow older behind these prison walls,
I lost my family; I lost it all.
I have found love and love found me,
At the cross, it's what helped me to see.
Jesus loved me through all of my sin,
And a life of drug abuse now ends.
Living for God is what's now important to me;
Living for him and those drugs I leave.
Thank you, Lord, for saving my soul,

And for delivering me from drugs that made me so cold.
(Barry Wilson, 10/06)

Was it jailhouse religion? Some might say it was. Certainly, I can understand how such a conclusion could be drawn as I've known many cases where prisoners declared they found God behind prison walls but lost him again when released. But I've met many others whose hearts and lives were truly changed during a time of incarceration. God's grace and forgiveness is not limited to those who remain free of bondage, either physical or spiritual. He doesn't reserve heaven for those who are humanly "good." In fact, Luke recorded the words of Jesus in Luke 5:31–32, "Those who are well have no need of a physician, but those who are sick. I have not come to call the righteous but sinners to repentance."

And as he hung on the cross between two criminals, Jesus responded to the thief who asked him to remember him when he became King, "Truly, I say to you, today you will be with Me in paradise" (Luke 23:43).

Jesus recognized the genuine remorse this criminal expressed that day. He was moved with compassion at the words of faith he heard in this one who was dying alongside him. So if Jesus himself did not reject sinners, criminals, or prisoners as outcasts unworthy of his grace, who am I to disqualify anyone? In fact, all of us have sinned and fallen short of God's requirements to enter heaven, which is why every single one of us require a savior.

With all this said, I'm convinced that while many people, even prisoners, have genuine intentions to change their ways, some lack the commitment to actually live out the life they've declared to live. A changed heart requires something more than just human will. It requires the internal presence of a Holy God—the Spirit of God living inside the human heart to direct his thoughts, his steps, his responses to natural events and challenges. No human has ever been able to change his own human nature. Only God can do that. He does it by giving us a brand-new heart, thereby transforming everything about us. If we could do this on our own, we wouldn't need a savior. If we can do this on our own, then Jesus died in vain. The fact is we are desperately wicked and helpless to recover without the Lord.

My brother had a drive for success, a drive strangely sabotaged by a force inside him that none of us could see and which even he was helpless to understand. His self-control button had malfunctioned or gone missing. Any old excuse was all he needed to justify in his own mind why he needed a drug or alcohol fix. A little pain here or a harsh word from a friend or loved one there—any stressor at all—was the only excuse he needed to pop a handful of pills to dull the pain or help him forget a disappointment. He lived each day only to get himself to the next one. Even two years inside a prison wasn't enough to convince him that drugs were not the right response to his anxiety.

The thing he consistently failed to grasp was that one taste of the drug served only to reignite the trained endorphins in his brain to create another wave of insatiable cravings that he was helpless to control. With each return to the drug, the more intensely entangled he became in the web of addiction that was slowly destroying every part of him. As I watched in horror and heartbreak—unable to get through to him—I likened it to an insect entangled in a spider's web, which slowly becomes so tightly squeezed by the tiny strands of the sticky web that it can never break free. Little by little, the cords wrap round him. Slowly, but surely, they engulf the entirety of his being. Short of a stronger outside force to intervene on his behalf, the insect dies right there in silence in a great big world with many onlookers who don't care or dare to take the time necessary to help set him free.

I saw Barry slowly grow worse over the years. With each new challenge, he tried to overcome by the strength of his own will. He tried over and over again to prove himself and his worth, but the more he tried, the more he seemed to fail. With each human effort to overcome the addictions that bound him, he became more entangled and helpless to break free. He needed a rescuer. He needed an overcomer stronger than himself and the forces that were binding him.

True change requires a power greater than that found in human flesh. I knew that *if* Barry ever truly changed—*and I must admit I had all but given up*—the fruit of change would be evident in his actions. Repentance reveals itself through an attitude of humility. *And, on this day, I recognized it!* It was genuine.

He was broken to the very core of his being. The things he said were unlike anything I'd ever heard from him before. No longer did he blame others for his failures or his current state of being. The remorse he felt for the pain he had inflicted on others was genuine. He recognized that every bad decision had been his own to make. He was grateful, truly grateful, and humble for God's grace and forgiveness, and he was determined to do everything humanly possible to right the wrongs he had committed.

I was elated. In that moment, I declared the only words my heart could formulate: "Oh, God, what mercy! What grace! Thank you!" Only God could bring him to this place of humility, and the gratitude I experienced that day was not unlike the gratitude I felt the day I experienced God's grace and forgiveness in my own life. Nothing else in this world feels like this. And it's personal.

As I bowed beside my bed that night to pray, my heart grieved at the thought of where Barry's broken life had brought him. Why had it taken all these years for him to get to this point of brokenness? The tears streamed down my face as I cried out in prayer, not really knowing the right words to pray. I've learned by studying the scriptures that when I don't know how or what to pray, the Lord will help me with that.

Romans 8:26 says that the Holy Spirit intercedes with God on our behalf with groanings too deep for words. Isn't that amazing—God hears our groans and understands what they mean. I continued to thank the Lord for grace and mercy that had transformed my brother's heart in the midnight hour of his life. I thanked him for preparing Barry's heart to face this hour. I prayed that his faith in God would not fail!

THE NOTEBOOK

As I prayed, the Lord reminded me of *a message* he had given me several years earlier. It was a message that I had long since forgotten, but the memory of it came flooding back in that moment. The message, I recalled, had come to me in a dream. It doesn't happen frequently, but on rare occasions, I have dreams that are so vivid with detail that I can't shake them. In my spirit, I sense a distinct message with meaning deeper than what I sense happening in the dream.

I recalled feelings of deep sorrow mixed with a strange sense of joy. The dream had moved me so deeply and convincingly that I wrote down every word of the message in a notebook—verbatim, just as I had heard it in the dream. I was convinced that God was telling me something that I would need to remember later. How much later, I didn't know. No time frame was given, but I sensed imminence. I remember rehearsing it over and over in my mind for days and weeks. Months even. I was afraid to tell anyone.

I further recalled the confusion in my mind when weeks turned to months and my sense of hope turned into anguish. The message I received in the dream had seemed to become void as we began to experience the nightmare that followed. That nightmare was not a dream. It was our life.

Barry came to live with us later that year and was with us for about seven months. The pain of this recollection caused the raw emotions of today to take on yet another dimension. Waves of pain and hurt from the past washed over my soul so intensely. A new nightmare.

I strived to recall where I might have stored the notebook; but at that moment, my mind was so jumbled I couldn't bring it forward.

Weak from the events of the day and the mental strain of the past few hours, I crawled into bed and fell asleep with a heavy heart and the message on my mind.

On Saturday morning, September 1, 2018, I awoke with the heaviness unabated. It had been a restless night. The thought of "the message" was still strong in my mind as well. I couldn't shake it. I knew I had to find that notebook.

Sitting up in bed, I prayed, "Lord, I have no idea where I put the notebook. If I need this, you will have to show me where it is." Waiting no longer, I got out of bed and went to the first place I could think of where I might have put it: my *library*. I walked into the tiny room and scanned the shelves. Books and journals lined them along with lots of other clutter that badly needed culling. As my eyes moved from shelf to shelf, I noticed a stack of notebooks on a lower one. I picked up the first one, opened it, and read a few lines. That wasn't it. Another notebook, one with a pink snakeskin pattern on the cover, caught my eye. Something about it seemed oddly familiar, so I flipped it open.

The page that fell open was near the back of it. At the top of the page, a title was written: "The Prodigal Son—A Eulogy." It was dated October 17, 2012. The noted time of entry was 3:25 a.m. At once, I knew I had found it.

The message was almost six years old at this point. Although I was convinced at the time of that dream that I would have to deliver this eulogy in 2012 or soon thereafter, I had later dismissed it. The events and circumstances that unfolded over the months and years that followed ripped my soul apart. He seemed destined to live his life completely in opposition to the message expressed on these pages.

I know that time has no meaning for God. He remains *timeless*. Yet he remains *true*. True to his Word. True to his promises. The Scriptures say this:

> But do not overlook this one fact, beloved,
> that with the Lord one day is as a thousand years,
> and a thousand years are as one day. The Lord
> is not slow to fulfill his promise as some count

slowness, but is patient toward you, not wishing that any should perish, but that all should reach repentance. (2 Peter 3:8–9)

I pondered the words on the pages. I reflected, too, on the unfolding of our lives over these last half-dozen years. Putting all of this into spiritual and physical perspective, this six-year-old message revealed a whole new perspective of God's power and divine intervention in our lives. I'm reminded of a scripture in Isaiah which states:

For as the rain comes down, and the snow from heaven, and do not return there, but water the earth and make it bring forth and bud, that it may give seed to the sower and bread to the eater, so shall My word be that goes forth from My mouth. It shall not return to Me void, but it shall accomplish what I please, and it shall prosper in the thing for which I sent it. (Isaiah 55:10–11)

In 2012, when the message was fresh, I thought I understood its meaning. I thought the time of fulfillment was imminent. *Had I heard God clearly?* I knew I had! *But had I misinterpreted the meaning of it?* I didn't think so! Yet the reality of Barry's life that had played out since that time just didn't add up. How could this message have any meaning given what we were seeing and experiencing?

From an eternal perspective, what is a period of six short years compared to one's lifetime?

It's but a moment, the blink of an eye.

If I am completely honest, though, I must admit that doubt had pretty much replaced all hope I had embraced from the message received. Doubt creeps in like an uninvited guest and steals our hope. My hope had all but faded away as I watched Barry's life spiral further out of control after his return from Florida. He seemed only to grow worse with time. It looked nothing at all like the message—a story of a life transformed. Transformation of this man's life, *I knew*, would require a miracle.

A miracle. Yes, indeed, a miracle had occurred. Two, in fact. One had taken place in my brother's heart. His was a miracle of a lifetime. The unfulfilled miracle had been revealed to me six years earlier in the message. The second miracle had just occurred right here, right now. I realized that I was holding it in my hands. The second miracle was instantaneous, unlike the timing of the first. I stood there for a moment staring at the words on the page, a bit shaken at the powerfulness of the moment. Chill bumps still run the length of my arms as I recall it, even now as I write. I'm reminded of the words of the Prophet Isaiah, "The grass withers, the flower fades, but the word of God will stand forever" (Isaiah 40:8).

I love Jesus's words written in the book of Matthew, "Heaven and earth will pass away, but My words will not pass away" (Matthew 24:35).

As I read "the message" again, the tears flowed unstoppable. I sensed that the time had come and the promise was unfolding. It seemed the last few grains of sand in the hourglass were trickling through the narrow opening. God's work in Barry's heart was almost complete. What I had perceived as a delay in the transforming work of Barry's life had actually been occurring all along—it was just hidden from plain view. Sometimes we can't see all the Lord is doing in the lives of people around us. It can also be difficult to perceive what he's doing in our own hearts too. But looking back, it's plain to see how he has worked out the details of our lives in unimaginable ways.

Soon I would have to share *the message* with my family and with the world. This message was not just one of action, but it was also one of promise and full of hope. How can one hope when death seems so final, so irreversible? Except for Jesus Christ, we would have no hope at all.

God gave me his promise six years earlier, but the promise didn't fade with time. It remains true and unchangeable even today. It may have been kept hidden away in a notebook on a shelf awaiting its proper time to be shared, but his Word is firm, unchangeable, complete.

This was no ordinary eulogy. It was a message of life. Life filled with promise to ignite a miraculous reunification of a family shattered by broken promises and broken lives. This was the beginning of healing from the inside out—physical, emotional, and spiritual. As I continued to ponder the most difficult task of delivering this message, I still didn't know exactly when or where it would take place. God's timing is his alone to determine.

I stood there, soaking in the reality of all that must take place before the time came. It meant that my brother would have to die. Yes! His life and his story on this earth were nearing the end. As difficult as it was to accept the reality of this truth, I realized that something even more significant was taking place. *That is, the Lord God is always faithful to fulfill every promise he makes. His words are truth, they are timeless, and they never return void without accomplishing all that he intends.* God's Word was spoken, and Barry's fate was decided six years earlier.

But, more than that, God's promise for the reconciliation of my family had also been sealed with his Word at that same time. Everything had been set in motion, and the unfolding began.

Broken Promises

My mind was transported back to 2012 and a series of events that began in the spring of that year, which continued to unfold for more than a year. As I read and reread my journal notes recorded during those months, I recall the many whispers and nudges of God's voice that gave me direction, wisdom and courage along the way. It was an extraordinarily dark time.

I'm reminded of early morning awakenings, including one in September and another in October 2012, with vivid urgent promptings to pray, to take action, and to write down things intended for future action. More painful to recall are the many months of trial, hardship, and testing of my faith. Painful words spewed from the mouths of people I trusted. Words that left scars on my heart and distrust that still need healing. Most of the hurt is a distant memory now. Yet I firmly believe those difficult experiences solidified my faith and trust in God. They confirmed his faithfulness to me and provided the strength I needed to endure greater trials to come.

I am convinced that every trial and challenge we face in this life prepares us for the next greater one that lies ahead. I shiver to think of what my response might have been during this season if there had not been periods of testing and refinement before this one. The fires of life will either destroy a person or make him stronger. It all depends on what we are made of. More than that, it depends on where our faith rests.

Do you have faith? Do you have hope in a power greater than your own? Or do you give in to every temptation or painful experience and allow them to dictate your responses?

> These trials will show that your faith is genuine. It is being tested as fire tests and purifies gold—though your faith is far more precious than mere gold. So when your faith remains strong through many trials, it will bring you much praise and glory and honor on the day when Jesus Christ is revealed to the whole world. (1 Peter 1:7)

This process of testing and refinement continues our whole lives through. If we stand firm in our faith in God, determined and full of hope, we grow stronger and more resilient as the trials intensify. Each test, each temptation, becomes easier to overcome. Every hateful word spoken against us begins to bounce off like a ping-pong ball on concrete.

*****

What is it about the month of September? Repeatedly, it seems to set in motion a myriad of things and dramatic events in my life. It's the ninth month of the year, at least according to the Gregorian Calendar we follow today. It's the beginning of autumn in the northern hemisphere. The word September comes from the Latin root *septem,* meaning "seven." If you're curious like me, do a little research regarding the origin of the word September. It's a bit too deep to go into here, but I find it fascinating.

September is, for many, the month that signals the end of summer, the beginning of autumn, and a time of harvest and preparation for the winter months that lie ahead. I'm intrigued as I reflect on these facts and all the things that have occurred in my life over the years. On a most personal note, it's the month in which I was born. More than that, the number of turning points that my family and

I experienced during the month of September over the years is too significant for me to ignore.

The following segment will highlight some considerable events that occurred in my brother's life. Several of these events led to the writing of this story. Some might argue that it's only a coincidence that many of these events occurred in the month of September and perhaps that's true. Or maybe it isn't. Consider the pattern as you read on.

Seven years earlier—2011

September 2011. Jimmy had great plans for him. The meat cases were full and looking better than they ever had. His customers loved him. His boss loved him. He was finally getting his life together *again*. His customers loved him because he had such an infectious personality and a smile that matched it. His skill as a butcher and market manager caused his customers' mouths to water as they browsed the meat cases that lined the local grocery store. His were certainly the best-looking displays of beef, pork, and poultry they could find anywhere. He took great pride in his work. His boss also loved the significant contribution that Barry's hard work added to the store's profit margin.

It was Barry's greater hope that this job would prove to his family that he had his life together. He hoped they would love and forgive him once he proved himself able to hold down this job. Surely, *this time*, they would come running back to him with arms wide open. He would prove to them how he had changed.

At first, he worked forty hours a week, but that quickly turned to fifty, then sixty, and more. Payday was his delight. Seeing all those digits on that check made him feel worthwhile, accomplished, and able to conquer the world. He ran the numbers in his head. If he could make Jimmy $50,000 this month, then surely he could expand the meat market's production and reach $55,000 next month. He would ramp things up and get to $60,000 in month three, and so on. He consistently strived for more.

All of this hard work would mean a great bonus for him, and then everyone would *have to* love him even more because of his accomplishments. Or so he thought. Maybe then the girls and their mother would see that he was successful, that he had *really changed*, and they could all be together again.

Immersing himself in his work was a kind of addiction diverse from any other. He worked hard and was the best at his chosen trade—the best, at least, until the long hours began to physically exhaust him. He needed help to keep up the pace and increase it even more. He worked longer hours and more days each week until he was stretched so thin he had little time left for the rest his body required. He was constantly thinking and dreaming about faster production, more money, and proving his worth to others.

As the long hours and intense pace continued, the exhaustion he tried hard to suppress began to impact his ability to stay alert and keep pushing himself beyond normal human limitations. He had to be superhuman just a little while longer! "I can do this!" he told himself. *I just need a little help*, the silent whispers in his mind convinced him. *I won't overdo it this time—just a little pick-me-up to help me stay awake so I can work longer hours, make my boss happy, and make a little more money!*

This was his self-justified intention. The argument seemed plausible enough to make him believe it. "All I want," he rehearsed to himself one more time, "is to see my girls grow up, to spend time with them, to prove myself to them. I will be a good daddy, but I need money to make that happen. Yes, I've failed them so many times before, but this time will be different. This time, I'll show them!"

Oh, to see the proof of this statement. If I had ten dollars for every time I've heard this statement come out of his mouth, I could buy a yacht and ride the waves of the wild blue ocean for a decade.

But, this time, just as every time before, his little "pick-me-up" turned into a daily ritual. It once again awakened the endorphins in his brain that craved *the drug* and *the high*. The euphoria he had been determined to suppress—that sleeping beast which had relentlessly entangled and imprisoned him for years—was aroused yet again. *This time*, she awakened even stronger and with more intoxicating control than ever before. He was helpless to stop her. He needed more and more of the drug to get him to the required level of achievement. The escalation of the beast with its insatiable appetite is a most frightening controller. She was untamable.

The nightly dark alley visits to his dealer cut deeply into his weekly paycheck. He quickly felt the financial squeeze. The drugs seemed to burn a hole in the bottom of his pocket. Feeding the addiction was more costly than feeding his entire family. It wasn't just the financial squeeze that made him anxious. He feared being caught by the police with drugs in his possession. Beyond that, he feared for his physical safety as he made his way back to his apartment each evening in the low rent section of town. He could afford better living quarters, but somehow, he felt strangely hidden from the truth of his condition in these places. Many were his fears, but none of them were enough to suppress the craving or deter the beast that raged inside him.

He had to find a solution to the constant drain of money. If he couldn't keep any money in his pocket, no one would ever believe he had changed. This war of competing interests waging inside him was too much to contemplate. What could he do? He asked himself this question and pondered on that for a little while.

"No! I can't do that! Not again!"

He had promised himself that he wouldn't do it again. But, again, here he was in the same condition—a new day, a new city, a new job, but the same old rotten predicament. He was desperate, and this was the only solution he could come up with. He would have to resort to the same trick he had learned from the past. After all, he had gotten away with it a few times. Maybe he could again. *Even drug dealers have to eat*, he thought, *and there's nothing they love more than a good steak or a couple racks of ribs.*

A quick text, then a knock at the back delivery door let him know that his package was ready for exchange. *No one will ever know,* he convinced himself. *Besides that,* he rationalized, *I'm making this store so much money that surely I'm justified in taking a steak once in a while to keep making Jimmy this much money.* He stepped across the line he had drawn in the sand after losing the last job. No turning back now. The deed was done.

The long hours, the excessive drug use, and the burning of his candle at both ends distorted his thinking. He continued the pace he had achieved for a little while longer. His boss remained ignorant of a few packages of meat that slipped out the back door. But he grew a bit sloppy in the exchange of packages.

His body was exhausted, spurred forward only by the drugs. His otherwise cheery personality turned to hatefulness and impatience, particularly with his employees. He screamed and yelled at his workers—workers who, too often, had their own problems with drugs and law enforcement. Some had discovered his dirty little secret. He tried to keep them quiet by sharing a few hits off a joint with them here and there or threatening them with disclosure of their own dirty little secrets if they ratted him out.

As his altered personality continued to fuel heated exchanges with his workers, his threats against them for sloppy work or not showing up on time became more frequent. He fired one, then another. The workers shared stories, watched him closely, and plotted to expose him. They not only shared stories with each other but also with their own dealers. This created an even more significant risk of bodily harm against him, a danger far worse than that of losing his job. Blackmail from those people closest to him prompted even more backdoor exchanges. He had to buy out his own drug dealers as well as his employees and their drug dealers.

Paranoia consumed him. He felt hunted by his dealers, mocked by his workers and betrayed by those he believed were his closest friends.

Gradually, he lost all sense of safety, security, and hope of accomplishment. Why had he allowed himself to fall into this same trap *again?* Another job. Another place. Another chance. The same disgraceful ending.

The more he tried to hold everything together, the more he felt it all slipping away. The fear of getting caught or killed consumed his every semi-lucid thought. His mind raced continually, partly triggered by fear and partly by the drug-induced state.

Then came the crash! He tried to open his eyes. The lids felt as though they were held shut by weights tied to each eyelash. He couldn't move. He couldn't get out of bed. One day passed, then two.

He called his boss and told him he had the flu, but he would be back to work soon. The hollowness in his sunken eyes and the pallor of his skin revealed more truth than he could explain away with flu symptoms.

Mama called him, as she always did, periodically checking in to see how he was. She convinced herself that he was just working too hard and not eating enough. *Surely* she recognized the visible appearance and the pattern of actions she had seen so many times before. She loved him more than she did her own life. She worried and she prayed. In her soul, she knew but rejected the notion.

"Barry, I need to see you in my office," Jimmy called over the intercom.

It was his first day back at work, and the sound of Jimmy's voice sent a cold knowing chill down the entire length of his spine. *He knows! It's over! I'm done!*

As he slowly walked to the front of the store, he had a minute to concoct another story that he hoped would cover him until he could get back on track. That's all he wanted—just to do the right thing and keep his job. The look on Jimmy's face when he walked into the room said it all. He could forget reciting the story he had just prepared in his head. The purchase orders and the sales tickets—everything was all laid out on the desk in front of him. "I need your keys, and you need to find another job. You're fired!" Jimmy didn't even ask any questions. Other workers who knew the true reason behind his sudden illness had been more than happy to share with the boss where the missing inventory had gone.

Another job gone! Where...when would he find another?

*****

Barry's lifestyle had advanced into a predictable pattern. He craved human acceptance and a sense of accomplishment amid his self-loathing. From the time he graduated high school in 1980, he gained and lost more jobs than he could count, some lasting longer than others. He was engaged in a sustainable career that offered significant benefits. He had great skill as a butcher. He knew how to market himself and his skill to achieve the highest sales. He was married and divorced three times, and he fathered two beautiful daughters. His love for those little girls was genuine, no doubt. But his body's craving for the drug consumed every fiber of his being, a craving so powerful that his wife and children had to settle for second place or not at all.

Except for the drug addiction that plagued him for more than three decades, I have no doubt that this story I now write would have been much different. Perhaps there would be no cause or need to write it at all. The facts are what they are, no less. Every person's life story is a winding road. Ups and downs are inevitable. We run in circles at times. It's where we end up; however, that makes all the difference.

I'm quite content in this moment to write of these events because Barry's end-of-life story is one to instill hope for the wayward, the lost, and for us all. My intention and greatest desire is that this writing will help those, maybe even you, who are caught up in patterns of addiction that have rendered them hopeless. I long, as did Barry in his last months, to help the hopeless find a path to freedom.

I have no desire whatsoever to tarnish the memory of my dear brother. Rather, I hope to expose the darkness, the very depths of pain and agony through which drug abuse will take a man (or a woman). Please hear me loudly and clearly here: *No written words are sufficient to describe the extent to which the beast of addiction will destroy the lives and relationships of individuals and families, robbing them of their best years, their greatest dreams, their deepest loves.*

It is my intention to reveal how the incredible power of an all-loving, all-knowing, all-sustaining God can completely transform the one who has taken this dark path all the way to its end. A beating heart has hope.

Please, I beg you, *read on.*

HOMELESS AGAIN

"**M**ama, I'm so lonesome. I just can't live by myself. I don't want to be alone," he pleaded. "If I just had somebody to help me. Mama, can I move in with you? I'll help you. You need me! You don't need to be alone either. I'll get another job and I'll help pay the bills."

The same story. A different day. She had heard it so many times before.

He went to the one and only person he knew who would even listen to his sob story again. She was the only person he could even hope would take him in each time he lost another job and ran out of money and out of luck. She was the only person who believed his stories or had any faith that he might ever change his ways. That's what a mother does. God designed us this way. We connect with our children in ways no one else can—emotionally, spiritually and physically. Most of us have this innate sense of knowing when something isn't quite right with our children, even when we are not in the same room or the same state. One day, I'll ask God about that. It's a mystery.

Once again, she came to his rescue. More than believing anything he had to say, she felt sorry for him. She couldn't bear the thought of his being hungry, alone, or homeless. She feared that turning her back on him now would lead to his certain death, and she knew she couldn't live with herself if that happened. Rather than administer tough love that would force him to grow up and take responsibility for his repeated actions, she melted and opened her house to him once again.

We admonished her over and over, but she never listened. "This time, he's different," she told herself and us, just as she had multiple times before. "This time, the Lord will change him. I'll make sure to pray harder. He will go to church with me, and the Lord will surely change him. If he can just find some good Christian friends, that will help too. That's what he needs—someone who can be his friend and who will spend time with him." She prayed and believed that this would be true. She suppressed thoughts of all the broken promises he repeatedly made and forced herself to believe in him again.

His personality, when drug-free, was delightful. He was a real comedian and could bring tears of laughter to whomever his audience happened to be. Even children loved his childlike musings and fun personality. He had a killer smile and sparkling blue eyes that said, "You can trust me."

He talked a good talk, but walking the talk was often a problem. The local cops recognized him, and they often pulled him over for little or no reason. They knew he had no valid driver's license. He had lost it several years earlier, and the effort required to reinstate it was more than he was willing to undertake.

His record of accomplishment for turning bankrupt meat markets around and making their owners more money than they had ever imagined possible preceded him. Small-town grocers in south Alabama and north Florida knew of him—the good *and* the bad. They had heard of his reputation for drug use and abuse. For that reason alone, it became increasingly difficult for him to convince one of them to take another chance on him.

With continuous pleas for "just one more chance," he was finally able to convince a long-time acquaintance for one last opportunity to prove himself worthy. This time, though, the owner was more observant than before. He watched closely, doubting the promised good behavior. At the first sign of trouble, he was out the door. Another job gone, then another. Two jobs in less than two weeks was a new record.

All out of options, he knew he would have to find a new location where no one knew him if he ever hoped to find a decent job. He contacted every lead he had, but no one would listen to him anymore. He had become too much of a liability for them to take on.

Then call came in from my mother, "Diane, he needs help. He just needs someone to believe in him and give him a chance! He's so depressed and he is doing so much better. Maybe David can help him. Maybe he could come there and work with him for a while."

"Sis, I promise this time is different!" He begged, "I don't know where else to turn. I'm so depressed. I just need a chance. I just need somebody to give me a chance."

These words resounded in my head like a broken record. I've lost count of how many times I heard them. The heartbreaks, the disappointments, and the anger that inevitably follows them rushed to my mind as I heard them again.

"Why must I endure this yet again?" I asked myself, "He will never change!"

"What about you?" I asked God. "What would you do? I can't help him if he refuses to help himself."

My thoughts screamed in my ears, *No! No more of this!*

My heart counter-argued, *This could be you. The only difference between you and him is one wrong choice on any given day.* What makes one person choose one thing over another and another person the opposite? God gives each of us the right to choose. I wanted him to make the right choice, just once. If he could do it once, then maybe he could do it a second time. And then a third.

I caved. "Maybe this time really will be different," I told myself.

After talking it over with David, we agreed to let Barry come and live with us for a while. He could work with David in his new landscaping business. David could certainly use the help. Ten dollars an hour wasn't much, but it was more than he was making sitting on the back porch, smoking cigarettes all day.

David and I had only been married for about six months at the time. I was still trying to adjust to having another person living in my 1,500-square-foot house. It would be a real challenge with a third person in such a small space, but we decided to give it a shot.

Barry proved to be a hard worker even in this setting. His zeal for hard work had never been a question. If anything, the pace at which he worked was extraordinary. He always seemed to be either wide-open or completely shut down, no matter what he happened to be engaged in. There was no happy medium for him. He poured himself into his work with every ounce of energy he could muster. He and David got along well, and they seemed to make a great team.

Spring cleanup and planting time is very busy in the lawn care business. So they stayed very busy and spent some long hours doing manual labor. But every good thing has an end or at least a lull. Springtime also brings with it spring rain. Rain meant no work. No work leads to boredom and restlessness.

I've often heard that old saying, "An idle mind is the devil's workshop." And it's true. Barry soon found an outlet for his restlessness when he went looking for something to do on rainy days. The local bowling alley and a pool hall offered some entertainment. In those places, however, he found other people with idle minds. Some of those people had much in common with him. The difference between them at the time was that he had a little money in his pocket, and they had something to sell. The merchandise they were selling was the last thing he needed. I saw the signs that began to unfold. Trouble was brewing.

One day in early April, Barry made the mistake of taking out his frustrations on me. He quickly discovered that I wasn't his mother. Our heated exchange ended in his swift and angry departure. He verbalized his intent to leave and never come back, which was perfectly fine with me. He thought I'd beg him to stay like Mom always did. I didn't! When he was out of the house and on the road, he realized what he had done. I ignored his calls and pleadings to let him come back. My charity offering had run its course, and I simply had no tolerance for his games.

Not surprisingly, he made his way back to my mom later that day. That's where he stayed for the next month or two until he found someone else who would believe his story. And his pattern of life continued.

A CLOSE ENCOUNTER
WITH DEMONS

S everal months passed, and he found himself in one of the lowest places I'd ever known him to be up to that point. A great deal occurred between April and September 2012. This is the first of a number of September events that send shivers up my spine when I think about the many crossroads we faced. This was also the first of a number of future exchanges and events about which I chose to keep a record. My anger with him from our last exchange five months earlier had subsided by now, although his behavior had only worsened.

Barry: I'm sorry if I sounded rude the other day. My life is so messed up. I don't know what to do. I'm prayin' for wisdom, please pray for me.

Me: I know that, dear. I offered you wisdom. I truly believe that God wants you to stop running, face whatever the messes are, and let him sustain you through the consequences. In order for you to gain any peace, you have to be able to look forward without the need to worry about what may be behind you or fear that someone is after you. Regardless of the consequences or the price that may have to be paid, the peace of God beyond our understanding can be yours if you want it. God never promises that we can escape the consequences of our actions, but he does promise to love us and forgive us and to be with us if we turn our hearts completely to him without holding anything back for ourselves.

Barry: I don't know where to start.

Me: Just one step at a time. Let the Spirit lead you. Don't fight it. Be sweet and submissive. I love ya!

Barry: That's the reason my life is in a coma. Thanks anyway; no answers.

Me: Begin by dealing with the issue that's facing you right now. Whatever you have to do to get that behind you...do it!

Barry: Deep depression. I have no one but me, my mind, and time.

Me: That's not true. There are plenty of people reaching out to you who want to help, but you choose to hide yourself away. You can't keep doing that. You push people away who want to help and who try to help. Until you decide in your own mind that you are going to do some things differently and make positive steps in that direction, there is nothing that any of us can do to help you get better. Do you want to come up here and check into a hospital for a while?

Barry: I wish I didn't feel so depressed, worthless, and alone. Someone who could understand. I'm so depressed. I've took two showers in three weeks.

Me: That's not good! Why do u think u are this far down? What's changed?

Barry: Many things; can't go into it all, I love you, goodnight.

Me: Trying to find a treatment center close by. I'll send you the number when I find it. Okay?

Barry: Don't do that, my life is almost over. Let it go...

Me: I won't let it go! First of all, you have to decide that you want help. If you do, we will get it for you. But, if you don't, well, then, I will just keep right on praying like I've been doing. I'll pray that you decide you want help and will reach out for it.

Barry: I did that my whole life, I guess prison is all that's left. I shouldn't have bothered you. I've tried to tell people what's wrong. No one understands.

Me: I understand u are depressed. You feel like nobody understands. But they do. What I do know is that hiding away isn't going to help. Do I need to come down there and take u somewhere?

Barry: There's so much more than that. That's why I stop talkin'.

Me: I know there is. I'm not listing everything either (on purpose), but u have to start somewhere, and I'm convinced that u need help from a third party who has no family ties to you; someone who has experience dealing with all these issues and can get to the root of the problem.

Barry: I give up.

Me: That's a good start. You do need to give up, because YOU CAN'T FIX IT! It's too big for you!

Barry: I'm so sick of my life. I shouldn't have texted and bothered u.

Me: U r not bothering me. I wish I could fix u; but I'm bright enough to know that I can't. But David and I are going to stop right now and pray that God will show u the first step to make toward recovery tonight.

Barry: It's too big. I don't even understand it all.

8:31 p.m.

Me: God has it. He understands. He has the answer. And he will show u. He's about to show you.

Barry: Don't sell me out.

Me: Sell u out? What r u talking about? I just prayed that he will dispel the enemy and all his forces that have u bound and to help u reach up for His hand that's reaching for u right now.

Barry: Never mind. Thanks for ur prayers.

8:56 p.m.

Me: There's a place called Faith Farm Ministries in South Florida. It's a nine-month program and it's FREE. Are you interested?

Me: The center I recommend is on a farm in Okeechobee, Florida. I can fill out the application online. Also, you can call and talk to them at 863-763-4224. If u want to go and they agree to accept u into their program, I can come down and take u there.

Barry: I fell asleep. Maybe we can talk later. I don't sleep much anymore. A lot of things to think about. Maybe we can talk tomorrow. Just pray I know what to do.

Me: Ok. Call me tomorrow.

Barry: Ok. Thanks, Sis. I know there's no quick fix. It's just too much: it's overwhelming, and I don't want to be a burden. I hate my life!

Me: I know. But where there's a will, there's a way.

Barry: No one seems to believe the pain I face every day, and it's so frustrating, and the state don't care unless u got insurance. I can't take much more.

Me: I'm so sorry. I know u r.

Barry: Thank you for caring.

Me: Try to sleep. We can work on this tomorrow. Nite ☺ Love ya.

Barry: Maybe so. I luv u!

Me: Blessed be the God and Father of our Lord Jesus Christ, who according to His great mercy has caused us to be born again to a living hope through the resurrection of Jesus Christ from the dead, to obtain an inheritance which is imperishable and undefiled and will not fade away, reserved in heaven for you who are protected by the power of God through faith for a salvation ready to be revealed in the last time (1 Peter 1:3–5)

*****

My mom called earlier that day to talk about Barry. He had moved out of her house about two months earlier. She had been to see him on that particular morning. She told me he was living in a tiny travel trailer in a trailer park in Dothan, Alabama. "He's in a really bad place," she said as she described his living arrangement and his state of mind. I could tell from the tone in her voice that she was more worried about him than I've ever known her to be before. He asked her to leave him alone and not come back. She was brokenhearted. I was concerned for her health as much as I was for his—maybe more.

What am I going to do?
What can *I do?*
I have to do something!
I can't just let him die!
I can't allow this to destroy my mother. She loves him so completely.

Another text message exchange began in the evening. He never responded to my message from earlier in the day.

Barry: I'm scared and weak. I don't know which way to turn. I'm afraid I'm going to die.

Me: I'm coming down there. Can you tell me what's happening?

Barry: My mind is totally messed up. It's over my head with too many thoughts.

Me: Can you tell me if u are withdrawing? Or is it something else? I need to try and figure out how I'm going to help you. So I need u to be very open with me about everything.

Barry: So many things. Maybe I'll be okay tomorrow. I ain't moved in 6 days.

Me: I'm going to head out in the morning. I'll do something. I don't know what, but I'll figure it out. Have you taken anything? If so, what and how much?

Barry: I'm exhausted mentally. That's not what's wrong, but I have been out of my meds for a few days.

Me: Have u ever been this low before?

Barry: Don't come here. I'll make it.

Me: I'm coming.
Barry: No!

Me: U can't keep doing this.

*****

I was so scared for him. I felt helpless and afraid myself, and I couldn't imagine what he must have been feeling at that moment. I could sense his utter despair. I went to sleep praying for God to show me what to do, whether to wait another day or just how I should respond. If he was unwilling to listen to me, what good would it do to go?

As I struggled that evening with the decision of what to do, it suddenly occurred to me. *It's September. My birth month. I was supposed to renew my driver's license three days ago on my birthday.* If the things that were happening around me weren't enough to completely wreck my sense of peace, I had added another stressor to the list.

I worried about driving 350 miles to Dothan, Alabama, without a valid driver's license. I'm a rule follower. I fear what happens when I fail to follow the rules. It's just how I'm wired, I guess. This may sound like a non-event to many of you reading this, but for me, this was a big deal. Getting a speeding ticket is bad enough, but to be caught with an expired driver's license would be the worst law violation I'd ever committed. Yes, I get it. Some of you are rolling your eyes or shaking your head at this. But go with me.

I questioned, *Would God really want me to go on such a long journey, knowing that my driver's license is expired?* Surely he wouldn't.

September 9, 2012; 3:00 a.m.

A frequent occurrence of late occurred again this morning. I awoke out of deep sleep at 3:00 a.m. I was wide awake and feeling anxious. I sensed an urgency to pray for Barry, so I crawled out of bed and knelt beside it. I asked God to watch over him, to protect him, and to show him the way out of the darkness. I prayed for his protection, his salvation, and his release from the addiction that was destroying him and everyone around him.

*****

In recounting these 3:00 a.m. occurrences to a friend recently. She shared something with me that I've never heard before. She said this hour is known as the "devil's hour" or the "witching hour." Some believe that it's the preferred time of day (or night) for devils and other paranormal beings to conduct their evil activities. Whether there is any truth to this or not, I can't say for sure. Nevertheless, I can attest to the fact that it is at this time of the morning that I'm often prompted to pray about something specific or to read scriptures in search of peace for my own heart.

I'm fully aware that there's a dimension that exists which can't be seen with the natural eye, a force at work in the spiritual realm. I'm convinced that evil promotes itself against good in this realm. I believe it's a place where angels and demons wage war over men's souls. I fully embrace that it's a dimension of our lives that's just as real as the physical one, only more powerful and determinative of our future existence. It's outside our human control. I can't touch it, but I can certainly feel it, and we can see the effects of it, even if we don't understand it.

The fact is that we are spiritual beings. The evidence of it is revealed to us through thoughts that enter our minds. Those thoughts, together with the exhibition of our will and our emotions, move us to action. So it makes sense that the spiritual part of our existence is at work in and around us all the time. The manner in which we approach life, choosing good or evil, and the forces against which we must contend all depend upon which spirit we choose to follow.

The presence or absence of God's Spirit within each person can generally be discerned quite easily by watching the person's actions and listening to their words. Some tend to make a mockery of this idea and seek to discredit anyone who believes it, but that doesn't change the fact one iota. One need only walk to the end of life, the very point where this physical life ends in death, to recognize the truth of the matter. The saddest part of this reality is for those who refuse to believe in a God who can change everything about them. When once the sudden revelation of the truth appears, it's much too late for them. It's too late to undo the disbelief.

For the soul who believes in God and that he created all things and controls all things, there exists an internal sense of quiet peace. We believe that there is life beyond this one. There is a purpose for our existence and an answer to every question. All this is true for us even though we may not fully comprehend it all right now.

I have to ask, *what harm occurs in believing?* And then I ask, *what harm might occur if I disbelieve?* If I believe but happen to be wrong, then I'm no worse off than if I had not believed. At the very least, I have lived and loved. I've found meaning and purpose. Living with hope allows the believer to face the most difficult things in life and still find joy. On the other hand, if I disbelieve and I'm wrong, then I've missed out on an eternity of life, peace, joy, and everything good. Not only that, but I have doomed myself to an eternity void of life, peace, joy and everything good—a place of darkness, pain, and death that will never completely die. We will all spend eternity somewhere. Our spirits don't just sleep endlessly when our physical bodies die.

Ask yourself this one question: when you reach the end of this life and look back over it, will you regret the decision to believe?

I declare to you this *truth*: there is life that exists beyond the grave; there is one God and one true Savior, Jesus Christ the Lord. No, I've not seen him with my physical eyes yet, but I am convinced that I will. My heart is full of hope, and I have peace in believing that he has done just as he promised in preparing a place for me and for everyone who believes in him.

So, with this in mind, I will continue to share this story of heartache and brokenness, bad choices, and pain. But I do so with a joy that can only be explained by the very hope that's within me and knowing that the brokenness will be mended and the pain will cease.

*****

I fell asleep again, praying all the while. At 6:00 a.m., I awoke with a startle. I sat straight up in bed as I sensed an urging to "get up and go!" Have you ever had one of those moments when you just knew what you must do? Your struggle to know the right path to take, the right decision to make, it's gone in that moment.

There was no longer any question in my mind. No doubt whatsoever remained. I got up, showered, and told my husband, "I have to go!"

He said, "Okay," yet I could tell by the reluctance in his voice and the look in his eyes that he didn't really want me to go. I asked him to make me coffee while I packed. Graciously, as he always does, he honored my request without question or argument. By now, he trusted me to follow my instincts and to do the things I felt strongly compelled to do.

With a small bag of essential clothing and toiletries in hand, I grabbed a bag of new clothes that David had bought me for my birthday and a large cup of coffee and got into the car. It was 7:30 a.m.

My plan at that point was to go find a place where I could admit Barry, a place of safety and help. Once I accomplished that, I'd turn around and head back home. I guessed it might take me a couple of days. I wasn't sure whether we would end up at Faith Farm Ministries or whether I might find some mental hospital or some other place closer. I was simply trusting God to show me the way.

I felt prompted to call my mom to let her know I was on the way. My plan was to meet her at her house, and we would go together to where Barry was living because I had no idea where that was. I called and explained the plan to her and asked her to contact her friend, Bob. I felt like we might need another person, a man, with us. She explained to me that Bob and Barry had recently had a serious argument, and she hadn't seen him in a while. It must have been quite an argument because she seemed quite confident he wouldn't agree to go with us.

Sensing the urgent need, I called Bob myself. He didn't answer. I left him a voice message, explaining the situation and my plan. I told him, "I don't need you to say anything or do anything. I just need you to be with us and to pray."

I hung up the phone and continued to drive. Since I wasn't sure if he would respond or even show up, I called my mom again. I asked her to go on to church and if she felt strongly about asking another person who could go with us to pray to please ask them to come. I let it go at that point. I knew we were in good hands. I didn't stress or worry about that.

My estimated arrival time was 1:30 p.m. As I drove, I prayed that God would keep me safe and that I wouldn't be stopped by any patrolmen. Although I sensed the urgency to get to Barry as quickly as possible, I felt just as strongly that I should drive the speed limit, and not one mile per hour over it. That was quite unusual for me, and I've never been one to let the grass grow beneath my feet. I did mention that I'm a rule follower, right? Well, for whatever reason, driving a few miles per hour over the speed limit wasn't something I felt completely wrong about. Of course, that still doesn't make it okay.

With this strong urge, I set the cruise control to the posted speed limit and drove on. I just drove, prayed, and listened to praise music for six hours. I didn't stop for anything, not even food or more coffee. I hoped I wouldn't need a potty break.

My mind began to wander a bit as I thought about all the other roles in my life. My current responsibilities both at work and at home were weighing on me. I thought of the endless tasks that needed my attention at work, my nonprofit fundraising event that was imminent, our small group meeting scheduled for that evening, and a dozen other things. But, at this moment, all of that fell several notches down the priority list. Nothing else was more urgent than saving my brother. Everything else would have to wait.

At some point, at an hour or two into the trip, Bob called. He assured me that he would be at my mom's house, waiting for me. I spoke to David a couple of times along the way, stopping only once to go to the restroom and grab a bottle of water. I also sent text messages to several people, asking them to please pray for my safety and our success in finding a place for Barry—friends, coworkers, and small group members from church were all willing to join me in this mission through prayer and encouragement.

*****

I refer to prayer a lot. It's an essential part of my life. I don't refer to it lightly or irreverently. I've found it to be a source of strength, no matter the challenge that lies ahead of me. Please understand that each reference to prayer is intended to relay the true urgency of the moment and my reliance on God himself, the greatest of all power available to humans. It's not used here (nor would I ever use it) as an empty cliché or word that could be substituted for mere *wishful thinking*. Too often, people use the term *prayer* very loosely, not realizing the magnitude of power that genuine prayer releases into a situation. Prayer *was* and *is* my key to unlocking the power of heaven over my earthly existence. It's been the essence of my survival on many occasions, particularly at those times when I've slipped into a world of despair without a visible means of escape.

Prayer—genuine heartfelt prayer and a cry for help to the God of all creation—is an invitation that opens the door that stands between God and man. The Bible tells us in the book of the Revelation 3:20, "Behold, I stand at the door and knock; if anyone hears My voice and opens the door, I will come into him and will dine with him and he with Me." When we pray and invite the Lord God into the intimacies of our lives, things change. Hearts, minds, situations, and all manner of things change, which we in our own human power are helpless to achieve.

So when I refer to this term, please understand the context. For in the following chapters of this book, you will see an unfolding, a beautiful transformation brought about through prayer and the mighty hand of God at work in Barry's life, my life, and in the lives of my family and others with whom we interacted. Prayer is powerful. God is real and at work in the earth. And neither of these things should ever be approached in a loose or irreverent manner.

*****

I arrived at my mom's house at precisely 1:30 p.m.—six hours after I began the trip. Mom and Bob were waiting for me. I took just a moment to change clothes, and then we got in the car and headed to our ultimate destination from Hartford to Dothan. It was about a half hour trip from there. Mom directed each turn as I drove. She suggested that we call him to let him know we were coming.

I told her, "No!" I don't know why. I just sensed that we shouldn't alert him.

2:00 p.m.

We entered the small campground where Barry's RV was parked. The campground was in the south part of the city. I noticed that the grounds were kept neat and clean. His RV was very small and appeared quiet with no movement whatsoever when we drove up.

I asked the two of them to stay in the car and to please pray. I said another quick prayer myself and then cautiously, but with firm resolve, went to the door and knocked. Barry quickly opened the door and allowed me in. He didn't seem too surprised to see me. I'm not sure why.

What I found inside took my breath for moment. It was heartbreaking. He was secluded inside a tiny living space so small that there was barely room for one person to turn around. He was very quiet. I quickly surveyed my surroundings, feeling closed in, and encircled by deep darkness like I'd never felt before. It sent chills up and down my spine.

I saw that he had nailed blankets and other materials to all the windows to keep all light from entering and, I assumed, to keep anyone from seeing inside. His paranoia was extreme. T-shirts were nailed to the walls as his décor. I saw a few other things—compact discs, a hammer, some posters, and few food items on the small counter space. I spotted a calendar on which he had circled certain days, some of which I noted were days that he was to receive an unemployment check. His small television was on, and a golf tournament was airing.

He was small, frail, and shaking. He sat on a small bench with his head bowed, the same bench on which he had apparently been sleeping. I sat down beside him, and he leaned against my shoulder and began to weep. He clasped his hands together and held them between his shaking knees.

I wrapped my arms around him and said, "Just let it out!"

He sobbed. "I don't know what to do!"

The desperation in his voice was intense. He had obviously reached the end of his rope. He told me how his mind was racing with all kinds of random thoughts and how he was unable to put any cohesive thoughts together in his head. I learned that this day was the first time in seven that he had left the trailer. He had been out before I got there. He had gone to the common showers at the campground, taken a shower, and washed his clothes. I spied a small clothesbasket on the floor.

I don't know when he had last eaten. His eyes were dark and deeply sunken, as were his cheeks. Death was lurking all around us. I sensed it just as strongly as I sensed my own heart beating in my chest. I sensed the presence of evil spirits living in this tiny dark box with him.

Surrounded by the armies of heaven and covered by the prayers of many saints of God, including my mother and Bob, I wasn't afraid. That may sound strange, but it's true. I felt covered and strong, kind of like David when he stood before Goliath in the book of Samuel. Don't get me wrong, I'm no David. But I serve the same God as David, and he supplies me strength to face the Goliaths in my life. Today was a Goliath-facing kind of day.

"Do you want to be free of this prison?" I asked him.

"Yes!" came his reply.

I asked about his medication and any other drugs that he might have taken. He insisted that he had been out of meds for a few days and had taken his last pill (purchased, I assumed, from off the street) on Saturday. He was an avid liar, but sometimes, when in a place of desperation, more truth than normal poured from his lips. I sensed truth in his words. He said that a "friend" (I use that term very loosely) had texted him about buying five Lortabs that morning. "I'm just too tired and weak to go and get them," was his added comment. At that moment, he had about $60 to his name.

I had no doubt that if I had delayed my coming, he would have spent his last dollars on those five pills to try and ease his pain and probably to finally end all his pain on this side of life. This was how deeply in despair he had fallen.

I suggested that we gather up enough clothes for a couple of days and go to Mom's so that we could talk and try to sort things out. He agreed without hesitation. Before leaving the RV, however, I asked him to get on his knees and pray with me. The floor space in the middle of this RV was barely wide enough for the two of us to kneel together but we did anyway. I showed him how to position himself in a posture of surrender by opening his hands palms up in front of him. This is how Pastor Chip had taught us to pray. Open hands show that we are releasing and not holding back anything, and at the same time, it's an invitation for the Lord to give us back whatever he may choose to give.

As we began to pray, I asked the Lord to break the strongholds and chains that held him. I prayed many things that day. Bold prayers of faith and for his deliverance. My brother was in the deepest darkness I'd ever known, and the chains that held him in this state were too powerful for him or I to break. I asked for freedom and for peace. We prayed for several minutes, asking God for help and direction. Barry cried and prayed, palms open, on his knees before the Lord.

I can't say what Barry may have felt or heard from the Lord that day. All I know is that God hears us when we call his name in our desperation. We don't have to have it all together. It doesn't matter what we might have done the day before or even ten minutes before. If we seek his help with a humble heart, he will show up!

Barry gathered the things he wanted to take with him—some clothes, his phone, a briefcase with some papers, etc. Looking around, it didn't appear that much else in this place had any real worth or meaning. We locked the RV and went to my car. Mom and Bob were there waiting for us. We drove quietly back to Mom's house, and I continued to quietly pray for direction about what to do next. It was about 4:00 p.m. by the time we arrived back to her house.

A trip intended to last two days turned into two weeks. On Monday morning, the real work of finding a place for Barry began. Mom had no Internet access at her house. We went to the only place I knew that might supply that. We ended up at the small public library in town to do our research. The librarian there knew Barry. In speaking with her, it was apparent that he had gone to her, seeking help in the past to file for unemployment or to do job searches. She had a sweet demeanor and was a great help to us—a welcome inspiration and breath of fresh air.

I was successful in finally making contact with someone at Faith Farm Ministries. We completed an online application. Phone interviews, lots of paperwork, and many other things had to be done before we finally received confirmation that they would accept him into their program. I was so relieved and thankful for this open door. I truly believed it was one more answered prayer. But it would be another week before I could physically deliver him to the camp at Okeechobee, Florida, a seven-hour drive even farther south.

My mind was plagued once again by the fact that I had no active driver's license. *Oh well*, I thought, *the Lord has brought me this far. He can take me the distance.* I could see impossible doors opening to us every day, both physical and spiritual doors. I was grateful.

The next several days were challenging. At night, especially, the spirits of darkness seemed to be all too present. This is impossible for me to explain to anyone who has never felt it, but I woke almost every night, frequently sensing the chill of a dark presence that I couldn't see. I prayed a lot! I knew that we were protected. I believed with my whole heart that the armies of heaven had been dispatched, and they stood as our defense every night and every day.

Barry and I prayed and cried together a lot. As we took the necessary steps to gather the things he would need for the next few months at Faith Farm Ministries, he told me stories, *crazy stories* which were nearly impossible for me to believe. You may have difficulty believing them as well, but I urge you. *Keep reading.*

THE LOTTERY TICKET TO HELL AND BACK

Over the days that followed the escape from the demon-infested RV, Barry talked to me a lot about his life and many of the things he had refused to put in writing in our text messages earlier. He shared with me this story of his adventures after leaving my house earlier in the year. As unbelievable as this chain of events may seem, they are true nonetheless. Police and lottery records exist as evidence.

"Sis, a few weeks after I came back to Mama's when I left your house in April, I met this girl at a yard sale. We got to be really good friends."

I don't recall this so-called friend's name, but Barry shared with me how the two of them hung out together a lot. They seemed to connect in a way that made him feel loved, accepted, and alive in some strange way. He told me of a day he gave her a ride to another of her friend's house and discovered that this other friend was cooking methamphetamines.

Crystal meth was always a go-to drug for Barry when he couldn't afford anything else. These people he had met offered a share of this a freshly made batch of poison with him. He watched as they made it. He recounted to me his intrigue since this was the first time he'd ever seen it made. He talked of melted batteries, Drano, Sudafed, rat poisoning, and ammonia.

My heart sank as I sat listening to this surreal account into a world so foreign to me that I could not fathom the utter depravity of it. How do people reach this point of desperation to inject such deadly substances into their bodies? I understand that it happens, but I couldn't wrap my mind around it.

He further explained that they mixed all these ingredients in a two-liter plastic bottle, periodically releasing the gases that were produced from it to prevent it from exploding. He recalled the horrid smell it produced. Ultimately, he said the liquid was poured onto a plate and cooled. Later, they scraped the dried residue from off the plate with a razor blade to create a pile of white crystal-like dust, which he described as having the appearance of snow.

I have heard many stories of how addictive this concoction is. It must be so. Otherwise, no one having rational thought processes would smoke or inject it repeatedly. Barry told me that over a period of two days, he injected about thirty needles of this drug into his veins. He recounted how the injections caused him to enter another realm, an alternate reality. He told me how he prayed to Satan in that realm.

My heart raced and my soul cried quietly within me as he shared this story, a story that on this day was much different than the promises he said Satan made him the day he was under the influence of the drug. He told me how he had prayed and told Satan that if he would give him lottery numbers to win some money, he would buy and use more methamphetamines. He said two specific numbers came to mind that day—the numbers 6 and 7. Following up on his prayer (not the kind of prayer that I described earlier but a prayer to the enemy of his soul) and his own promise to buy more drugs with any money he might win, he made a trip to a Florida convenience store where he bought a lottery "scratch-off" ticket. He scratched off the coating on the ticket, which revealed his winnings: $25,000!

(My mom had shared a little of this story with me earlier in the year, but she didn't have all the facts. All she knew was that he had won a significant sum of money on a scratch-off lottery ticket. It was part of this money he had ultimately used to purchase the RV where he was living when I found him. So while the full story that he was revealing to me now was surreal, I listened on.)

He told me that when he saw the value on the ticket, his entire body began to shake. He said, "I didn't want the money! I knew it was evil money." Nevertheless, under the control of a power he described as being helpless for him to resist, he went back to the same house where his new acquaintances were making the meth. He apparently shared with them what had just occurred because "They started feeding me more and more and more meth. Like handing candy to a child."

(I was curious but never asked why, in this obvious drug-induced state of mind, these people didn't just kill him and take his ticket. There might be a thousand reasons, but I'm convinced that it's because God still loved him and wasn't finished yet. As far down as my brother was, far from the heart and will of God, God still saw him and loved him and was divinely protecting him even then. We will talk more about this later.)

One of the guys agreed to go with him to Tallahassee to cash in the lottery ticket. I learned something else new. A lottery winning of this sum is more than the ordinary convenience store can pay out. It required that he go to the state's lottery headquarters in Tallahassee to retrieve his winnings. He told of the troubles the two of them had in getting to the location and finally retrieving the money. Apparently, a significant lottery winning requires one to jump through a number of hoops.

(I'll admit I still don't fully understand how all of this works. The written notes I made after he shared this story with me have a few gaps in the details because I really didn't know all the right questions to ask at the time. With that said, the major points and events that follow are accurate and significant to understand other parts of this story.)

He gave the man who went with him $1,500 to claim the winnings. He stressed his worry that his unemployment benefits might stop if anyone found out he had just won this large sum. And, no doubt, it would have. I'm sure there were other details about the matter that he chose not to share with me.

"Approximately $6,000," he said, "came off the top for federal taxes." Next, they found a hotel room to rent for the night. He went on to say that the guy running the hotel that night sold him $600 worth of cocaine. It must have been a sleazy place.

He recalled finding a pistol that his companion had brought along on the trip. Fearful that the guy was going to kill him and take the rest of his money, Barry took the gun and kicked the guy out of his room. He said he later took the man back to his house and ditched the gun, although he didn't say where. Sometimes it's best not to ask too many questions.

Over the next day or so, he told how he had decided to drive to North Carolina to see his daughters. He began that journey, but on the way there, he discovered that the older daughter was away from home at the time. His alternative plan was "to get high and take a vacation" that he believed he deserved. He spent the next several days getting high on an "8 Ball."

(This terminology was foreign to me, too, but I wrote down the things he shared. I have since discovered that "8 Ball" is a term used to describe an illegal drug, usually cocaine, with a weight of about 3.5 grams or an eighth of an ounce. This didn't make any sense to me either, especially after hearing the next turn of events.)

Barry recalled that he was "in the middle" of his 8 Ball when he became extremely paranoid. He was so strung out that he believed cops had surrounded his hotel. He said, "I was so scared and paranoid that I swallowed about two ounces of cocaine. I tried to throw up, but I couldn't." He didn't know what might happen as his body absorbed what was left of the cocaine.

He told how on the following day, he talked to a friend named Carolyn, and he decided to go and visit her. On the way to her house, the drugs he had swallowed the night before really began to "kick in." He said this made him even more paranoid than ever. He recalled passing a cop who was going the opposite direction. Seeing brake lights on the cop's car, he convinced himself that the cop was coming after him. He began to hallucinate and increased his speed to between 110–120 mph. He said he drove like a maniac for quite a while until a tire blew out on his car. At such a high rate of speed, he ended up in a ditch.

Another miraculous survival! How many would he have?

After finding himself in the ditch but still alive, he left the car and set out on foot to try and find someone who could pull him out.

He saw a house and headed toward it. He recalled it being around 4:00 in the afternoon. He said he must have passed out as he walked to the house he had seen because the next thing he recalled was waking up with the moon shining in his face. He looked back and saw blue strobe lights from a cop car and red wrecker lights. It was then that he realized that his car was being towed.

In the next instant, he panicked because *he had left $14,000.00 in cash* in a briefcase in the back seat of the car. He began running and yelling, "Hey! That's my car!"

State troopers, the ATF, and news media were already at the car. Not surprisingly, they arrested him and took him in for questioning about the money. Having found the money, the troopers and the ATF were convinced that he was a drug dealer. A logical conclusion, I must admit.

He sat confined in a jail cell for several hours while the authorities worked to confirm his story about the lottery winnings. I'm sure he didn't tell them the whole story, just the part about the lucky scratch-off.

He recalled how he believed God had spoken to him during this time. He felt at peace, and his mind was completely clear for about six hours. But he said God warned him about what would happen next. He explained how his mind began to race and his thoughts ran together when he no longer heard God's voice. He told how his tongue began moving rapidly, but the sounds and words that came out made absolutely no sense. The words were foreign to him. He never shared with me what God's warning was to him.

Using some of the money, he bonded himself out of jail and returned to our mother's home. He told how he was determined in that moment to use the rest of the money for a good purpose. He gave Mom about $1,500 to help pay expenses, and she also took $2,500 to pay off a credit card, which he had fraudulently obtained under a false name with stolen credentials. Using stolen credentials was a repeat offense for him, just one among a long list of bad acts that had led to estrangement between him and several family members. As short-lived as his decision turned out to be, at least a small amount of the money wasn't used to purchase drugs.

(If you've been calculating as I've told his story, you know that this left him with between nine and ten thousand dollars, which he asked Mom to put in the bank for him.)

As days passed, he began to demand withdrawal of the remaining funds. He used $1,200 to purchase the RV. In August, he moved the RV to the trailer park in Dothan, Alabama. He recounted his future plans to never come back to my mother's home but to die of an overdose in that very park.

He rehearsed how he didn't want to change his life. He was in deep despair. He did exactly as he promised Satan he would do. He used the lottery winnings to continue abusing prescription drugs, smoking crack cocaine, and injecting himself with crystal meth until the remaining $7,000 (*more or less*) was all gone!

*****

I want to take a bit of a detour for a moment.

For those of you familiar with the Bible and the stories of the wanderings of the nation of Israel, you may recall the names of some of the kings of Judah. One particular king who lived around the time 700 to 640 BC was named Manasseh.

King Manasseh began his reign when he was only twelve years old. He was the son of King Hezekiah, a faithful king of Judah who followed God with his whole heart. Hezekiah is famous for his powerful prayers and God's incredible responses to those prayers. Manasseh, his son, however, didn't follow in his father's footsteps but allowed himself freedom to mix and mingle with people who didn't know or follow God. His heart was enticed by those gods and the pleasures of the world around him. Soon Manasseh's heart was fully drawn away from God, which led to idol worship and pagan rituals practiced by citizens of these foreign nations.

The scriptures tell us that he built altars for all kinds of gods and even offered his own children as sacrifices to them. He practiced witchcraft, used divination, practiced sorcery, and dealt with mediums and spirits. His evil deeds went so far that he set a carved image of an idol inside the sacred house that Judah and Israel had dedicated to God in Jerusalem.

Manasseh's heart was evil, and God was very angry with him. Because of the unique covenant relationship God had made with Israel, and his divine protection over them, the kings of Judah and Israel were held by God to a very high standard. He expected them to follow his commands and lead the people to do the same. These were the very same commandments God gave Moses hundreds of years before Manasseh was ever born.

The Bible is filled with stories of these various kings and leaders of Israel, some who followed the law of God, and some who didn't. It's easy to see the severity of consequences when a king failed to follow God. If you read the story of Manasseh in the book of 2 Chronicles, chapter 33, you will note that God sent the king of Babylon—one of Judah's fiercest enemies—against Judah and against Manasseh. Manasseh was captured, hooks were placed through his nose, he was bound with strong bronze chains, and he was taken to Babylon. What is most amazing to me about this story, though, is that God didn't forget Manasseh. He knew right where he was and exactly what was happening to him at all times.

When Manasseh humbled himself before God, it is recorded in 2 Chronicles 33:12–13 what happened:

> When he was in distress, he sought the Lord his God, and earnestly humbled himself before the God of his ancestors. He prayed...and the Lord was receptive to his prayer. He granted his request and brought him back to Jerusalem to his kingdom. So Manasseh came to know that the Lord is God.

Manasseh made a U-turn. He abandoned his idols and followed the Lord God with his whole heart.

This story of Manasseh is a reminder to me that the Lord never forgets those he loves, those whom he has chosen and called. He remembers his promises *and* his covenant. He extends incredible mercy and grace to his chosen ones in order to allow them room to turn back and follow him. We must *choose* to follow him, however. If we reject his extensions of grace and walk away, we do so to our own detriment, and we have no one to blame but ourselves.

Barry abandoned the God of his father and mother and went his own way. He even exposed his children to unimaginable horrors, much like Manasseh. None of this brought him or them any peace. Rather, his life brought great sorrow, brokenness, sickness, and everything opposed to peace. But I'm here to report that not all was lost. God wasn't done yet. More sorrow and pain lay ahead, but God is faithful.

Although it didn't fully happen at this point, I can tell you that Barry ultimately turned and humbled himself before God. Like Manasseh, he made a U-turn. When he did, *everything changed*. As with Manasseh, Barry spent the most productive years of his life chasing after everything he saw in the world, things that he believed would give him lasting joy and peace. But, if you read on, you will see how God's divine protection remained over him, even as he continued to wander.

Now, back to where I left off.

Faith Farm Ministries (September 2012)

As we continued to press through the next few days, it felt as if the weight of the world was bearing down on my shoulders. It went beyond just the weight of my own little world but extended to include the weight of my brother's and my mother's personal pain. Their pain was deeper and darker than any I'd ever personally experienced.

I asked God the reasons. He chose to remain silent at the time. I could not understand why I had to walk this road. "I didn't ask for this," I told myself. Truthfully, I wanted no part of it. I was tired, weary, exhausted in every way possible—mentally, emotionally, and physically. "Why can't he just grow up? Be a man? Do the right thing?" Surely, I loved my brother *and my mother*, and I wanted both of them well and happy. But why did life have to be this hard? For them? For all of us? Why did he have to struggle with these demons *every single day* of his life? Why must demons persist in wreaking havoc in his life? Why were they determined to wreck the lives of every member of our family? It seemed they were relentless and inexhaustible.

*****

I recently heard a Bible teacher say, "God sometimes allows the thing that he hates to bring about the thing that he loves." She was referring to *suffering*. Some people suffer because of their own sinful acts while others suffer innocently. I had never considered suffering quite this way. Nevertheless, I've learned the importance of examining myself to know whether or not my suffering is a result of my own disobedience to God's commands. After I examine myself and know that my hands are clean and my heart is pure, all that's left for me to do is simply let go and trust the unfolding of God's plan. The unfolding sometimes takes longer than I would like, but during these times of suffering, I'm compelled to lean in a little closer. He wraps me in the magnificence of his grace, and an endless flow of his mercy covers my soul in a blanket of blessed assurance.

*****

Barry's emotional struggles were only a portion of the challenges we faced that week. He had legal issues pending that required a monthly check-in with his probation officer and the payment of some fines. All these personal and social issues loomed over us like a storm cloud on a Monday. We also needed the court's blessing and referral before leaving town. Otherwise, he would face even more legal problems later. When we considered the mountain of issues before us, it seemed to be an impossible climb. The entire ordeal pressed down on us with crushing intensity.

Overwhelming was the word for the day. The problems were bigger than any solution I could dream up. So I continued to pray for God to open the doors he wanted us to walk through. I prayed for the strength to overcome every challenge and obstacle that lay ahead of us, including the ones that remained unknown at the time.

As I prayed, I moved forward one step at a time in what I believed was the right direction. When I faced challenges greater than I knew how to handle, I fell on my face before God. He was the only one I knew big enough or powerful enough to handle them. He knew, too, how to handle me. The Lord is my refuge. He's the one "constant" in my life. He's my calm in the midst of chaos. Even when I can't see two feet in front of my face, I trust his promises that he won't leave me alone.

> I am with you and will watch over you wherever you go. I will not leave you until I have done what I have promised you. (Genesis 28:15)

> The LORD Himself goes before you and will be with you; He will never leave you nor forsake you Do not be afraid; do not be discouraged. (Deuteronomy 31:8)

> Surely I am with you always, to the very end of the age. (Matthew 28:20)

I spent the next few days contacting officers and court officials and pleading Barry's case for a referral and reprieve. After hearing the plan and that Barry was approved to enter a faith-based recovery program, they were more than willing to grant the referral. I still recall the encouragement and well-wishes they gave us that day. It was another prayer answered.

We had to sell the travel trailer, take care of the rent on the parking spot, redeem the title on his car (which he had recently pawned for a few dollars), and stay in close contact with the ministry to secure his bed. The plan unfolded day by day with little resistance. I gave thanks to the Lord for each victory, large and small.

Each morning I spent in quiet time with Jesus just praying and seeking his guidance. Having recognized God's hand from the beginning, I knew that he was my only source of strength. Without him, I most certainly would have failed. It's frequently easier to see God's hand at work in our lives as we reflect back and consider what he's been teaching us over a period of time. As I searched my journal entries to recall dates and events, I found an entry that surprised me. The entry was made just four days after the rescue from the RV and prior to taking Barry to Faith Farm, and it was only a few weeks prior to the dream that prompted the writing of this book. This entry reaffirms *the message* and the promises the Lord continues to whisper into the depths of my soul—promises of salvation, healing, forgiveness and hope for my entire family.

Prayer excerpt from journal entry dated September 12, 2012:

> O God, You are good and righteous in all Your ways. You are good to *all* in giving grace and mercy. Your mercies are new every morning. You are good to those who are pure in heart (Psalm 73)... O LORD, grant me wisdom and discernment and strength to see the mission You have for me today... LORD, I am overwhelmed in my spirit this morning, but I know You are faithful and true. You will see me through no matter the outcome. I believe in You, and I believe You sent me here to do exactly what I'm doing... I trust You to accomplish Your plan.
>
> I pray that my brother will be released from this bondage he is in...that he will cling to You in the dark hours of testing... Grant him wisdom, understanding, and discernment to know when Satan shows up to tempt him. I pray for pureness in his heart so that he will not be drawn away and fall.

Prayer excerpt from September 13, 2012:

> O LORD, thank you for awakening me early this morning so that I could spend time with You. Thank You for taking time to confirm Your love for me and to let me know that You are here with me every step of the way. I hear You say, "Be still, Child, and know that I Am God. Watch and see my salvation." I hear You say *my entire family will be saved through this process*. I know that all

things work together for good to those who love You and are called according to Your purpose.

LORD, thank you for removing me from the hustle and bustle of daily life that creates so much noise that I have difficulty hearing You. Thank You for Your gracious kindness that sometimes takes me places I never imagine myself going—a place that in my flesh I would never want to go—and You do it all in order to gain my undivided attention!

You are so, so good. I praise You for Your love and wonderful grace. Thank You for loving Barry and for the changes and transformation that is taking place in his life right now.

*****

We finally received the date of entry into the program: Friday, September 21, 2012. It would be another week before I could deliver him to begin what I believed was a fresh new start to a changed life. A new beginning. A renewed hope. My hope and prayer for him was the birth of a *new hope within him*, a new perspective, an about-face, a forward march. Though my body was weary from the physical and emotional challenges associated with the entire ordeal, the brighter side was that I was growing in faith, and I believed that he was too.

On Sunday, September 16, I wrote these words from Romans 4:20: "No unbelief made him waver concerning the promise of God"—words written by Paul the apostle regarding Abraham. "But he grew strong in his faith as he gave glory to God, fully convinced that God was able to do what He had promised."

I, too, was fully convinced of God's promises and that he was not only *able* to keep them but that *he wanted to* keep them. Experience had shown me that he is *unshakable, unchangeable, and unstoppable!* I've seen God's power in action. I've personally experienced his faithfulness. I know beyond any hint of doubt that he was then and is now in control of everything on earth and in heaven. Regardless of what he was doing or not doing in my brother's heart, I knew he was transforming my own. He was working to establish *my faith* and trust in his endless love. I guess this was part of the answer to my questions, "Why, Lord? Why must I endure this trial that's not of my own doing?" I was a willing vessel.

A willing spirit is all that God requires of us. He takes it from there. I have no personal power or wisdom, no knowledge or ability about which to boast, but I can always boast of him and of his power, wisdom, knowledge, and ability. And that's what I did and will continue to do as long as I have breath in my lungs. I prayed, "Give me eyes to see and ears to hear You. Break my heart for what breaks Yours. Move my hands and feet at the impulse of Your Spirit for Your glory and Your praise!"

*****

The trip to Okeechobee was long. A fifteen-hour 960-mile round trip in a day is quite an undertaking. *Determination* was the word for this day. We began very early before the sun appeared, and thankfully, as the sun came up, it was bright, and the day was warm. The interstate wasn't packed, but a steady stream of traffic accompanied us along the way. We talked and listened to music as we drove, stopping only for an occasional bathroom break and coffee. I was anxious, and I know he certainly was too.

Personally, I had no idea what to expect when we arrived, although I suspected he might have had a hunch. He had experienced a number of rehabilitation facilities over the course of his life. All I knew for sure was that my heart was saying, "This is the place God has chosen for him, a place of rescue to help him find faith and recovery." I believed it with my whole heart. No one could have convinced me otherwise.

We arrived safely and without incident just after lunchtime on Friday, September 21. When we walked in the front door, a sign caught my eye: "Welcome, Barry!"

"Ahhhh!" A sigh of relief escaped my lips at the sight of it. This was a reassurance that they anticipated his arrival and had taken time to roll out a welcome. *Surely, surely,* this was the right place for him!

We completed the sign-in process, met with several people for interviews, and then we unloaded his few personal items. He seemed fairly optimistic. For that, I was grateful. A part of me was apprehensive up to this point as I vaguely recalled the very first rehab center where I had taken him about twenty-five years earlier. That one had not gone well and ended after only two days. That thought made me a bit anxious. I recalled that he had entered that facility with much resistance. But he seemed to be onboard with this one. Although now, as then, he could check himself out whenever he might choose to, I sincerely believed he craved the help necessary to fully recover this time to be free, to start over with a fresh hope. It would take much longer than a few days away from his familiar environment to accomplish this.

We prayed. We hugged each other one last time. Then I left him there with God and these ministers to work through the rest. It was up to him now. *I had taken him as far as I could go.*

As I backed out of the parking lot, I considered getting a hotel room. My body craved sleep. I opted, instead, to make the seven-hour trip back to my mom's house. It had been a long journey since I left home almost two weeks earlier. I missed my husband and my home. So I refused to delay my return any longer.

This mission was accomplished. Soon enough, I would rest.

*****

Over the next several weeks, my mom stayed in close contact with the ministry partners, and she kept me up-to-date on his progress. All seemed to be going well. Interestingly enough, Barry had met a young man there from our hometown in Tennessee. They became fast friends. Although the other man was much younger than my brother, the tenuous connection to our former Tennessee roots brought them together somehow. I was a bit shocked to find, however, that the other man had a personal cell phone on premises.

I couldn't quite figure that one out as that was one thing I knew was not allowed at the facility.

My, my. Where will this lead? I wondered. I worried.

Grateful that my boss and everyone at work had been so supportive of my impromptu two-week adventure, I eagerly jumped back into my normal work routine. At night, I spent time with my husband, talking through my anxious thoughts, preparing for the holidays that were fast approaching, and in meditation and prayer. I knew I had to stay strong in mind, body, and soul to keep myself from worrying about what might be going on further south.

Still, anxious thoughts and fear threatened to overtake me. I fought to retain internal peace. I couldn't allow myself to fall back into the trap of anxiety again. I felt those old familiar feelings of depression trying to drag me under. I filled journals with prayers and spiritual insights as they were revealed to me as I studied the Scriptures. I sought understanding and knowledge from God through it all. I needed understanding and wisdom because I sensed there was so much more to this than what I could see with my physical eyes.

The events of the past few weeks, Barry's stories of all that had occurred over the past few months, and my own understanding of spiritual warfare affirmed that there was much more to this story than I knew. I can't explain it, but I sensed it.

I'm reminded in scripture that when we put our faith in God, we are hidden with Christ in him (read Colossians 3:3).

Jesus holds us in the palm of His hand, and Satan can't touch us or take us out of God's hand (Read John 10:28–30).

Jesus himself keeps every child of God safe, and he will not allow Satan to touch them (Read 1 John 5:18).

I love Romans 8:31–39, which says, "If God is for us, who can be against us." Nothing can separate us from God's love, and we are able through him to "overwhelmingly conquer," whatever challenges come our way. But when a child of God makes a conscious decision to walk away from God's protection, all bets are off. When that happens, Satan is quick to swoop in with every enticement and creative lie he's so craftily designed just for us.

You see, Satan has temporary and limited authority to rule over the earth and the people in it. He gained this authority because of Adam's sin. For those of you who might not know, Adam was the very first human God created and placed on the earth in the Garden of Eden. Adam listened to a lie from Satan and gave away the authority God had given him to rule over the earth. For sure, Adam didn't mean to give away the perfect life he had with Eve in the Garden nor did he intend on giving up the authority God had granted him. But after listening to Satan's lie, he began to doubt God. He sinned when he believed and acted on the lie. Certainly, he was enticed but made the decision of his own freewill.

We, too, give Satan authority to rule over our lives when we listen to his subtle whispers that sound so innocent and rational and then give in to them. As we listen, thoughts enter our minds. As we ponder those thoughts, we become enticed by them and allow our hearts to be drawn away from God. The next thing you know, we've crossed a line that leaves us broken and separated from God and away from his protection.

Satan's only power over us is a *lie*. If we believe his lies and reject God's love, he is able to control our minds and actions. His whole plan from the beginning was to remove us from the place of God's protection in order to steal our best years and destroy every part of what is sacred and beautiful in our lives. Mostly, he seeks to destroy any hope of our eternal destiny, the one ordained by God in the beginning. The Bible tells us that "the thief [Satan] comes only to steal and kill and destroy" (John 10:10). And it's true. This is exactly what he does.

The Bible also reminds us that God does not tempt us but "every man is tempted when he is drawn away and enticed by his own lust." Then, when lust has conceived, it gives birth to sin, the scripture says. "When sin is finished, it brings forth death" (Read James 1:14–15).

So Satan can only tempt a child of God when he takes his eyes (or her eyes) off God and focuses instead on *anything* else. This misplaced focus creates a desire for those things he sees, things he believes will fulfill him or give him physical pleasure. The craving for those things becomes so strong that he will do anything to get them, regardless of the cost. It is then that Satan uses his excellent lying skills and false promises of physical pleasure to trick us into denying God and following him instead. Pride and a craving for pleasure are two of Satan's most effective tools. Experience has taught him that humans love to be in control (or think they're in control) of their own lives, and they love physical pleasures. So he studies us and knows our weak points, and at just the right moment—in a real moment of weakness or when we are tired or lonely or angry or sick—he paints us a pretty picture, sets it right in front of us, and whispers a subtle lie to lure us into his web.

Have you ever watched a spider spin a web? The web is carefully designed by the spider to lure and trap its prey. A flying insect is lured into what appears to be a place of rest. It's feet or wings then stick to the invisible glue on the web. The more the insect wiggles, squirms, and tries to get away, the more entrapped it becomes.

Every time I see a spider with its web, lying in wait for its prey, I'm reminded of the enemy of our souls and how he lies in wait for us, patiently waiting to lure us into his trap so he can destroy us.

It's at these times when we are weak and vulnerable that we must remain alert and cognizant of the voices in our ear—the voices of truth and of lies. Become keenly aware of the voice of God and make careful distinction between it and the voice that tries to lead you astray.

If you've never heard God's voice, I urge you with everything within me to seek him out and learn the sound of it. Knowing and heeding his voice is for your protection. It will shield you and protect you.

If you seek him, you *will* find him. He desires to be found by us.

*****

Barry's fiftieth birthday, October 11, 2012, came and went. I mailed him a card of encouragement along with a book, some note cards, and postage stamps. I received handwritten notes from him periodically, and all seemed well. We all continued, thankful that he was safe and in a place where he could receive instruction and encouragement.

THE MESSAGE

At 3:25 a.m. on Wednesday, October 17, 2012, I awakened from what seemed like a dream—a nightmare, really.

I've read in the Bible where the Lord said that "old men will dream dreams, and young men will see visions." And while I have had a few dreams over the course of my lifetime, some which I sensed were strong signals of warning and messages of importance, I had never had one anything quite like this one. This episode included a very clear event. The matter seemed imminent.

As I lay there in the darkness, I could remember every word I heard, verbatim. I rehearsed it over and over in my mind, shaken but unsure what to do with it. I sensed the urgency to get up and write it all down, somehow knowing that I would need to recall it later. I was certain that the message of this dream was sent directly from God.

The Bible is filled with many instances of God revealing to men things he is about to do. In the book of Amos, chapter 3, verse 7, I found this scripture: "Surely the Sovereign LORD does nothing without revealing His plan to His servants the prophets." Now I'm no prophet. Let's get that straight from the get-go. But I also found in the book of Luke, "For nothing is hidden that will not become evident, nor any secret that will not be known and come to light" (Luke 8:17).

In Daniel 2:22, I read, "It is He who reveals the profound and hidden things. He knows what is in the darkness, and the light dwells with Him."

And, finally, I found in Deuteronomy 29:29, "The secret things belong to the LORD our God, but the things revealed belong to us and to our sons forever, that we may observe all the words of this law."

It is this last scripture where I find the most comfort and relevance to the message given me that night. The secret revealed—though painful and tragic on the one hand—would bring hope and healing to me and my family in the end.

The revealed *thing* belongs to us *forever*, the scripture said, and because of it, we will observe and do the will of God according to his commandments.

This was the dream and the message, which I have copied directly from my handwritten notes on that morning. Those notes were the exact words spoken in my dream:

The Prodigal Son—a Eulogy

I am with you. Draw your strength from Me. Be strong. Be courageous. Tell them all that I command you to say to them.

Remember My promises:

Your entire family will be healed through this process.

Barry's voice in the end will declare My glory more than his life brought shame in his disobedience.

You, Daughter, must be that voice which will declare My glory. You, Daughter, must tell them:

The time is short; Christ's return is imminent.

You came here today to pay your last respects to my brother—your son, your brother, your father, your nephew, your cousin, maybe even an old friend. What you came for is slight and so small in comparison to God's purpose in bringing you here.

You must each—hear me now—*you must each* examine yourself this day and decide whether you will give forgiveness and receive forgiveness.

Will you be reconciled?

Barry lies here before us now—actually the broken shell of his body lies before us. His spirit—the part of him that God Almighty breathed life into a little more than 50 years ago—is actually present with our Creator now. That Creator, the Righteous Judge and Compassionate Father, has sent me to tell you all this.

Barry's life is a picture of us all—every person in this room—as we stood (or yet stand) in the sight of God Almighty. We were (or are) broken. We were (or are) lost, hopeless, helpless, yielded to the prince of this world, doomed for destruction.

No, I am not here to paint you a glamourous picture of my brother, who he was, all that he accomplished, the principles he stood for. I can't in all good conscience do that, and I don't believe he would even want me to do that.

But, what I can do is to declare to you the saving, transforming, and unimaginable power of my God. For I have seen it! While brief, I got a glimpse of Barry's life in the end which is a picture of one who was (and is) redeemed, forgiven, full of hope and life and peace.

This is a picture of what God wants to do for each person under the sound of my voice today.

Do not weep for Barry, for I am persuaded that he stands before God today clothed in white and kneeled before Him in adoration and praise.

Weep, however, for yourselves if you don't know the Savior. Weep for your children. Weep for your neighbor to whom you haven't spoken in so long. Weep for those yet to be born into this broken world.

I pray that your hearts are broken for this world and the sin sickness that is consuming it.

God commands us to love one another, to forgive that you may be forgiven, to ask of Him and receive, to seek and find, to knock and have doors opened to you.

He declares that if His people who are called by His name will humble themselves and pray, and if they will seek His face, then He will hear from heaven and He will forgive our sin and heal our land.

So, the life that you saw lived out before you—a life of tragedy and failure for so many years—you must understand that this is a picture of how God views this broken world in which we live.

But the life of my brother, and the picture I paint for you now—the beautiful transformation of a broken vessel, reconstructed by the Master Potter's hand in his last days—is a picture of the grace and mercy of our LORD.

I was completely shaken. Had I just been told that my brother was about to die? Was God really asking me—*commanding me*—to share this message at his funeral? Wow!

Having written what I heard in the dream, I didn't know what I should do next. Should I tell someone? Should I talk to Barry and tell him about the dream? *How could I?* How do you tell someone that you believe they're about to die soon? *Was it my place to do that?* God didn't tell me to tell him about the dream.

As I considered it, I realized that the message was not for him. Rather, it was for my family and for the people who would attend his funeral, whenever that time should come.

What on earth? Was I losing my mind? Was all the stress I was under impacting even my dreams?

In spite of the sobering thought that someone I loved might soon pass away, I was reassured by the hope extended in this message—hope and a promise that even when my brother's life here on earth is over, his spirit will live on in heaven with God. This was a hope and a prayer I had prayed for him so many times but which I'd almost given up prior to taking him to Faith Farm. I heard the promise. I believed it. And I chose to rest in the peace of it although it meant we would lose him temporarily.

*****

More weeks passed. Thanksgiving came and went. I frequently thought of the message and pondered when the time would come, always expectant of a call. I was certain I had heard the message correctly. I couldn't make something like that up, even if I tried.

The holidays were here. It was a time of celebration and joy as we remembered the birth of Jesus and reflected upon why he came. As I tried to make preparations for family gatherings, my efforts were only half-hearted. Not a single day went by without anxious thoughts of how this news and my brother's death would impact our family.

Recent messages from Barry led me to believe that he was growing restless at the Farm. His positive notes were slowly turning to complaints and negative comments about the ministry. I feared that he might soon seek a way to escape it, an excuse of any kind to leave.

I continued in prayer, however, knowing that Christmas has always been a difficult time for him. For reasons I don't fully understand, the Christmas holidays have brought him to his lowest points. Severe depression sets in. His sense of self-worth, well-being, and hope always seemed to wane at Christmas. This emotional nosedive had consistently sent him searching for a way to forget his past and numb the pain of it, a past which he seemed unable to forget, personal regrets for which he was never able to forgive himself.

Christmas is certainly a time of year when most people want to be with their families, to share the blessings of the season, and to enjoy food, fellowship, and gifts. Whenever that can't or doesn't happen, it can trigger sadness and depression. I get it. I've walked through such times of sorrow myself. It can leave a person feeling hopeless, unloved, and alone. So my heart was breaking for my brother, anxious but hopeful that he would find a way to get through it without turning to his old way of masking the pain.

December 19, 2012

My cell phone rang midmorning. The voice on the other end of the line explained that Barry was sick and in the hospital. He had been taken there two days earlier. The minister told me how doctors at the local hospital had explained that Barry's heart was enlarged. They were quite concerned that he couldn't survive in this condition for very long. "He needs to be with his family," Mark said. "We need to send him home. I just need to know where and how you would like for us to send him."

Another kick in the gut from out of left field. I prayed. "Oh, God, how can I keep going? This is too much. What do I do? It's Christmas…his very lowest time of year. I don't know how to deal with this."

It wasn't that I didn't want Barry to be with his family if this was truly what was happening. Something didn't feel right about the conversation I'd just had with the minister. I sensed that there was more to the story. Still, in the back of my mind, the message loomed. *Could it be?*

Calling David, I debriefed him about the call I had just received. Knowing all that my mother had gone through with him over the past several months, I couldn't bear the thought of sending him back to her. He had no job nor money, and she didn't have the means to care for him.

"How do you feel about bringing him here to live with us for a while? They've indicated that they don't believe he has long to live."

David was quick to agree that we should bring him to our house. We had plenty of room after all, and David's schedule was flexible enough this time of the year that he could keep watch on things pretty well.

Barry's plane arrived in Jackson the very next day. We met him at the airport, nervous about how we might find him. Although a bit forlorn, he wore a smile and seemed happy to be with us. With that, the next phase of our journey began.

The Devil Moved In

We quickly emptied a closet and a chest of drawers in one of our empty guest rooms. He would have a nice soft bed and plenty of space to make his own. He would share a bathroom with his nephew, my youngest son, who occupied another bedroom across the hall. The master suite was on the opposite side of the house, and a large family room and the kitchen separated the two sides of the house. A fourth bedroom was vacant for anyone else who might happen to drop by during Christmas. And with these accommodations made, we settled in for the holidays.

We encouraged Barry to join us in the family room as often as possible in order to help him feel connected and part of our family. It was awkward at first, and he had trouble making our home feel like his own.

Mom came for Christmas, and the next several days were quite a blur with the flurry of activities as the final preparations for Christmas celebrations and festivities came together. Mom seemed pleased that he was here in a place where he could live in safety and receive help and encouragement from David and Jared. She knew he needed male companionship and encouragement. This is something he had lacked for a long time, at least the kind that was wholesome and free of temptations. She, of course, was concerned for his health in light of the report we received from the ministers at Faith Farm.

I still had reservations as I had not seen any evidence to suggest that he had heart problems at all. Except for a weak appearance, he seemed quite normal. He laughed and talked like he was going to live forever.

I thought about the dream and the message a lot, but I never said a word to anyone. If my dream was imminent, then surely, the diagnosis from the Florida doctors pointed to the fulfillment of it. If his condition was as they had described or if it worsened, evidence of it would appear soon enough. For now, he showed no signs of returning to his old habits. So I was confident that I could stand before my family and deliver the message I had been given.

*****

As the days turned into weeks, a new year began. Barry became stronger in body and much more bold in his approach. His physical heart condition, which was diagnosed as dire in December, became less and less apparent. There were times when he seemed unusually tired, but beyond that, there was no sign of significant health issues at all. Initially, his spirit was lively and his outlook bright, but he often whispered how he didn't want to be a burden to us. We tried our best to reassure him that he wasn't a burden.

As more time passed, his lively spirit began to darken. His state of mind became restless, and depression began to grow. His self-degrading words and slumped shoulders revealed it. His outlook was grim. He talked of hopelessness, worthlessness, and regret. He spent the long winter days recalling all he had once had and lost. Mostly, he talked about how much he missed his children and wanted only to be with them and to provide for them. At other times and outside of my presence, he shared with my husband and son things he would never have told me.

One particularly disturbing comment he repeated to them more than a few times was how much he just wanted to "get high." He allowed his mind to fill with thoughts of drugs and the sense of euphoria he believed they brought him. More and more, he focused on his regrets, which pushed him deeper into a state of depression as each day passed.

A sense of darkness and dread fell over our entire house. It was almost tangible. A creepy heavy feeling filled the house, particularly at night. There were times that the spirit of darkness seemed to suck the oxygen from the air. It was the same kind of creepy fear I had sensed in Barry's trailer the day I rescued him from it just a few months earlier.

I prayed, "God, please protect us. Help us to know how to help him. Give me strength. Without You, I can't do this!"

Fear and anxiety stole my peace and my sleep. I often awakened in the middle of the night with a sense of dread, darkness, suffocating darkness. I regretted the decision we had made to allow him in again.

As more weeks passed, I began to notice an unrest in my relationship with David and with Jared. Actually, it was more than unrest; it was the building up of anger and resentment inside of me. I asked myself, "Is it because there's an extra person in the house? Is it because I am the only person who has to get up each morning and go to work?" During the winter months, there was little for them to do in the landscaping business. My resentfulness grew to a point that I could barely look at any of them in the eyes.

Regardless of the cause, my soul was overwhelmed with a sense of despair that I couldn't pinpoint. I was severely sleep deprived, four to five hours a night tops, often waking up in the middle of the night, barely able to breathe. I worked long hours at the office, partly to keep my head above water there and partly to maintain my own sanity. My soul longed to avoid the looming darkness that seemed to cover our house. The feeling of heavy darkness and the presence of an evil spirit in the house shook me to my core. I spent a lot of time reading and praying for strength and wisdom just to get through each day.

Barry often spoke words of distrust in my ears about my family, all of them, words that made me doubt them. I failed to notice this pattern of negative commentary at first. The comments seemed "off-the-cuff" and not associated with any other subject matter we happened to be discussing. He stated a few times how he could talk our mom into anything. He commented how he knew just the right words to say to make her melt and get her to do whatever he wanted her to do.

It all made sense to me now. It made sense how he always managed to convince her to allow him back into her house, even after he treated her so harshly. I could only imagine how her heart must have broken each time. I wondered, *Was this what happened at Faith Farm? Had he been so determined to leave that place that he convinced them that he was dying? Or were they looking for a reason to send him home? Had he created an atmosphere of darkness there?* My mind was in a whirl, and I questioned *everything* and the motive of every person under the roof!

I continued to pray and ask God to show me what to do with him and about him. I struggled with finding a way to help him while protecting my family and my own heart besides. My fears came out in my prayers. I recall them now as I review my prayer journal from that time period.

An excerpt from a February 7, 2013, prayer:

> Oh God, My Creator, the One who knows me better than anyone else; the One who taps my heart early in the morning and bids me to come and cry out to You. You are the One who carries me through the dark places. I am in such a dark valley. Come and save me. Save me from the waves of darkness that cry out and threaten to consume me. Save me from the fears that steal my joy and consume my days and nights. Oh Lord, You alone know the fears that threaten to overtake me and leave me to die in this wilderness. I am weak. I am weary of this life.
>
> Oh God, my body is tired. I'm so tired of being the strong one day after day. I'm so tired of being the one expected to provide the daily necessities of life... I pour out my soul to You right now. Free me from this dark valley; bring me through it.
>
> Lord, there are so many frightful things that threaten to overtake my soul. The tempter lurks around every corner, and he loves to find me vulnerable. It is here that he seeks to deceive

me and to tell me things like, "You can't trust God—where is He anyway?" He tells me, "You can't trust David. You don't know all the things he does and says when you aren't around, and they all laugh at you behind your back and joke about how they are able to pull another one over your eyes."

Lord, these are the things the devil whispers in my ear. O God, I ask you to squash him and make him leave me alone and forbid him to steal my peace.

Your Word says you will never leave me or forsake me, and I know that I can trust You. You are always faithful. You always do what You say You will do. When others fail me, when others disappoint, I know that *You never will*. Lord, send me a few good and faithful friends—people I can trust, people who know You in Your fullness and power, mentors who can guide me and help me through these dark valleys; angels of light who can warm my soul when I'm afraid and feel all alone. Lord, I feel all alone right now. It feels as though I carry the entire weight of the world on my shoulders.

Oh God, take this burden from me. Help me to lay it all down at Your feet. God, give me a trusting heart. I need You.

*****

This and many similar prayers spilled from my pen onto the pages of my journals over the weeks and months that followed. All the while, I watched, prayed, and did everything I knew possible to ensure that no drugs were brought into the house. I tried to remain an encourager and strived to keep a pure heart and a clear communication line open to heaven. My trust in God was the only thing that sustained me through this time. He provided strength and courage through this most difficult season in my life—*the most difficult up to that point anyway*.

My greatest fear at that time was of Barry falling back into the trap of drug addiction, which I knew would bring down the fury of hell on all of us. He needed to leave our house and find a way to live his own life. I was afraid, however, that he would end up back in the house with my mother, and I couldn't bear to think of him going back there—not in this state of mind. Plus, I knew that if he left Jackson, he would have no job. With no job, he would once again be a burden on my mother. I feared for her, for her health and well-being. She had always been his safety net, and I knew that this time would be no different than all the rest, particularly if he started using drugs again.

He seemed doomed to repeat the sins of his past. The changes I began to see in his attitude, his perspective, and his restlessness were all signs of trouble. I had seen it all before from a distance but never this close up.

David and I continued to encourage him and my son to attend church services with us. His only hope of overcoming the addiction was to keep his mind and heart in the right place. During the first weeks after his arrival, he seemed to gain strength and courage from the pastor's teaching and the worship services. As the months passed, though, he began to find fault with the sermons and argued that he didn't like going there because people stared at his bald head. When these arguments failed to convince us, he made excuses that he was either too tired or there were too many people in this big church—a place that must be filled with hypocrites. This, too, was a pattern I had seen over the years.

As he filled his mind with negative thoughts of the past, the farther and farther he drifted into the same depressed world from which he had worked so hard to emerge. Could he not see it? Did he not recognize the repetition of his addiction? All of this took him further from the truth and began to create distance between him and the rest of us.

The further he drifted, the less he wanted to be around people of faith. He refused to talk of spiritual things. He seemed to find ways to separate himself from us as well. This was a problem, considering our living arrangement. It was obvious that he didn't want to face reality or the truth of his own problems. His thoughts remained focused only on masking the pain with a drug. It was like quicksand. He sank deeper and deeper. Just how deep he was sinking remained a mystery to me for far too long.

*****

Many of you who are reading this story may be skeptical of some of my comments, particularly those that tie the physical world to the spiritual. Unless or until you have walked through it, such experiences may seem unbelievable to you and out of touch with physical reality.

I've been where you are, and I can understand the skepticism. It's okay that some do not believe, although my heart cries for *all* to believe. Regardless of your doubt, however, I just encourage you to stay with me as this story continues to unfold.

As I'm writing it, my own spirit is troubled, too, because I'm forced to relive many unpleasant and fearful experiences. The hurt and pain of it all is not something that I enjoy remembering or regurgitating. How I wish to forget that any of it ever occurred. But, in recalling the past, I am able to empathize with others as I'm reminded that we all face many struggles in our lives. The manner in which we deal with these struggles are pages in our life's story. They can't be ripped out and thrown away nor can they be changed. They are what they are. Knowing that others have walked this way before helps us to know that we aren't alone in our struggles.

Our personal experiences shape our lives, our thoughts, our actions. Who you are today is a by-product of the experiences of your past. It's my prayer that something you read here will help you find courage to keep fighting the fight, knowing that your past experiences need not define you. It is my desire that these words, this story, will help you overcome your fears and allow you to rise above what you may perceive as an uncertain or hopeless future. Just know you are not alone. There is hope. You will see it as you read on.

*****

The darkness of the winter months turned into the bright new beginnings of spring and life. David's work picked up, and so did Barry's outlook. He was able to get out of the house, engage in physical work, and earn some money. The longer the days became, the more work there was to do.

The two of them spent an increasing amount of time together. When they weren't working, they were fishing or doing some other guy thing. I figured these must be good things. After all, David knew many of the stories of Barry's past, and he was solid in his faith. Much to my dismay, however, I later discovered that some of David's weaknesses and vulnerabilities were being tested during this time. On a few occasions, he failed the test.

Satan is a master deceiver. It's been so from the very beginning of time. He has not changed his tricks or his lies. He keeps telling them, and humans keep falling for them over and over again. It can happen to any of us, especially if we aren't consistently filling our minds and hearts with pure thoughts. I'm not immune, and neither are you.

Barry told me stories about my husband and my son that he knew I wouldn't approve of. He knew these things would break my heart, but more than that, he knew they would make me very angry. I'm still not sure what he hoped to accomplish by telling me these things. Perhaps he wanted to feel better about himself if others were guilty of something. But it seemed to be some sort of cruel game he was playing with all of us.

Now, from a spiritual perspective, I can see that he was a pawn in the hands of the devil himself. This is how he inflicts the most damage. He uses people as instruments of destruction. People, particularly those closest to us—those we love the most—are able to inflict lethal injections of distrust, anger, and resentment. The damage is devastating.

A sense of unrest and great fear settled over me personally, but it spread across the entire household. Everyone began to distrust everyone else. It triggered arguments and angry words that had not existed before.

I later learned that things he had told me as "truth" were actually a twisted web of lies and deceit. I also discovered that he was making similar comments to my husband and son about me—the same kinds of twisted lies. Everyone picked fights with everyone else, not realizing the root of the matter. All the while, Barry sat back in his room and reveled in his accomplishment. Or so it seemed.

I recall taking him to see my cardiologist one day. I wanted him to establish a medical relationship with a local heart doctor so that if he did have a heart issue, we would have a place to go and a person who knew what was going on. Some weeks later, David shared with me how Barry sowed seeds of jealousy and distrust of me by leading him to believe that I was flirty with the doctor. Nothing was farther from the truth. But, of course, my husband didn't know that.

Barry told me stories about girls he was sure David was watching and lusting after while they worked. The stories planted seeds of jealousy in me against David. He sewed seeds of discord with my son as well. He whispered lies to him about how his mama was trying to control his life by not allowing him to live it the way he wanted to. Jared bought into that lie too—hook, line, and sinker.

It wasn't until later that the three of us—David, Jared and I—discussed among ourselves the strange things that were happening inside our once peaceful home. Only then did the truth of what was happening really come into focus for us. It was all a bed of lies, and the instigator of it all was one individual.

I have struggled with an unhealthy sense of fear my entire life. I have suffered greatly because of it. Panic attacks, depression, and hopelessness were a significant part of my existence in my twenties and thirties. I struggled long with fears I couldn't explain. I feared literally everything. I worried that we might not have food on the table, although I had a great job making plenty of money. I feared that my children might be stolen from me and lost forever, though I had no reason to believe it. I feared living life alone, without love or affection, although I knew my husband loved me dearly. Many other things that would likely never happen filled my mind day after day, year after year. All these lies and targeted deception fed my tendency toward fear like Miracle Grow applied to my potted plants.

In an odd kind of way, this fear helped me begin to understand more about Barry's struggles. He obviously was dealing with his own fears. He just handled it differently than I did. I never sought to suppress my fears and struggles with drugs or alcohol. He did. I tried to empathize with that. I struggled to maintain my sense of joy and peace. My continued sleep deprivation only added to the problem.

Everyone around me could see signs of distress on my face. I sensed them watching me. Nevertheless, I pressed on, determined not to give in or give up. I tried hard to mask the signs until I found a way to overcome. I've learned a few things about coping with stress over the years. I've learned to fight the battle on my knees. And that's exactly where I landed—face down on the floor.

All of this was more than I could handle, so I took my heavy burden to the Lord. I wept. I begged to understand why this was happening. Where were Barry's words coming from? Why did he feel the need to pit each of us against the other?

Although I couldn't fully comprehend all that was happening or the reasons, I began to sense that the lies were actually coming from a darker spiritual realm. They came from a place I couldn't see with my eyes or touch with my hands. As I watched and listened, I perceived the devious work of a dark evil spirit—a spirit that seemed to gain more strength when I was at my weakest.

That's how the devil works. He watches us to see just where our weakness points are. He targets the places in our hearts that are the most painful. He knows that if he can find a way to control our minds and our emotions, he can take control over our mouths, our actions, and our entire lives. Having gained control over us, he uses our tongues to spill out of us words of distrust, lies, hatefulness, bitterness, and anger. And with that, our responsive action is to retaliate against the other. We hurt the ones we love the most. We doubt the ones we should trust the most. Strife and discord push us into isolation. In isolation is where he wants us to be. When we feel alone, he traps and binds us into his web of lies. If he can get us here, he takes control over our whole being.

Please hear me.

Please recognize that your loved ones are not your enemy.

The devil is!

It seemed to me—to all of us—that the devil himself had moved right into our house.

The longer Barry stayed, the more intense my fear became. I sensed a demonic presence. It had not been there before. I had felt something similar several years earlier as I struggled with depression as a young mother, but I never fully understood the source of it then. Now I was terrified. I poured myself into prayer and Bible study all the more. I knew that I was defenseless on my own. Only a stronger higher power could defeat a demonic foe like this one. My only hope—*and Barry's only hope*—was God himself.

Have you ever been there? Have you ever been faced with an issue so insurmountable that you knew you were doomed to fail? How did you handle it?

I couldn't just leave my house. I couldn't run from this problem. No one else was going to fix it for me. I had to face it, regardless of my fear. I'm a fighter. That's just my nature. When backed into a corner, I refuse to cower. I'm convinced that this is how we grow stronger. We have to be stretched beyond our physical and emotional limits if we are ever to gain any ground in this fight.

I needed to understand the opposition I was facing in order to deal with it. I had heard stories of others who had dealt with these kinds of demonic encounters. So I called my friend, Teresa. She had experiences dealing with such things when she spent several years in South Africa as a missionary. She was a devoted Christian and one of the strongest prayer warriors I have ever known. I could talk to her. I knew I could trust her. Although she was sick and dealing with her own fight for survival against pancreatic cancer at the time, she insisted that I allow her to come to our house. She talked with me, and we prayed.

Everyone needs a trusted friend, someone whom you know has an open line of communication directly into God's throne room. This becomes even more essential when facing something like this. I truly believe God puts people like this in our lives, allowing the paths of our lives to cross at a time when we most need them. Teresa and her husband, Steve, were gifts from God to David and me. How thankful I am that she was here when I needed sound advice and a calm perspective. Although Teresa is now in heaven, free of cancer and pain, I'm so very grateful for her heart of compassion and her willingness to share her life with me and the hope of Christ with so many people. My heart is glad as I write this paragraph because *I know* I will see her again one day.

Encouraged by Teresa and determined even more not to give up on Barry, I worked my way through the book of Romans during the month of March. As I meditated on the deeper meaning of the scriptures and the promises in them, I found strength to get through each day, one at a time.

On March 8, 2013, I recorded Romans 15:13, "Now may the God of hope fill you will all joy and peace in believing, so that you will abound in hope by the power of the Holy Spirit." I noted these reflections:

God is the God of hope, not of despair. He is able, and desires, to fill us with joy and peace. We are able to abound in hope by the power, which God himself sent to fill us with joy and peace—the Holy Spirit. It's a gift straight from God's throne room in heaven.

Wow! If we could only grasp the magnitude of this gift, nothing in the world could ever get us down. For if we believe in Jehovah God and that he truly loves us unconditionally, there is nothing for us to fear—*absolutely nothing.*

*****

On a hot summer day in late June, I received a call from David. "I need to you to come and get Barry. Something's wrong. Maybe he got too hot or something, but I think he needs to go to the hospital."

Quickly closing my computer, I grabbed my purse and keys, told my assistant where I was going and ran out of the office. At University Medical Center's emergency room, we shared with the attending physician about Barry's medical diagnosis from the Florida doctors. He showed signs of dehydration and possible heat stroke, so they connected him to IV fluids and admitted him for tests and a more thorough evaluation in light of his history. After a couple of days, doctors at UMMC explained how his heart was in perfect condition, and there was no sign of an enlarged heart.

"What? No! This can't be! They must have missed something. Someone missed something either here or there." There's no way that he could be on the verge of death in December and in perfect health in June. Human hearts don't just heal like that. Not without some miracle, and certainly no miracle had occurred at our house over the past few months. Yet, all the tests showed that he was in picture-perfect health.

That gnawing feeling of doubt about his initial diagnosis from Florida emerged once again. Was there no truth at all to anything he said or did? Was his connection to the dark side so strong that doctors couldn't explain the change in his physical ailments from one part of the country to the next? I know that Satan has no power to create life or to heal a body of ailments. But how could this be? Surely the medical tests and the diagnoses could not be this far apart.

Few answers were provided to my many questions. I only knew that something was amiss, but I couldn't explain any of it. Deeper trouble was brewing, and I was helpless to stop the progression. I seemed caught in a dark world that I wanted no part of but was helpless to escape.

Doctors dismissed him from the hospital after a couple of days, and he went right back to work, just as though nothing had happened. Making money seemed to be his new focus. He wanted to work all he could to make as much money as he could. Pacing himself didn't enter his mind.

A few more weeks passed, and the angst continued to grow. His room became his haven. He rarely left it, except to go to work, and I'd noticed an increased tendency to escape the house in the evenings with some of David's other contractors. His story was, "We're going bowling." *Uh-oh! Not that again.*

He kept the details of his activities to himself for the most part. I wasn't aware of his real purpose in spending so much time at the bowling alley or wherever it was they went. Later, however, I would learn that local drug dealers can often be found lingering around the bowling alley. He also spent a lot of time on his phone and walking the woods around our house. I found this odd.

Late one afternoon in July, Jared warned me that he had overheard one of Barry's phone conversations. He believed that he was about to make a drug purchase. He thought the exchange was planned to take place on a road near our house. Furious at the very thought, I watched and waited, feeling every beat of my racing pulse and the blood rushing to my head.

All three of us were constantly aware of his every move each day. We shared with each other what we saw or heard. He was growing more confrontational with me, more than I had ever experienced in the past. Of course, it had been years since I had lived in the same house with him day after day.

He and I engaged in a heated exchange of words that evening. I even told him to straighten up or get out! He spewed words of hate and anger back at me, using language I didn't allow in my house. I was *done* with being taken advantage of and disrespected in my own home. The last words I recall saying to him were, "Keep it up, and I'll call the cops!"

Not the right words to use with someone who is already paranoid of cops or under the influence of a controlled substance.

*****

The trip to Orlando promised to be a much-needed escape from the daily stress that David and I had been under for the past few months. We needed time to reconnect and to be refreshed. The trip had been planned for weeks, and we were both looking forward to the escape. I knew that most of my days would be spent sitting in lectures about insurance law and compliance, but David and I would have the evenings to spend relaxing, reconnecting, and restoring. It would be good for all of us—including Barry and Jared—that we get away from one another for a while.

I was somewhat uneasy about leaving the house with all that had emerged of late. Nevertheless, I trusted that the Lord would keep everything intact until we returned in four days.

11:30 p.m., July 22, 2013

"Mom! Mom!"

Startled out of a deep sleep, I heard Jared's voice at my bedroom door.

"Something's wrong with Barry! He went stumbling outside, mumbling. He's out there now, and I don't know what's wrong with him!"

David and I quickly put on our shoes and ran outside to find him completely out of sorts. He was barefooted, and his feet were bleeding from something he had tripped over. His tongue was thick, and his words were a jumbled mess. I had never seen him like this before. I had never seen anyone like this, so it scared me.

The emergency call button on our alarm system was our quickest source for help. Within minutes, an ambulance arrived and transported him to the hospital. Soon after the ambulance left, a sheriff's deputy arrived to take a report.

Surveying his room for clues as to what might have happened, we found an empty pill bottle and some other strange paraphernalia in his room. As suspected, we soon learned that he had overdosed on a drug that we didn't know he possessed nor did we know where he had obtained it.

Seriously! Could this really be happening? Our bags were packed and our flight was scheduled to leave Jackson at 6:05 a.m. *What now?*

We never saw him leave the house the night before to make the purchase we had suspected he planned to make. I was furious! We searched his telephone messages for clues as to who his supplier might be. We found a few local numbers and some messages from one person we knew locally and several others between him and a girl from Alabama, a former like-minded acquaintance. It was evident from the messages from her that she had mailed drugs to him at our address.

Angry and upset, we discussed what to do next. Should we cancel the trip or grab our suitcases and head to the airport in a few hours? Neither of us had had much sleep. But before making the final call, it was important that we know he was okay and able to survive yet another overdose.

When we arrived at the ER, I was escorted to where he was being treated. He was unconscious, but they assured me he would survive. They shared the list of drugs they had found traces of in his body. I was blown away as they recited the list of more than a dozen different things, many of which I had never heard the names. Where he had gotten these remains a mystery to me to this day. In hindsight, we probably should have cancelled our trip. Instead, I explained to the attending nurses that I would be out of town for a few days and gave them instructions about what to do if they released him before I returned.

We left the hospital and went home to give Jared some final instructions about the next few days' work and what to do if Barry called him. I told him that whatever he did, he must not allow Barry back in the house until I returned. We got no more sleep that night, and we headed to the airport early.

More questions. More fear. More things to worry about.

A day and a half later, as I sat, eating my lunch and waiting for my next session, a call came in from the hospital. The nurse told me they were releasing Barry from the hospital. They needed to know what to do with him. A wave of fear washed over me once again. I thought he would either be hospitalized until I could get back home or else that he would be arrested and taken to jail. Either scenario was just fine with me in that moment of anger and frustration. Neither of these scenarios played out.

I couldn't imagine allowing him back into our house with my son and David's nephew there without us. He had no car, no phone, and no one to call. I couldn't bring myself to ask Jared to go and pick him up. Recalling my last words to him, and knowing his incredibly angry reaction, I just couldn't do it.

I heard myself say to her, "Tell him to go to a local shelter, and I will find him when I get home." Those were the only words I could utter in that moment.

I waited until I knew they were home from work before I called Jared to warn him that his uncle had been released from the hospital.

"Lock the doors, and don't allow him in the house should he show up. I don't think he will, but you never know."

In the middle of our conversation, the tone of Jared's voice changed in an instant.

"Mom," he said, "Barry just walked in."

"Oh, dear God. What? How? Please, God, help us!"

At my request, Jared handed the phone to Barry. I ordered him out of the house. He was very angry at being left at the hospital without shoes or a phone. He spewed more hateful words at me and refused to go. I hadn't intentionally left him without shoes. It just happened that when the ambulance showed up, he was outside without any shoes on. The thought of taking him shoes had never crossed my mind.

He was angry at me even more because he had to walk two miles to our house. I learned that the hospital or someone else there had paid for a cab ride. The cab driver had brought him close to our house but refused to go farther than he had been paid to go. He dropped him off about two miles from our house.

I hung up the phone after giving Jared final instructions to take him to the local bus station and get him a ticket to wherever he wanted to go. Then I called the sheriff's office. I was frantic and I asked that they send someone to our house immediately to remove this man from the premises. I actually hoped that they would take him to jail. At least if he was in jail, he couldn't hurt himself or anyone else.

(What I'm about to tell you next may surprise you. It certainly shocked the shoes off me. It took away just a little more faith than I had already lost in the men in blue. Although I am a lawyer, I never knew that the law could render the innocent no help when help was certainly needed. I do trust our police officers, for the most part. But I've witnessed times when there was more that could have been done to provide help to someone in need, but that help was not fully extended. I mean no harm to anyone's reputation in what I'm about to describe as our situation and outcome that day. I tell this only so that you will be aware of how the law can sometimes constrain even our law enforcement officers in a way that protects the guilty more than the innocent. In this particular case, I believe the officer crossed a line that he shouldn't have.)

Since a record had been made about the events from two nights earlier, I was fully expecting cooperation with law enforcement. I felt certain that the officer who took the report about Barry's drug overdose and witnessed his erratic behavior would have him arrested or, at the very least, have him removed from our house. Not so!

A deputy did show up all right. But rather than remove the perpetrator (my brother), the deputy threatened to arrest my son if he so much as tried to "force this man out of *his home*."

Jared explained to me later how the deputy defended Barry, saying that this was his established residence and that we could not force him to leave without some advanced eviction notice. That would take weeks if he refused to go on his own accord. The officer had gone on to tell my son that he would arrest anyone, including me, who tried to force him to leave.

I could hardly believe my ears. We had opened our home and our hearts with the best of intentions to help a person who was sick, at the point of death (or so we thought), down on his luck, and needed a family during the holidays. Yet he had now become the victim and we the villains.

How could I have been so wrong about the change he professed a few months earlier? How could the message I thought came from God eight months earlier be true? Even if he died today, I wouldn't be able to share the message I had been given.

I was worried sick for my son. I felt so helpless and so incredibly naïve. How stupid can one woman be? My much-needed vacation had turned into an endless nightmare. Not only did I regret my decision to proceed with this trip, but now *the message*—the one I knew I heard so clearly in my spirit—couldn't be farther from the truth. All we had lived through over the past months and all were witnessing now couldn't have been any farther from the truth of the message.

*****

It would be months before I saw him again. By the time we arrived home two days later from Orlando, he was gone. Jared took him to the bus station the following day, and just as I had feared, he went straight to my mother's house in Alabama.

The thing that happened next crushed my heart almost to a point beyond repair. Barry carried with him to his next destination the lies and deception he had used on us. An evil spirit bent on destroying him and everyone connected to him controlled his mind, his tongue, and his whole body. It didn't take but an hour or two of truth-twisting to convince our mother that he had been mistreated in our home. He did as he had boasted before of doing—he said just the right things to make her believe what he wanted her to believe. She bought into his lies, just as she always had before.

I heard *his words* and accusations come spewing out of *her mouth*, and my heart sank. Furthermore, I was in complete shock. After all we had done for him for more than a year, and this was the thanks we got. The more her angry words and accusations came through the phone, I simply couldn't listen anymore. I hung up the phone while she continued to rant. I lost complete control of my emotions. The tears ran like faucets down my cheeks.

"Dear God," I moaned, "where will this all end? I can't bear up under the weight of so much brokenness and hurt. My family, already so fragmented over years of dishonesty and wounds too deep to express, is continuing to crumble. I'm helpless to fix this. My heart, though firmly fixed on the hope of Your power and ability to transform, is failing me now. *Please*, God, help us!"

Rather than allow my mother's accusing words to pierce my soul and make me bitter, I chose to fight this battle, too, *on my knees.* If I allowed these words to trigger fear or to take root as bitterness in my heart, everything I had believed God for up to now would all be for naught. I knew there was little chance of convincing her of what actually happened from 350 miles away. So I simply committed her and her angry accusing words into God's care. I asked him to watch over her, protect her, and help her to see and know the truth. I had gone as far as I could go now.

As time rocked on, she did eventually recognize that his claims of a changed heart were empty words. Nothing had changed inside him at all. She never apologized for the hurtful things she said nor admitted that she didn't believe the lies he had told her. But I forgave her anyway. I saw her as another victim of Satan's attack on our family.

I stored the notebook away and forgot all about the message. I must have been mistaken.

Rich in Mercy

Still, God, who is so very rich in mercy, watched over Barry as he continued to run. His eyes were always on him, even in those dark places he dared to go. Surely, heavens angels were busy protecting him throughout his lifetime, and certainly, they are present with him now. Running from God headstrong into a world filled with all manner of temptations took my brother down the darkest of paths, inflicting great pain on himself and others who tried to remain close to him. And though his careless actions could easily have killed him years ago in a hundred different ways, God extended incredible mercy and grace to secure his soul. These mercies followed him through every hellish venture of rebellion and every period of regret and remorse too numerous to recite.

The LORD is compassionate and gracious, slow to anger and abounding in lovingkindness. He will not always strive with us, nor will He keep His anger forever. He has not dealt with us according to our sins, nor rewarded us according to our iniquities. For as high as the heavens are above the earth, so great is His lovingkindness toward those who fear Him.

As far as the east is from the west, so far has He removed our transgressions from us. Just as a father has compassion on his children, so the LORD has compassion on those who fear Him. For He...knows our frame; He is mindful that we are but dust.

As for man, his days are like grass; as a flower of the field, so he flourishes. When the wind has passed over it, it is no more, and its place acknowledges it no longer. But the lovingkindness of the LORD is from everlasting to everlasting on those who fear Him, and His righteousness to children's children, to those who keep His covenant and remember His precepts to do them.

The LORD has established His throne in the heavens, and His sovereignty rules over all. (Psalm 103:8–19)

I found this written in one of Barry's notebooks. It is dated August 24, 2018:

I got news today about a CT scan of my lungs. I quote what she said: 'We found a large spot on your lungs.' I said, 'i know.' But, i didn't know.

God had already prepared me for that news. He saved me 4 mo. ago. I told her, 'I can except [sp] whatever happens because i know God saved me.' 6 mo. ago i couldn't have handled that news, but today i can. God is great. I know he loves me and has forgiven me of all my sin. That brings so much comfort to me.

Whoever may read this now i pray you will find this hope i've found in Jesus.

The Bible says by his stripes i'm healed. Today i rest in that verse and i claim it for myself. Whatever may come, i'm ready to face it. Praise be to God my Father and Savior.

To my children i pray you will see what God has shown me. He loves you Jaz and Destini. Trust him. He will give your life hope and meaning and eternal life.

Mom i love you. you've been my rock. you've always been there for me. You did all you could to help me, but the best thing is you prayed for me. Praise God, i'm saved.

"Ole Miss is up 14 to 7," I wrote. This was my effort to see what frame of mind he was in the day following his physical receipt of the radiology report. He loved to watch college football, and I thought he might be watching the game.

Barry: Who they playin'?
Me: Texas Tech.
Barry: I thought they played last nite.
Me: Nah. This morning. Not sure if they're done. I had to run an errand.
We play tonight. Hey, I'm listening to Ole Miss now on Sirius radio. Miss 30, TTU 17.
Barry: Awesome! Thanks for the update.
Me: Now 20.
Barry: Oops!
Me: Third Quarter; 36 to 20.
Barry: Lookin' good!
Me: Boom!

Barry: U watchin' the game?

Me: I was at Kroger. How they doin?
Barry: I'm thinking about things I've really never considered.

Me: What things?

Barry: Probably what anyone would think with the news I got; but, without fear and depression. I have a wonderful outlook and expectation.

Me: That's awesome. I do want to talk to you at some point. Just doing some pondering of my own. I'm overwhelmed by God's grace and his mercy. I found my notebook from 6 years ago when I took you to Okeechobee.

Barry: I tell u, what I've been shown in the last 6 months blows my mind. It's been between me and God. I have something inside that I've wanted my whole life. I just didn't know what until the last few months. Words can't explain it.

Barry: You don't need to explain it to me—I found it about 8 years ago. I fell so in love with Jesus that I couldn't get enough. Just wanted to spend time with Him and get to know Him more and more. It's sort of like falling in love with a person, and you just want to be with them all the time, getting to know what makes them happy, so you can do more of those things; and what makes them sad, so you don't do those things. The Word of God is like finding the best thing you've ever tasted and you just want to keep eating it and never stop. The Holy Spirit is like fresh, cold water from a mountain spring when you're thirstier than you've ever been! You just want to drink Him in and never stop drinking.

Barry: U just described it perfectly. And, God prepared me with the love I've never known. I'm so excited.

Me: I'm so happy about that. Overwhelmed really. I'm just so happy to know that someone in my family knows what I'm talking about. I want all of them to know, and I've been praying for it!!

Barry: That's what I told Mama, that I wondered if anyone knows what I'm talkin' about. Now I know u do. I go around now and I'm reminded what God's done, and can't help but throw up my hands and give Him praise no matter where I am. People think I'm crazy, but I can't help it. It's so good!

Me: So awesome!

Barry: Boom! I never had this before. I'm so, so grateful God showed up this way before I got that news last week, because no one can say anything, and the devil can't mess with me. Truth is, I'm right with God for all the right reasons.

Me: Yes! What a GIFT!

Barry: I'm reading *A Place Called Heaven* by Dr. Robert Jeffries. He's been preaching over 30 years. The book is awesome. Makes me want to go now!

Me: I'm ready any time!

It's incredible the number of rainbows I've seen this year alone. They're so vibrant and beautiful. Constant reminders that God has made promises to us that he will not fail to perform. I sent Barry some of the snapshots of today's rainbow. I'm always amazed at the sight.

"We have rainbows in Mississippi," I wrote a caption for the photo. "God's promises are beautiful and amazing!"

Over the next several days, I worked diligently to clear my desk of urgent issues that needed to be complete before I could be out of the office for several days. There was barely space to breathe on my calendar. The little bit of spare time I had was spent making last minute preparations for Jared's wedding set for September 15 in Tennessee. Immediately following the wedding on Saturday evening, I would have to pack everything and head back home on Sunday in order to make my next scheduled work trip. David and I had an event near the gulf coast beginning on the following Monday evening. This trip would keep me occupied for three more days following the wedding.

To add more stress into this already full schedule, David and I agreed several months earlier to go with a church mission group on a trip to the Dominican Republic. That trip was set for two weeks following all these other things. Too much was happening too quickly. My calendar was too full at a time when I needed it to be clear. Why do things like these always seem to happen when you can't seem to fit one more thing into your life? It's at these times that the clock's hands seem to spin rather than tick-tock.

I found it impossible to focus on any one thing. My mind was full of scattered thoughts moving in a dozen different directions. My heart was pulled right along with each one, not knowing whether to laugh, cry, or run for my life. Each obligation required its own level of high priority. I hoped, but couldn't be sure, whether any of my efforts were fulfilling the requirements necessary to achieve each goal. I was caught in a whirlwind of impromptu decision-making, and I was helpless to escape the cyclone. So I allowed myself to be carried along by these unseen forces.

I tried to make contact with Barry every day or so, not wanting him to feel alone or afraid. Yet I could only imagine—*and that not well*—the thoughts that filled his mind. I didn't want to overwhelm him with too many questions or motherly smothering, so I attempted to judge his mental, emotional, and physical condition from 350 miles away only as often as it seemed necessary. He had made it abundantly clear that he didn't want to be watched or smothered by anyone.

He consistently shared with me how peaceful in spirit he was and how his faith was growing stronger by the day. He spent a lot of time with his pastor who seemed to be the one person on the planet that he most trusted.

As I pondered "the message," I prayed for peace and for his faith not to fail. Strangely, I was unable to pray for his physical healing. I attributed that to "the message." I wanted him to know what I already knew, but I was afraid of how he might respond. So I carefully protected my words, waiting and listening for the right time to open my heart to him and share it all. In one particular exchange, I dipped my toes a little deeper into the subject, trying to find a way to tell him without wrecking his hope or negating his faith.

My text message on September 3 began with a scripture quote, and then I added: "You're on my mind constantly! I love you."

Barry: Oh, I have such peace, and my faith is stronger every day. Yesterday was an awesome day.

Me: Just know that your faith also helps to strengthen the faith of all of us! And that is truly incredible.

Barry: That's what's incredible!

Me: I know! As strange as it may sound, I believe the Lord has promised to heal our family thru this whole thing.

Barry: That's strange that u say that.

Me: Why?

Barry: For some strange reason I know something wonderful will become of this. I can feel it. This thing has been stirring for years. He said he would save us and all our household. I claim it. No weapon can overcome, but we overcome by the blood of the Lamb and by the words of our testimony. Matt. 18:19—my verse I love!

Me: Yes! And verse 20 is the best of all *'and there I am with them.'*

Barry: Vs. 21 shows us how willing he is to forgive. That's so good!

Me: Oh man! Scrumptious words. I love feeding on this!

Barry: Man! I can't get enough. His words r health to my bones. I never thought this life could be so good; it's exciting; always expecting something good is about to happen.

We continued this exchange a bit longer before he told me he needed to go mow the lawn. So I decided not to take the discussion any further that day. He wasn't quite ready.

Around 8:30 that evening, he sent me a message saying he was going to bed. He was having severe chest pain and difficulty breathing. He said, "It feels like it did when I had pneumonia. It hurts to breathe." Sensing his fear and empathizing with that, as well as his pain, I prayed for physical comfort, for mercy, and for peace.

*****

I checked on him the following morning. He had slept well but was still in tremendous pain. He had talked to a nurse who told him to go to the ER. At the time I spoke with him, he hadn't even told Mom he was hurting or of his pain the night before.

Bless her heart. So much was happening so fast, and he was trying his best to shield her from it as much as possible. She *is* a *worrier!* She's also a *fixer!* From my own mother's heart, I can only imagine the magnitude of "motherly smothering" that must have been going on inside that house over the past few days.

By 11:00 a.m., he sent me a message saying he was headed to the ER and promised to keep me posted. Mom was taking him, but it must have been with much reluctance that he asked her to do it. He wrote "She stresses me out!"

I heard nothing more directly from him until the following morning around 10:00 a.m. (September 5), although I had stayed in touch with Mom the whole time. He sent a message asking me to call him.

He explained how he had entered the ER, still holding the unexplained, unconfirmed radiology report he had been given a few days earlier. This day was Wednesday, and his appointment with the pulmonary doctor wasn't until Thursday. I believe he instinctively knew that pneumonia wasn't the problem, although he had convinced Mom that it was. Perhaps he was in search of answers to all the questions he had from the radiology report, more than seeking relief from his pain. He was no stranger to pain.

Medical professionals ran more tests and did more X-rays before the attending physician ultimately confirmed "no pneumonia." Rather, he told Barry, "The tumor (as if he believed Barry knew what tumor he was referring to) is pressing against your lungs and causing the pain you're experiencing. We will give you some medication to help relieve that. What else can we do for you? We will do whatever you ask and will try to help you every way we can."

Although no official diagnosis had yet been given, the doctor had unknowingly affirmed our deepest fears, and in that moment, he seemed to be extending an offering to provide whatever medical remedies that were available and within his power and authority to give. The unspoken words between the lines seemed to say, "We will do our best to relieve your pain. That's all we can do."

*****

Later in the afternoon on September 5, I received this message: "Hey, Sis. Feeling lot better. Love U."

"Wonderful!" I responded. "That makes me happy on my birthday."

That day was indeed my fifty-fifth birthday. It did make me happy that he had relief from the pain; but over the next few minutes, I regretted saying anything about my birthday to him. He kept sending me messages about how sorry he was that he had forgotten. He said he hadn't been able to remember anything for the past few days.

I assured him that he should let this small thing go; I wasn't upset, and certainly, with all he was going through, the last thing I would have expected him to remember was my birthday.

Thursday, September 6, 2018

I was anxious to get some news about the day, the diagnosis, and Barry's state of mind. I sent my first message to him at 9:07 a.m., "What time is your appointment?"

At 9:46 a.m., he replied, "Well, just got out, and at least I know a little more than I did. When u can talk, call me."

I immediately picked up the phone and called him. The doctor had explained to him that there was a mass in his chest, but until they did a biopsy and ran more tests, they wouldn't know precisely what the tumor was or how best to treat it. He confirmed that the mass was attached to his spine and was growing around his heart and lungs. A biopsy was scheduled for the following Monday, and they would also do another CT scan on Wednesday to see if the tumor was confined to the chest area or whether there was more cancer in other parts of his body. He told me he would fax a copy of the X-ray so I could see everything he was seeing.

The e-mail message with the fax attachment came through, and I opened it. Tears filled my eyes, and a lump rose in my throat. "Dear God, please *help!*"

The x-ray confirmed the truth of the fabricated image drawn in our minds after reading the radiology report. It appeared that the mass covered the majority of his chest cavity. How his heart pumped blood and his lungs filled with air was more than I could fathom as I sat there staring at the page. Every inch of space around his heart and lungs looked as if it was filled with the malignant mass. Mustering all the courage I could in that moment, and striving with all my might to remain positive, I wrote "I got it. I can see everything pretty good. I'm going to ask our doctor to look and see what he thinks."

Our resident doctor, Dr. D, would be able to help me understand. I knew that he had walked alongside several people as they battled various forms of cancer over the years. I also knew that several of these instances were terminal. Without giving him any background as to the patient's identity, I attached the X-ray to an e-mail and asked him if he would mind reviewing and let me know his thoughts. Moments later, he called me.

In his best doctor voice, he began to describe what he believed to be lung cancer. He, of course, noted that a biopsy would be necessary to fully determine the type of cancer it was and the prognosis. He asked, "Whose is this?"

Swallowing the lump in my throat, I told him about my brother. Then I shared with him the corresponding radiology report. He gave me some potential diagnoses and treatment options but stopped short of diagnosing anything himself. He didn't have to. I already knew it was bad. There was no way what I was seeing couldn't be bad!

Barry focused on what he knew in this moment—that God loved him dearly, and he alone controls the number of our days. At one point, he asked me, "Do you think I should tell the girls?"

I encouraged him to do just that. I also quizzed him about who else knew of his condition. He seemed to be keeping the news as private as possible. It really wasn't my place to share it unless he asked me to. As difficult as it was for him to accept, he was having a difficult time trying to determine the best way to tell anyone at all. I encouraged him to share it with the rest of our immediate family soon.

He seemed very reluctant to do that, replying to my prompting, "I don't know about that." I followed up by asking him to think about it and to imagine himself in their shoes.

He told me he believed they would understand. "Right now anyway," he pointed out. Then he added, "No need to talk about something that won't be there in a few days anyway."

From this statement, I knew that he wanted to take a firm stand of faith for supernatural healing of this cancer. This worried me a little. I know that God is certainly able to heal any disease. But the message was also in the back of my mind—a message I had not yet shared with anyone either. It was my firm belief that my brother's physical healing would not occur this side of heaven.

I had already given Dad a heads up, although I had told no one about doing so. I couldn't bear to think of how hurt he would be if this went on for weeks and no one made him aware. I told him because I knew how I would feel under the same set of circumstances if someone kept such a thing from me. I asked him to please keep it to himself until Barry felt comfortable talking to him. He was obviously concerned and very sad. I could hear the pain in his voice as I shared with him what I knew. He agreed to my request. The stress and strain of Barry's forty-year battle with drugs had taken its toll on their father-son relationship, which had become even more strained over the past few years as Dad took steps to try and assist him financially.

As in the past, Dad's most recent efforts to help him were more of an exercise in futility than anything else. Barry's inability to manage money or his life in general was painful to watch. Dad's efforts ended in a loss of more funds but with no lasting effect on Barry's financial stability or future. This left their relationship further scarred, creating more distance between them.

Barry's relationship with my brother and sister was also strained as his with me has been from time to time. It seemed that his relationship with his children and his ex-wives had long ago been broken beyond repair. It breaks my heart to think now of all the wasted years, broken relationships, unthinkable wounds, and incredible pain and hardships he and our entire family have endured as we've walked through one crazy nightmare after another. And, now, here we were, facing another battle. *Likely the last one*, I thought in that moment.

Over the years, I had envisioned Barry dying in many tragic and sinister ways. I've imagined intentional and unintentional overdoses; drug deals gone terribly wrong; drug-induced car accidents; or a successful suicide attempt. All these had been highly probably based upon his activities. Each of these events had occurred *multiple times* yet without ending in his fatality. Cancer was perhaps the most remote of all the possibilities in my mind. *Oh, but how I had hoped and prayed regardless of what event took his life, he wouldn't leave this earth and meet God unprepared.*

Recalling once again *the message*, I was reassured of God's promise to me. I was convinced that Barry was now spiritually prepared for death if this was really the time. I was unsure, however, about his (and the rest of the family's) mental preparedness to walk through the most difficult season of life—physical death. Nevertheless, I resolved in my own heart to face whatever came and promised to be with him through it all, regardless of the final diagnosis or any treatment that might be needed. I thanked him for trusting me to walk with him through this challenge. I was determined to be his constant positive encourager.

*****

His mind reeled over the next several days. His communications with me were sparse, but as they came, I could tell that he was inwardly reflecting. I can only imagine the thoughts that must have filled his mind. One day, he sent me this message: "Do U remember in the 6, 7, 8 or 9th grade tryin' so hard to live right, but scared to tell others that U were a Christian. But, U really wanted to, and when U did, people made fun and U would get into arguments with them? And, if you did any little thing wrong, U had to make it right?"

"Yep!" I replied. "Those were tough years. I think it was worse for us because we were PKs." I smiled.

"Ha!" he said. "But God has been showing me awesome things about those years, and later not so good about how and why I made the choices I made."

"That's awesome! A lot of those people have actually turned around too." I told him how I had recently reconnected with one of our old classmates who had shared with me that some of the guys he knew and ran with as a teenager had made a complete turnaround in recent years.

He noted further, "I see how God was really happy with me as a young kid. I just always thought he was mad. Insecurity brought a fear and loneliness, and then many other false emotions, not feeling that I could be loved by the other sex."

I reminded him of what he had already discovered. "Yes, the devil was the liar in that equation."

*****

It's so true. The *enemy* of our souls works endlessly, relentlessly day and night to steal our peace, our hope, our joy, and our very lives. If he can make us believe that we're unlovable, worthless, and unredeemable, then he's had a good day. But the *lover* of our souls says to you and me, "I love you! I've loved you from the beginning. I loved you so much that I gave My only Son for you; to be the perfect sacrifice for your unrighteousness; to fill up the gap where you are not enough; to rescue you; to redeem you; to make you My own child!"

Jesus Christ longs to show you how dearly loved you really are in his eyes. Unfortunately for some, it takes getting all the way to the end of life before they look up and realize that Jesus sees them as worth saving. Still more concerning is the soul that looks around and believes he has *his stuff together*, is self-sufficient, and not in need of anything, especially a savior. It is this one who, blinded so much by the world and all it has to offer, rarely comes to know Christ's love because his life and hope is in temporal things.

For Barry, it was the case of getting to the very end of his rope—and unfortunately, his life—before fully realizing the power and love of the Savior. He bought into the devil's lies that he was unworthy, unlovable, and unredeemable, and it cost him everything in this world. It almost cost him his soul as well. But the great news is this: at the end of a frayed rope suspended over the darkest pit of death and hopelessness stands one who says, "It's not too late for you!" This place doesn't have to be your end! Where there is life and breath, there is *hope!* For the one who looks up, cries out, and sees the hand reaching out to them, a welcome smile greets them with these words: "Come to Me, and I will give you perfect rest."

I'm convinced that if Barry were right here, right now, this is precisely the plea he would make to you. Since he isn't, I'm pleading with you, don't give up! And I make this plea fully convinced of the hope of endless life that fills every inch of my soul. My own story, while I took a much different road than my brother, is not so unlike his in many ways. I, too, have believed in times past that I was unworthy, unlovable, and unredeemable. I dare say that most of us experience these feelings from time to time. And we *all* need a Savior. We *all* need hope. The great news is that both are available to us if we only ask, believing.

FULFILLING HIS PURPOSE: NOT IN VAIN

Barry: Hey, I was asked to give my testimony to 25 recovering drug addicts tomorrow at a luncheon. It kinda' scared me; then, I thought about it. What a great way to honor God now. It brings me joy. Pray that I have wisdom to know what to say.

Me: Ok. It will be given to you in that hour. Just be like Paul and tell your story of life change.

Barry: If my words can help one lost soul, my life will not be lived in vain.

Me: It's going to be a good day! Thinking of you and praying for you today.

Barry: Already is.

Later that evening, he simply told me that his luncheon speaking event was *awesome!*

His message popped in: Thanks for the faith words and resources. You're such a blessing and friend. God always knows our needs and concerns, and puts people in our path just at the right time, full of mercy and forgiveness. I got things to tell u later on. We'll talk tonight.

Me: Sounds good.

7:41 p.m.

Barry: Call when you get a min.

I picked up the phone and dialed his number. He was so excited as he shared with me how amazing his day was on Sunday and the things he was able to share with the people he spoke to. He said, "They listened, and I believe I helped some of them!"

He spoke to them of how he had walked through life's tough experiences like drug addiction. He told them how he had found freedom. He believed this had allowed him to tell his story in a way that others knew that he understood their pain, and so they listened.

Personal experiences are powerful. Sharing them with others who have had similar experiences can impact them in ways that no one else's story ever could. A person who has never experienced drug addiction can't ever fully empathize with the addict's pain, feelings of inadequacy, or internal sense of rejection by society. It's proof that God can use our brokenness and the broken roads we have traveled in ways we never imagined. Regardless of the road we may have taken in life, the road isn't so broken that we can't use our stories to help others find the path to freedom and redemption. Never be ashamed to tell your freedom story!

MENDING

At 11:26 a.m., he let me know what was happening at his doctor appointment and how he was embracing his faith. "They're putting the medicine in me. Now I wait an hour to let it go through my body so they can scan my body. It's called a PET scan. Google PET scan, and it will probably tell about it. So now it's on, and 'no weapon formed against me shall prosper. Amen!'"

"Amen," I acknowledged back to him. "Praying! Love you!"

4:18 p.m.

Me: Everything go okay? Never mind… I know it did!
Barry: I'll know in a couple days; but, it's ok!

*****

I left for Tennessee the following morning. My son's wedding was in three days, and I had a ton of things to do once I arrived. So many thoughts filled my mind, and my *to-do* list contained more than what one person could adequately accomplish in a week, much less in three days. My heart was full to the brim and overflowing with mixed emotions.

We had rented two cabins large enough to accommodate the dozen or so family members who would be arriving over the next two days. Once I arrived, I had to stock the cabins with food then help Jared and Katie finish preparing the wedding venue. I also had to finish the groom's cake, which I promised Jared I would make.

Thankfully, caterers were prearranged to provide the wedding meal, and Katie assured me that the venue was mostly preset and needed little or no added decorations. But I needed to see it for myself and take note of any last-minute necessities.

As we drove the five and a half hours to Davy Crockett State Park, my mind drifted to other things that the next three days would likely entail. Barry planned to share everything about his condition with our immediate and extended family while everyone was together in one place. His message to me read, "I will talk with everyone and try and make my amends with them. That's what I feel led to do."

I knew what he meant. He wanted to repair some seriously broken relationships, particularly with my dad and our younger brother. So much troubled water had gone under the bridge between them. And time was running out. He wanted most of all to share with Dad the revelation he had about how and why he had taken the broken road.

For such a long time, Barry had placed blame on so many people, including our dad and many others, for his poor choices. But God had revealed to him the truth about his choices in a way that no one else had been able to help him understand, though many had tried for years. He wanted, once and for all, to make things right and to mend these shattered relationships. Only God's glue can bring such pieces together into a brand-new beautiful masterpiece. I hoped and prayed that all would go well, and that he would be able to finally repair this breach.

Friday, September 14, 2018, 7:27 a.m.

I sent Barry this message of encouragement from the Psalms. I knew that he and Mom were either on the road or they would soon be.

Me: 'My flesh and my heart may fail, but God is the strength of my heart and my portion forever.' Psalm 73:26. Here's wishing you a good trip. Love you!

Barry: Yes, and pray that I get the wisdom I need to obey God.

Me: I will! No worries. He's got you!

Barry: I got the results.

My breath caught in my throat.

Me: What did he say?

Barry: Mostly good.

I accepted the positive note with a sigh of relief.

Me: Did he find another tumor?

Barry: Hadn't spread. All other organs look good.

Me: Good. So will he biopsy that one next week through your chest?

Barry: Yes. Wednesday. I'll explain when we get there.

The next several hours are pretty much a blur in my mind as I write this now. Family members began to arrive. I did my best to focus and finish the groom's cake, quickly regretting having agreed to take on this task of making my son his favorite carrot cake with cream cheese icing. From scratch, no less. I did make this promise, though, and I was determined to keep it. Even if it killed me. It was an incredibly hot September day! I was convinced that the cream cheese icing would surely melt and the cake would fall apart.

We had planned a cookout for the evening everyone arrived at the cabins. Again, a poor decision on my part. In hindsight, we should have just planned to meet everyone for dinner at the park restaurant. I took on too much of the responsibility for making this a perfect weekend.

Oh, *hindsight*. How clear is the vision.

Evening came, and dinner preparations began. We grilled burgers and hotdogs. All my family was there, except for Mom and Barry, who had made prior plans to meet my mom's sisters and brother at a nearby restaurant. They soon joined us, however, and brought along my aunts and uncle too.

Working hard to stay focused on the positive and enjoy the time with my family, I prayed that God would unite this diverse group in a way that only he could do. I longed for the fulfillment of his promise to bring my family together as one cohesive unit. That's how it's supposed to be.

Soon I saw Barry alone with Dad. I knew that Barry had anticipated this moment for several days and had rehearsed all that was in his heart to say to Dad. They talked quietly, and I saw smiles and hugs. Sensing all was well, I breathed a sigh of relief! I watched him interact with everyone as the evening went on. He wore a genuine smile that I sensed was coming from a heart full of unshakable faith, peace, and assurance. One more thing *accomplished!*

We all talked and laughed until late in the evening like we hadn't done in years. It was a perfect time—well, *almost perfect.* The gnawing *knowing* building up inside my soul over his diagnosis cast a shadow over my heart, which was otherwise full of joy.

MOVING FORWARD

I rose early on Saturday morning. It was the wedding day! The cake wasn't quite finished, and so many more things were still left for me to do. A last-minute request last night meant that I also had to pick up the bride's cake and transport it along with the groom's cake to the wedding venue. Jared and Katie had chosen a wedding barn about a half hour away in a small community near where he grew up. The rising temperature and humidity in the air promised a sweltering day. *Will this cake ever hold together in this heat?* I wondered. I had serious doubts.

"Oh, well…either it will or it won't. But it is what it is!" I told myself, trying not to fret. Regardless of any cake or no cake at all, at the end of this day, my youngest son would have a new bride. He would begin a brand-new chapter in his life. All that's required of any of us is to put one foot in front of the other and keep moving forward.

Moving forward seemed to be the general theme that was developing all around us. That's precisely what time does. It marches forward, *tick-tock*, *speeding by*. There's no stopping it. It seemed as though the clock's hands were whirling past me, outrunning my desperate attempts to keep up. I felt the panic of the pace. On this day, everything inside of me screamed, "Slow down! Stop! I want to get off this runaway train for just a little while!"

*****

In Barry's journaling, he wrote:

> Sat. 15th, 2018. It's a good morning.
> Drinking coffee, watching deer on the deck. Went
> on a walk with Steve Wilson. We went down to the
> lake. Walked back. Got some good exercise… I'm
> feeling good this morning. Meditating. Praying
> and asking my Father to help me do what's right
> for everyone. I'm seeing my hometown that I once
> loved being destroyed by drugs. It's not the same.
> It's really devastating. I found out who killed ?
> I'm so grateful my Father Jehovah saved me and
> opened my eyes. I love Jesus so much. The Father
> and the Holy Spirit.

Being back on his old turf, particularly at this point in his life, must have aroused some old feelings, old memories, past guilt, and shame. So much of his teenage and young adult life remains a mystery to me and my family. He lived in a world quite foreign to the rest of our family in this very town during his teenage and young adult years.

The question mark he left in his journal puzzles me even now. I have no clue who was killed or who did the killing. He never revealed the information he received about the matter. I sense in his writing, though, the regret and remorse of this and other past experiences. I sense the anguish, as well, of seeing his hometown devastated by the very thing that enslaved him for most of his life. Drugs and addiction stole his best years, and he mourned, seeing how it continued its devastating advances across the lives of others he knew. At the same time, I'm refreshed and comforted by the sense of peace and joy I read in his words. He had broken free—free from his past; free from the guilt; free from the addiction and the pain; free at last.

*****

Four o'clock arrived much too quickly. Friends and family gathered to celebrate this day with us. It was good, even though not everything was perfect. Weddings bring out the best (and sometimes the worst) in people. I love looking back to laugh at some of the most imperfect moments and remember. These memories of imperfections are the best ones of all!

The wedding vows were spoken. Photos were snapped to memorialize each moment. Food was consumed, even the melting groom's cake, which they tell me was *so delicious* (I didn't even get a bite). Each step of each dance was taken, and then they were gone—gone to begin their own lives together.

This day flew by too quickly, like the brevity of life. *Time, please slow down!*

*****

Regardless of the endless details and meticulous plans we make, an end to each thing will come. Time moves swiftly forward, bringing an end to our best days and years much quicker than we want. Time rarely, if ever, brings the end without significant things left undone and important words left unspoken. We speed through the days of our lives, packing as much as we possibly can into each one, hoping that at the end of it all, we've accomplished something worthwhile and made a difference in at least a few lives along the way. Yet, no matter how carefully we plan or how many of our plans don't come together quite like we might hope, still the end will come.

June 2019

As I sit, propped up in bed in my mother's guest room on a Thursday evening, typing these words *when I should be sleeping*, I'm reminded once again how quickly time passes. It's late June 2019, nearly seven months since Barry passed over. This crazy week began for me on Sunday when I left home to drive nearly six hours to my mom's. I picked her up, and we drove another six hours south to visit her brother who was fighting his own battle with cancer. Seventy-six years passes much too quickly as I'm sure his wife and children would attest to. It was difficult hearing the diagnosis yesterday as I stood next to my aunt when the oncologist repeated to her the details of the CT scan and the grim diagnosis.

It makes no difference how well-prepared you *think* you are. Nothing prepares you to hear a doctor say these words: "The drugs failed. The cancer is back and growing quickly. There's no cure. Do you understand what I'm saying? We will do everything we can to manage the pain and keep him comfortable, but please understand that's all we can do at this point." The earnestness in the doctor's eyes and voice when she said, "Do you understand what I'm saying?" was unmistakable to me. I'm not sure that my aunt really grasped it in that moment. I really doubt it.

Hearing these words again so soon after having heard them in September 2018 ripped my heart open all over again. The recent memories came flooding back with a vengeance. It took every ounce of strength I could muster up to hold back the tears and maintain my composure.

They had so many plans, my aunt and uncle—plans that will never be fulfilled. As the scriptures say, "Man makes his plans, but the Lord numbers his days." Our plans may be incomplete in this life, but these plans and dreams don't have to define us or the purpose of our existence. The good news is that not all is lost if you know the Savior.

As I sat there, listening to Uncle David declare the praises of his Lord and Savior, despite the tremendous pain that filled his body, I was reminded once again of the hope that we have in Christ. I was also reminded of the words and the praises on my brother's lips in his darkest hour. Uncle David told the people in his room yesterday, "I know where I'm going! I know where my Daddy and my Mama are! I know where my nephew is! Thank you, Jesus! Everyone please wake up and be ready! Tell everyone you know that Jesus loves them too!"

The peace in his heart and the joy he felt in that moment was unmistakable. Only a true child of God can say these things with such conviction at a moment like this. The smile on his face said it all! His faith spilled out into that hospital room without shame or hesitation, like a mountain spring pours out its cold, clear, refreshing water on a hot day in summer.

Sunday morning! On Sunday morning, I rose early as I usually do. While everyone else slept, I quietly walked out onto the balcony of our cabin to grind my coffee beans. There's nothing like fresh coffee beans ground to perfection to brew the perfect pot of coffee. What a beautiful day to begin this brand-new week! The air was crisp and fresh so early in the morning. It ignited in me a fresh hope of better things to come.

With my coffee in hand, I stepped out onto the balcony. I just wanted to drink it quietly and meditate on yesterday, ponder the events of today, and think about what lies ahead of us. I found Barry doing the same on the cabin porch next door. Exchanging "good mornings," we decided to take a walk in the park.

This was the first time I'd had a chance to walk and talk with him alone. He had recited to me bits and pieces of things on his heart over the phone, but I hadn't yet had a chance to discern for myself the look in his eyes as he spoke. This, for me, would be the tell-tale sign as to the truth of the change he professed.

Over the years, I'd been able to detect pretty quickly whether the change he touted would last a day or two or whether he might endure for a month or more. Most often, I found his newly professed changes to be temporary. The look in his eyes and the words he used to describe the purpose and plan were usually enough to help me make a pretty good assessment. Too often, his professed "change in heart" was more of a momentary "change of mind," which lasted until the next wave of disappointment came or until he had achieved some selfish purpose. I had often seen this temporary change of mind when he was in trouble with the law, in financial desperation, home-less, or lonely because his children weren't around. He longed for and sought for peace, for something to satisfy the longing in his soul. But these things didn't exist in the places he looked for them. His mind went there, but his heart did not follow.

"Is this going to be another one of those times?" I asked myself. God himself only knows the pain of a heart that's been crushed too many times to count. He only knows the scars and pain left behind. The doubts that accompany them, the fear of when will be the last time. The greatest pain of all, I believe, is in knowing your loved one really does want to be better, but the self-control and discipline it takes to get there continues to escape them. I've experienced the pain, too, of seeing the final straw loaded onto a fragile heart—the one last straw that tips the scale to the point that it can no longer bear the burden. It breaks. It crushes beneath the weight of it. It gives up all hope and walks away.

Many who loved him gave up hope long ago that Barry would ever change. Only a small ember of hope still burned within my own heart. My hope was that *this time,* the fire of change inside his soul was real. A change truly ignited by the Spirit of the Lord and a genuine transformation of his heart—not from the outside in but from the inside out.

*****

We walked for an hour or more, stopping at times to snap a photo or just to look at one another eyeball-to-eyeball with intense heartfelt emotion about the greatness of God's grace. As we walked, he shared in great detail the moment when he knew he had reached the end of his rope with the drug use and abuse.

There came a day when the verbal clashes between him and my mom reached a level so intense that he feared for what might happen next. I never want to believe that he would have hurt her physically, but I sensed in his tone that he knew that was a real possibility if something didn't change—and soon. He had reached a point where he knew he had to have help or a greater tragedy was imminent.

I wondered about what was different in that moment. What was it that hadn't occurred before but was present then? I can't say for certain, but I believe it was a sense that he had no escape. He had nowhere else to go. He was trapped by the addiction. He didn't have the physical strength to work nor the financial means for self-sufficiency. He had exhausted all his friends and all his resources. My mom and her house were his only means of survival.

She, too, had reached a point of desperation about the same time as his. She had told me how she cried out to God one day, "God, take me or take him! I can't live like this anymore! Do something!"

She demanded of him a respect to which his drug abuse wouldn't yield. They were at an impasse. Something had to give, and he knew it.

As he continued to tell me his story, I recognized in his tone, the look in his eyes, and the very words he used a true sign that a genuine change of heart had occurred. He had sought out help on his own. No judge demanded it for his freedom. No family member required it in exchange for room and board. He had reached a point within himself where he made a personal decision that the drugs had to go. He finally recognized that the very thing he had used for years to dull his pain and mask the unsatisfied longing in his heart meant certain death for him. And perhaps for her.

He shared how he met with his counselor week after week to talk through whatever was on his mind on any given day. Layer by layer, they scraped away at the callousness encrusting his heart. Past hurts had created gaping wounds. The wounds healed over time, but they left scars upon scars. With each failure, his heart had hardened. Bitterness and resentment filled the space that God had originally designed to be filled with love and affection and belonging.

A turning point was triggered on the day the counselor pointed out the fact that his problem was not the fault of his past hurts and failures. Rather, it was spiritual and nothing more. He recalled how very angry he was at hearing this for the first time from his counselor. He had certainly heard this assessment before, but it was from the pulpit or from the people closest to him. Too often, we refuse to hear the truth from those closest to us. It was certainly the case with Barry.

So why now? Why did he receive the truth from a total stranger? I believe the counselor had built a "trust relationship" over a period of weeks that was strong enough to enable her to speak truth to him in love. Not in judgment but in unbiased perception and genuine acceptance. For that reason, he didn't walk away.

She was a person on the outside looking in. Objective. A person who had no insight into his past or deepest thoughts, except to the extent that he shared them. She had no reason to reject him. She was not afflicted or influenced by his painful past. She could call a spade a spade without judging how it became that.

He knew that he could simply walk away if he chose to without angry words or repercussions from this person. At other times, he *had* walked away, even run hard in the opposite direction when others said the exact same words to him. Was it the tone? Was it the knowing? The knowing eyes piercing deep into his soul in a way that rejected the notion? Perhaps he knew of their own sins, their own failures. At those times, however, he was running from those who knew him best, from those who loved him most. He knew nothing of this counselor's past issues or failures. He was merely free to receive the truth, to take it or to leave it.

The mind, the heart, the emotions are strange *and complex.*

This is one of the photographs from our walk in the park on that September Sunday morning. It hangs on my living room wall to remind me of his surrender. Here he stands with his arms held high and his face lifted to the heavens in praise to God. His eyes seem to peer right through the clouds above him and lock onto the eyes of his Savior. It was a spontaneous moment perfectly captured in this timeless photo. It's a daily reminder for me of the genuine expression of his changed heart and his gratitude to God for grace—*perfect, everlasting, unimaginable grace* that never let him go! It never lets me go! How eternally grateful I am for that day and for several that followed.

In his journaling from that same September morning, I found these words written:

> When I remember what my Father has done for me, I lift my hand in praise to him, for he is worthy of all our praise. He's a Good Father. An Awesome GOD. He's my friend. Jesus is my brother.
>
> I pray that all my kinfolks will see what God has shown me. God's not MAD. He loves all [of] us so much. If all people could see just how much their Father in heaven loved them, they would want to know more and more. He is Awesome. Read the word. It is truth.

He prayed, "Father, I pray you will reveal yourself to my family. May they not be deceived. Life is not worth living without God as our hope and life."

He continued:

> Heaven is real.
> So is hell.
> God is trying to tell you he loves you. Hear him.
> Please hear him.
> Destini, please listen. God is real.
> Jazzy, he's real. Please listen to me.

Get in church. Read your Bible.
He's coming back soon. Listen to me.
Everyone knows the life I lived. How could I
have changed so much?
Listen. Only by God. Only by Jesus.
Listen. Jesus died so I could live.
Please listen, everyone. Ask Jesus to come into
your heart and live and give you purpose. He will.

As soon as we arrived back at the cabins, others were up and making preparations for their trips home. Final check out time was 11:00 a.m., so we all had to get moving. We gathered for one last meal together at the park restaurant before parting ways. It had been many years since I last ate there, but it was the same as I remembered it—a delicious Southern buffet breakfast simply cannot be beat. We laughed. We talked. We loved being together, just as a family should on that day. It was good! It felt right! It felt like we had all come home again.

*****

David and I made it back to Jackson by sundown, completely exhausted from the trip and the events of the past week. We unpacked, changed into our PJs, and sat on the sofa for a little while, just loving on our pups. They're always so excited to see us when we come home. It doesn't matter if we've been gone ten minutes or ten days—their greeting is as though they've not seen us in weeks. Barry fell in love with Samson (our Morkie) when he lived with us in 2012. He gave him a nickname, "Side," because Samson gets so excited when he hears the word *outside*. So the nickname Side stuck with him.

I sent Barry a quick photo of Samson sitting totally relaxed on my lap that night.

His response: "That's the one of love. He's my Side!"

Later that evening, he sent this text: "Thanks for the time you made possible for all of us. It was truly a blessing. I'll never forget the good memory you made for everyone. You're really special. Thanks."

My own heart was full of gratitude for this special time I was able to spend with my family, particularly under the present circumstances. I knew it would likely be the last time that all of us would be together as a family. I thanked the good Lord for making this event possible for us.

The wedding was one we worried would not last, and as I sit writing this, I can confirm that it didn't. Regardless of this fact, I'm forever amazed at how the Lord orchestrates our lives so beautifully, even when everything seems to be going so wrong. The Bible says, "And we know that God causes all things to work together for good to those who love God, to those who are called according to His purpose" (Romans 8:28).

So I'm convinced that even though my son's marriage was short-lived, the time we all spent together over this weekend was not all for naught. Something good came from it, and for that, I'll be eternally grateful.

David and I crawled into bed, knowing we had to *repack* for my business trip the following morning. That meant another three-and-a-half-hour drive in less than a twenty-four-hour period. I closed my eyes, willing myself not to think about it. I knew that if I did, I would cry. So I emptied my mind and fell asleep.

Monday, September 17, 2018

While I attended my daily meetings, David slept. He slept, awoke, ate, and slept some more. Sleeping is one of his favorite past times, but after the week we had had, he definitely needed sleep. And I needed him to sleep. A safe trip home in two more days would require an alert and focused driver. I knew that certainly *would not* be me.

Barry's biopsy was scheduled for Wednesday morning, so thoughts of him filled my mind constantly. I was unable to find any peace of mind. It was as though a cloud of gloom followed me everywhere I went. As I sat through the hours of meetings, I recall thinking how futile and unimportant the topics were. Everything is relative. The importance of things in our lives tend to shift in relation to our experiences. I considered the things I saw and heard that day against the backdrop of my brother's life clock, and I wondered, *What am I doing here?*

Have you ever found yourself in a place like that, where you knew that you should be somewhere else, but the expectations of others seemed to pilot your coming and your going?

How often do any of us really take time to consider how much time we waste on the *unimportant* while the truly important things are pushed aside for a more convenient opportunity? Most of us tend to believe that *somehow, somewhere, someway, someday,* we will find the time to give those most important things and people the attention they need and deserve. I recall seeing those words written on a greeting card many years ago—*somehow, somewhere, someway, someday.* They seem to promise us something, a future just beyond our reach. But it's like groping to catch the wind.

How often do we ponder the fleeting hours and days of our own life clocks? Not a single one of us knows the amount of time left on our own clocks. If we did, I'm certain we would spend every moment much differently.

Barry was a little concerned about the upcoming biopsy. His Monday message read "I'm wondering how much danger is involved in that 6-inch needle being shot between the two aorta vessels?" He referred to the doctor as he added "He sounded worried when he talked to me before the PET scan."

I encouraged him: "Everything will be just fine. Rest assured that it will be. I'll pray that the Lord will guide that needle to just the right place."

Wednesday, September 19, 2018

I woke up early with a prayer on my lips. It was as if I'd been praying unconsciously then awoke in the middle of that prayer.

I don't recall exactly when I first noticed it, but this awakening in the middle of a prayer began for me several years ago. It happened once, and then again. As time went on, I noticed that it was happening much more often than not. It was a peaceful sense, and I was grateful for the shift from anxiousness to peace. For years prior to this, I often awoke exhausted from the anxious thoughts that filled my mind and my dreams overnight. My jaws ached from clenching my teeth during sleep. How pleasant and refreshing it is now to awake with a prayer and a praise instead. Just knowing that I don't have to face the challenges of my day in my own strength is revitalizing.

The Lord has promised that he is always with me and that he won't ever leave me alone. Do I forget sometimes or fall back into a slump where fear tries to take over my senses? Of course. But, when this happens, I know that all I have to do is stop and pray, and a sense of peace returns. I draw my strength from him when I'm weak in body or in spirit. He supplies the wisdom I need for every question, every challenge. I don't always know the answer to each problem or question ahead of time, but when an answer is required, I have found that it comes at just the right time.

The secret, I have learned, is to lay everything that burdens my soul at the feet of Jesus in prayer. I lay it down by praying and asking the Lord for his help. Sometimes I just need help knowing *how* or *what* to pray. Too often, we flippantly say things like "I'm praying for you" or "Prayers for you." But do we really mean what we are saying? I really doubt it. The evidence of the truth of these words can be seen in the way we live them out. When we say them, do we actually pause and ask God to meet the needs of a friend or even our own need?

I must admit that there are times when I take a burden to the Lord in prayer but, immediately after the *amen,* pick that burden right back up and carry it along with me to the next room, the next meeting, or the next day. The anxiousness doesn't leave me. The heavy feeling in my chest weighs me down even more. I rob myself of God's promise of peace when I'm determined to carry my problems myself. I'm sure there have been times, too, when I've told someone, "I'll pray for you,"—*and I actually intended to do that*—but once I walked away from them, other thoughts or needs filled my day, and I simply forgot. Now when I tell someone, "I'm praying for you," I pause right there in that moment and do it, lest I forget.

My habit is to begin each morning in a quiet place with my Bible, a journal, and a pen to record the thoughts that come to mind as I read the Scriptures. I'm revitalized as I draw near to the heart of God in prayer and as I meditate on the truth of his promises. It's like searching for and finding nuggets of gold buried in the pages of this Holy Book, nuggets that can't be found anywhere else. The treasure is not found merely in reading the words. Rather, it's found when we allow those words to seep deeply into our hearts and to change our entire perspective about life and the future. The promises found in the Scriptures are bursting with meaning and personal application. The warnings and the promises transcend time and space. They are applicable to every human who has ever lived and even those yet to be born. The Word is powerful, transforming.

*****

This particular Wednesday began no differently than any other day. I got up extra early and spent my quiet time in prayer and Bible reading. I searched the scriptures for nuggets of encouragement and promises I could hold onto. Time seems to fly with lightning speed in the mornings. Before I know it, I've been sitting for an hour or more and have to rush to get dressed for work.

I checked on Barry before walking over for my final day of meetings. I sent him this message, which was based on my morning meditation: "So He said, '*Go forth and stand on the mountain before the Lord.*' And behold, the Lord was passing by. And a great and strong wind was rending the mountains and breaking in pieces the rocks before the Lord; but the Lord was not in the wind. And after the wind an earthquake, but the Lord was not in the earthquake. After the earthquake a fire, but the Lord was not in the fire; and *after the fire a sound of a gentle blowing.* When Elijah heard it, he wrapped his face in his mantle and went out and stood in the entrance to the cave. And behold, a voice came to him and said, '*What are you doing here, Elijah?*'"

This scripture reminded me that we hear the Lord speak to us more clearly when we are quiet and still without distractions of any kind. My experience has been that when my life is filled with noise—whether physical noise or just the noise of too many competing thoughts—I can't sense God's presence or hear what it is that he wants me to know. He rarely reveals himself noisily, but he does so quietly. *Still moments.* In these moments, I can hear him speaking to *my heart* and *not my ears.*

This scripture also reminded me that even in the middle of the storm we were facing with Barry now, the Lord saw us. He knew where we are hiding. He knew every anxious thought we had, every fear that interrupted our peace, the demons that stole our sleep. Nothing was hidden from him. He cared about us, so he whispered, "Hey! What are you doing in here? You're not alone, child. I'm right here with you always."

On this Wednesday morning, I wanted Barry to know that he wasn't alone in this storm.

Me: 1 Kings 19:11–13. Nothing has the potential to change your life like the whisper of God. Nothing will determine your destiny more than your ability to listen for and hear the sound of His still, small voice. It's close. It's intimate. He loves you like crazy! You're in my thoughts and prayers, especially today… He gives you strength!

Barry: I heard that voice last night while walking. It was so good. It was like I was dipped in a river of peace and love. It was so real!

He went on to remind me that this particular day (Wednesday, September 19, 2019) was the most holy day of the year according to the Jewish calendar. It was Yom Kippur. He wrote "It's a shadow of things to come. Like the Passover was a shadow of Jesus being our Passover Lamb, Yom Kippur is a shadow of the second coming. I'm learning more. It's so awesome!"

*****

My mind wandered as I sat listening to others in the room. They talked about all the things that we had come there to discuss, things that were relevant for business, for success in business. But the more I tried to listen, the more I realized that these ideas and plans had only temporary significance. They promised to bring about only temporary success. In fact, if I were to assess the importance of them on the grand scale of life and eternity, they were meaningless. There was no eternal significance whatsoever!

Why was I here?

Why wasn't I somewhere else doing something that mattered more?

Was I making a difference here?

Anywhere?

Was God asking me, "What are you doing here, Diane?"

Life.

I was realizing more and more every day that *life* is as the Scriptures declare it:

> Like a vapor that appears for a little while and then vanishes. (James 4:14)
>
> Like a breath...like a passing shadow. (Psalm 144:4)
>
> Like a wind that passes and comes not again. (Psalm 78:39)
>
> All flesh is like grass, and all its glory like the flower of grass; the grass withers, and the flower falls. (1 Peter 1:24)
>
> We must all die; we are like water spilled on the ground, which cannot be gathered up again. (2 Samuel 14:14)

These thoughts about the brevity of life, if considered in isolation, could leave one feeling hopeless and elicit a belief that life itself is without significance or meaning. But as I keep searching the Scriptures, I find verse after verse, and story after story that points to the significance of life, an existence that goes on forever to a hope beyond this life, a hope for something grander, life that exists beyond the grave.

The life we have on earth is only *part* of our story. Yet, what we do with *this part of life* and the choices we make here have eternal significance. It matters! It matters because it determines whether we will live forever in eternal light or eternal darkness. Eternal peace or eternal pain. Eternal joy or eternal suffering. What lies beyond this life is our *forever existence.* It will have no end. So the opposing existences are of the utmost concern for us. Consider these few scriptural references:

> You make known to me the path of life. In Your presence there is fullness of joy. At Your right hand are pleasures forevermore. (Psalm 16:11)

> Before the mountains were brought forth, or ever you had formed the earth and the world, from everlasting to everlasting, You are God. (Psalm 90:2)

> Of old You laid the foundation of the earth, and the heavens are the work of Your hands. They will perish, but You will remain. They will all wear out like a garment. You will change them like a robe, and they will pass away, but You are the same, and Your years have no end. (Psalm 102:25–27)

> Then the righteous will shine like the sun in the kingdom of their Father. (Matthew 13:43a)

> And this is eternal life, that they know You the only true God, and Jesus Christ whom You have sent. (John 17:3)

> And these go away into eternal punishment, but the righteous into eternal life. (Matthew 25:46)

> In My Father's house are many rooms. If it were not so, would I have told you that I go to

prepare a place for you? And if I go and prepare a place for you, I will come again and will take you to Myself, that where I am you may be also. (John 14:2–3)

For God so loved the world, that He gave His only Son, that whoever believes in Him should not perish but have eternal life. (John 3:16)

Then I saw a new heaven and a new earth. For the first heaven and the first earth passed away, and there was no longer any sea. And I saw the holy city, new Jerusalem, coming down out of heaven from God, prepared as a bride adorned for her husband. And I heard a loud voice from the throne, saying, 'Behold, the tabernacle of God is among the people. And He will dwell among them, and they shall be His people, and God Himself will be among them. And He will wipe away every tear from their eyes; and there will no longer be any death. There will no longer be any mourning, or crying, or pain. The first things have passed away. (Revelation 21:1–4)

And there will no longer be any night. And they will not have need of the light of a lamp nor the light of the sun, because the Lord God will illuminate them. And they will reign forever and ever. And He said to me, "These words are faithful and true." (Revelation 22:5–6)

Except for the hope of a *forever*, suffering and the overwhelming cares of life would completely crush us. Such cares would press us to the point of giving up.

In his poem titled "A Psalm of Life," Henry Wadsworth Longfellow wrote,

> Tell me not, in mournful numbers,
> Life is but an empty dream!
> For the soul is dead that slumbers,
> And things are not what they seem.
>
> Life is real! Life is earnest!
> And the grave is not its goal;
> Dust thou art, to dust returnest,
> Was not spoken of the soul.

Surrounded by the pain and tragedies that life often brings can cause us to believe that life is futile, an empty dream. But something inside each of us yearns for life to continue. What is that? Where does this yearning come from if all we are meant for is to live briefly, then die? We constantly seek out ways to extend our youthfulness and retain physical strength. Is it all a futile attempt? Is it meaningless? I dare say it isn't. Herein lies the source:

> He [God] has made everything appropriate in its time. He has also set eternity in their heart, without the possibility that mankind will find out the work which God has done from the beginning even to the end. (Ecclesiastes 3:11)

We may not understand all the workings of God, yet hope remains for our souls. The truth is this: that though our physical bodies will someday return to dust, our souls never will. That part of us that yearns for life. That part that hopes, loves, and dreams will live eternally—somewhere.

The scriptures assure us that the soul of man will one day return to the One who created it. We will stand before God, the Author and Creator of all things, and we will be judged according to the choices we make in this life.

"And as it is appointed unto men once to die but after this the judgment" (Hebrews 9:27).

Most of us don't like this thought of being judged. In fact, we resist and bristle at the idea altogether. Do we not say to one another, "Don't judge me"? Yet we all tend to judge one another either silently or aloud.

The sobering truth is that one day, every single one of us will be required to give an account of how we live our lives. No one will be exempt. The Lord, the only perfectly righteous Judge, will assess how we have lived as humans. The measuring life will be that of Jesus Christ, the only perfect human who ever lived. Yes, he was and is the Son of God, but he laid aside his deity for a brief time and humbled himself in the form of a man. He lived perfectly, and then he laid down his own life and poured out his own innocent blood in sacrifice for the sins of all humanity. He is our example, and we should seek to follow that example. But the amazing news is this: by accepting Christ's sacrifice for our sins and surrendering our life into his hands, he becomes our righteousness. We grow in grace day by day, and we become more and more like him as we walk in the truth of the gospel. So on that day when we stand before God to give an account of how we lived, Jesus will be right there, standing beside us (*having never once left us alone*). He will be our advocate—our lawyer who has never lost a case—who will defend us and point to the payment for our sins, which he has already made!

If we believe this and accept his forgiveness, then we will be judged as righteous before God when we stand before him one day. God will see only the pure innocence of Jesus that covers us. On the other hand, those who reject him and reject his forgiveness, they will have no covering for their sin. It will be fully exposed to God on that day, and because they rejected Jesus, the price of their sin will be left for them to pay with their own pain and eternal suffering.

Therefore, the most important decision we will ever make in this life is the one about Jesus. This one choice will determine whether we live eternally free or eternally condemned.

Recently, I listened to a lecture by a well-known apologist, author, and defender of the Christian faith, Ravi Zacharias. He said this, "The day you were born is the most important day of your life, and the second most important day is the one in which you find out why."

Sadly, many people never discover the true reason for their existence. Knowing the reason presents purpose. Living our purpose requires that we weigh each choice presented to us with more clarity and decisiveness. We reject those things that do not fulfill the purpose, and we embrace those things that do.

If I truly believed that my soul and spirit would simply vanish into unconsciousness on the day my heart stops beating, then I would try to find a way to fill every day with things that make this brief life pleasurable. I would live it like there's no tomorrow.

The reality is, however, that *there is a tomorrow!* What that *tomorrow* brings about for us will depend upon the choices we make *today*. I implore you, *choose wisely!* I urge you, find out *why* you were born and live for that ultimate purpose.

> "For I know the plans I have for you," declares the Lord, "plans for welfare and not for evil, to give you a future and a hope." (Jeremiah 29:11)

> He has caused us to be born again to a living hope through the resurrection of Jesus Christ from the dead, to an inheritance that is imperishable, undefiled, and unfading, kept in heaven for you. (1 Peter 1:3–4)

> Our citizenship is in heaven, and from it we await a Savior, the Lord Jesus Christ. (Philippians 3:20)

> The Lord your God is in your midst, a mighty one who will save; He will rejoice over you with gladness; He will quiet you by His

love; He will exult over you with loud singing. (Zephaniah 3:17)

May the God of hope fill you with all joy and peace in believing, so that by the power of the Holy Spirit you may abound in hope. (Romans 15:13)

But they who wait for the Lord shall renew their strength; they shall mount up with wings like eagles; they shall run and not be weary; they shall walk and not faint. (Isaiah 40:31)

The sufferings of this present time are not worth comparing with the glory that is to be revealed to us. (Romans 8:18)

And now, O Lord, for what do I wait? My hope is in you. (Psalm 39:7)

*****

The meeting ended, and my colleagues dispersed, each to his or her own next destination. David had the car packed by the time I arrived back at our room. I took one quick look around to be sure we hadn't left anything behind. Then we were off.

It was a relief to have one more task behind me. My "to-do" list was growing shorter. Soon I could focus on my plans to make Barry's last days his best days. We stopped for a quick bite of lunch near Mobile, and around 1:30, I sent him a message to see what news I could hear.

No response.

Soon after we left Mobile, my phone rang. It was Mom. She was with the pulmonary doctor. She put him on the phone with me. She wanted me to hear what he had to say. The one and only thing I was able to conclude from the five-minute conversation was this statement: "We know there's a cancerous mass, but we will not know how to treat it until we receive the results of the biopsy." Beyond that, he indicated a belief that the mass was malignant. *This* we had already surmised on our own by viewing the X-ray and considering the invasiveness of the mass shown in the image.

I have found, more often than not, that doctors have a tendency to avoid straight talk, especially when they have bad news to share. I can appreciate their desire to offer hope to patients and their family members, promising to do everything possible and within their ability to help cure every ailment. But there comes a time when we just need to know the hard truth.

Shortly after I hung up with the doctor, Mom called again. She kept repeating, "It's bad! Very, very bad!"

The doctor had apparently been a little more *matter-of-fact* with her, speaking to her in terms she could understand. Our conversation was brief as Barry was in recovery and would soon be awake, so she didn't want to tarry long. I shared the news with David, and we rode on in silence.

I didn't call or text Barry that night. I worried that doing so would only add more stress and pressure to his day. It had certainly been a difficult day. I would wait for tomorrow.

I tried to imagine the silent personal thoughts and emotions of a person who receives a diagnosis like this. An impossible attempt. When face-to-face with one's own mortality, I envision a strong desire to run and hide. It must be true, though, that there is no escaping the reality, no matter how far or fast one might run.

Life is real! Life is earnest!
And the grave is not its goal;
Dust thou art, to dust returnest,
Was not spoken of the soul.

SING WITH ME

"Sing with me this song," I texted him the following morning. "I'm alive... I'm alive because He lives. My life, my future is in His hands! The ridiculous truth of His grace is that we are fully known by Him. Still we are loved by Him. When fear tries to creep in, He whispers, 'I've got you. Rest completely in the truth of My endless love.'"

He wrote, "He loves me more than we love our own. He knows all our failures, yet He loves me. I love my girls, even though I know their mistakes; and nothing they could do would change that. Our Father is full of agape love. Awesome..."

This was his only comment until I checked in on him after I got home from work.

In the evening, I received this message:

> Living by faith alone today.
> They must've had a party inside me yesterday.
> Coughing up blood. It hurts to breathe.
> God and me, we will overcome.
> 18 needles; yeah! Swiss Cheese.

Later still, he added, "Encourage Mom."

I reminded him of Isaiah 26:3, "The steadfast of mind You will keep in perfect peace, because he trusts in You."

He responded, "Oh, yeah, that word brings comfort and peace."

We each learned from an early age that during those times, when all we want to do is give up, we must choose to look up. We look to the Author and Finisher of our faith, to the only One who is able to help us through the most difficult trials of life.

As I reviewed my personal journal from this September day, I found this entry:

> "Save me, O God! For the waters have come up to my neck. I sink in deep mire, where there is no standing; I have come into deep waters, where floods overflow me" (Psalm 69:1–2).
>
> Life with Jesus is a never-ending discovery of His love and power, if only we will trust Him. I can point to specific times in my life when I was in deep mire and deep water—so deep that I would have sunk if God had not responded to my cry for His help.
>
> Sadly, we are prone to withhold our pleas to God for His help until we find ourselves in a desperate situation. Whether our flood or mire is physical, financial, mental, or some other overwhelming thing, God stands waiting for us to stop trying to fix the thing by our own power. We can simply ask him to meet this need.
>
> I'm always amazed at His response when I let go and let Him take control of my problem. He works in ways I could never imagine.

September 21, 2018, 6:43 a.m.

Barry: Agree with me now, Sis. My chest hurts bad!

6:49 a.m.

Barry: He's tryin' to paralyze my prayers.

I knew what he was saying. He spoke of the enemy of his soul, the devil himself. Barry recognized the spiritual attack from past experiences. His faith in God was under attack. He was being severely tested. He wanted to overcome the fear and doubt that was rising up in waves that threatened to overtake him. He felt pressured to give up in that moment.

I didn't see his message until almost an hour later. He was struggling, and I could feel it. I stopped what I was doing in that moment, and I prayed. I poured out my soul to God with bitter tears.

I know beyond any doubt that the Lord God hears the prayers of those who sincerely cry to him for help. He knows our weaknesses and our pain, and he supplies the strength we need for every challenge. The scriptures teach that God bends down his ear to hear us.

As I prayed, I visualized God leaning toward earth with his hand cupped around his ear, listening for my faintest cries for help. My brother was in a dark and frightening place, and he needed immediate help.

As soon as I said my "Amen," I told him, "God's got you and He will never let go! The Holy Spirit will be your comfort when the pain is too much for you."

A few minutes later, he responded, "Thanks! I'm better now. Thanks so much. He heard us."

7:52 p.m.

Barry: Feelin' much better. Thanks for your prayers. It works!

We chatted briefly before we each finished our day with an exchange of "*goodnights*" and "*I love yous*."

September 22, 2018, 8:18 a.m.

Me: Happy Saturday, Bro!

9:09 a.m.

Barry: And that's what I choose it to be!

We made small talk periodically during the day, but the exchanges were brief. Over the past several weeks, he spent a great deal of time reading or listening to encouraging messages by various speakers. I spent a good amount of time alone in quiet reflection, *this being* the source of energy propelling us forward.

September 23, 2018, 4:25 a.m.

Barry: Please pray; I'm so sick.

7:04 a.m.

Me: Just woke up, but I've been praying for you throughout the night. Praying now! How are you now?

7:09 a.m.

Barry: At this mmmennt im trrying to figurre out what happen to me between 3 and 5. I cant seem to put my thoughts together.

It was obvious that he was having trouble putting together his message. I could tell from the way he spelled the words that he was struggling.

Me: Is your mind mixed up? What can you remember?
Barry: "Confused. I woke up about 2 and I got so sick. I threw up clear stuff with blood all in it, and then a pile of green stuff. Now I cant hardly spelt [speak]. So sick. I can't think. May go tn hos.

He managed to put these statements together over the next few minutes. I tried to research the symptoms he shared with me. Possible causes I found listed for the nausea and bile included everything from food-poisoning or a bowel blockage to an issue with his pancreas or liver. I gave him the brief list of possibilities before asking, "They did say that the cancer hasn't spread to your pancreas or liver, right?"

He said, "Very possible; but I ant much."

I couldn't decipher exactly what he was trying to say with that last message, but I encouraged him to try and get something on his stomach in case the frequent vomiting over the past few hours had simply emptied his stomach leaving only bile to be expelled. He seemed desperate and confused, saying "I can't text."

I tried as gently as I could to get information from him as I needed to know whether Mom was awake or whether he had even told her how sick he was. The only other message he sent was "Pray that I'll get wisdom."

He was struggling with the pain, with mental confusion, with doubt over his faith. I could read it between the broken lines of his messages. My heart ached for him. The message (and the promise) continued to resound over and over in my thoughts. His time was short, and I knew it.

Not knowing what else I could do, I headed to church about an hour later with a very heavy heart. I needed strength and courage if I was to be any help to him on this continuing journey. I couldn't encourage him if I was weak and full of confusion myself.

Before time for worship, I met with my prayer group, as I do almost every Sunday morning. On this particular morning, I poured out my broken heart to these women. I shared with them the detail of all that had transpired over the past two weeks. They were consoling and willingly poured out heartfelt prayers of faith for strength and for healing.

Oh how I longed to believe that physical healing would come for him, to give him time to share the true story of his faith. I longed for a miraculous showing of the magnificent power of the Lord, one like I'd heard of but never before witnessed with my own eyes. I've heard stories of people who were instantly healed of deadly diseases. To see it for myself would be amazing.

I was earnest in my desire for his healing; yet, I had difficulty praying for that kind of miracle. Down deep in my heart, I somehow knew that Barry's miracle was in the healing and transformation of his soul, not in the healing of his frail and broken body. I sensed in my spirit that he would meet Jesus face-to-face in a few short days, possibly weeks. All the pain and struggles of this life would be over for him. He would have complete rest and a brand-new body, one that would be healthy and whole. He would no longer struggle with the pain of addiction. He would have a new voice and a new pep in his step. He would sing and dance and praise his Savior like never before.

*****

I was torn over what I should do, whether to go and be with him and my mom or wait a few days longer. My work schedule was still so full. The schedule had been set long before I had any clue of Barry's illness, my calendar for October and November each year are generally filled with business trips and work obligations, and this year was no different. Added to this already full schedule was the need to complete a long list of urgent tasks in advance of a week-long mission trip that had been planned months earlier to the Dominican Republic.

The noises of life screamed in my ears.

What a dilemma!

What a tearing of my soul—first one way and then another!

"What," I asked myself, "is the most important thing here?"

"What," I asked God, "are you trying to teach me in all of this?"

I prayed, "How can I possibly fulfill all my scheduled obligations *and* take care of my family too? I'm only one person, and I'm weak. I don't understand, but I'm trusting you to show me. If you don't give me strength and wisdom to deal with it all, I will certainly fail. At everything! Help me! I need you above all else."

Around noon on that September Sunday, Mom called to let me know she had taken Barry to the emergency room. They were admitting him at that very moment. I knew from the prior week's exchange that he still hadn't received the results of his biopsy, and I expected that would be coming very soon. I wanted to be there with them when this news came. Furthermore, I needed to know what we were facing as far as treatment options. I needed to hear it with my own two ears.

Given Barry's state of mind and Mama's difficulty in understanding and translating all the facts to the rest of us, I decided that I couldn't just sit here. After mulling it all over in my mind a little while longer, I decided I had to go. I tend to be an impromptu reactor to the need of the moment. So I quickly packed a bag, texted my boss, and kissed my husband and each pooch goodbye. An hour later, I was on the road to Dothan, Alabama.

*****

A seven-day gap is found in my text message exchanges with Barry from September 23 until September 30, 2018. This period proved to be a true turning point for all of us. So much about the future and all we would be facing in the coming weeks was revealed during this time. Decisions were made that set us all on a predetermined course for which there was no avoidance or turning back.

My mind still swirls as I think of each event that unfolded. What's more, I learned that Barry had only shared bits and pieces about his illness with his daughters. I had encouraged him to share with them earlier, but things had progressed so quickly, he wasn't mentally or emotionally prepared to do that. Now I knew they needed to know, and I had to tell them. I called them as I drove, shared what I knew, and promised to fill them in once I knew more.

His Decision

I arrived at South East Medical Center in Dothan, Alabama, on Sunday evening, September 23, 2018, right about 8:00 p.m. Broad smiles lit up his and Mama's faces when I walked into his hospital room. I sensed the smiles were more a sigh of relief than that of joy at actually seeing me, each exhaling the internalized stress built up in his or her own spirit.

I knew that each one struggled daily with stresses and fears all their own that they dared not speak aloud to each other. Each one had shared enough with me in separate conversations that gave me insight into their individual fears and the anguish that weighed heavy on each one's heart. Neither of them seemed able to comprehend the fear of the other or to fully sympathize with the other's personal pain. So here I was to be a mediator, a counselor, an encourager for each of them. And I was determined to do just that to the best of my ability.

We didn't know it at that precise moment, but we were about to embark upon the most difficult phase of this journey so far. We were entering the darkest valley we had ever experienced.

Over the next hour or two, they did their best to fill me in on the events of the day—the tests, the questions, and the coordinating efforts of a host of medical professionals. Each one's recollection and understanding of all that had transpired during the day differed. There were clear expressions of impatience and frustration between the two of them. I tried my best to diffuse the rising hostility and create a sense of peace and safety in the room.

No official diagnosis had been disclosed by any of the medical professionals, although the buzz in the room when nurses and others came through the doorway was all the evidence we needed as to the seriousness of the situation. I could easily see from their facial and verbal expressions that they knew more about his condition than they were saying. Their words did not match their actions or facial expressions. Reading between the lines, I found the real truth about his condition evident in their nonverbal queues. His condition was far worse than they were willing to tell us. The atmosphere was somber at best.

We each slept as best as we could that night in the cramped space of the tiny room. The constant coming and going of nurses and others throughout the night to take vital signs and administer medications allowed only brief periods of uninterrupted sleep. By morning, we were all thoroughly exhausted and anxious about what the day would reveal.

A flurry of activity began very early. Although months have passed since that day, it's all still vivid in my memory. I can still see the faces of each doctor, one after another, as they came by to talk with us and to give advice concerning their own specialized area of medicine. I lost count of the total number of pulmonary specialists, oncologists of varying degrees, and their many overseers who passed through his room that day. The thing that I still find incredibly disturbing is that they, like the nurses, possessed knowledge they were reluctant to speak in clear terms. I sensed it but was careful to watch and listen before pressing them for the raw truth.

Before today, I didn't know that there were specialties in oncology, and each doctor sticks to his or her own special practice. They may share notes with each other in order to treat the patient, but each one is careful not to invade the other's territory. Our family's medical history is fraught with heart disease, *not cancer*. Therefore, I had no idea that one oncologist specializes in radiology treatment while another specializes in chemotherapy treatment. Some specialize in the treatment of breast or liver cancer, far removed from those whose specialty is treating leukemia, and in our case, *lungs*. Who knew?

A new dimension of unknown things about cancer began to be unveiled to us. The varying treatments and all that comes with that was new to the three of us. My very limited experience with cancer came from arm's length encounters and stories shared by friends and acquaintances. I had known people—extended family, friends, and colleagues—who had walked this journey, but cancer had never touched any member of my immediate family.

The radiology oncologist was the first to arrive. I recall precisely where he sat that day at the foot of the right corner of Barry's bed. He quickly launched into his prepared speech about the radiology treatments he planned to start immediately. I listened carefully, but I had a bit of trouble comprehending everything. He never asked, "Do you understand what this is for?" or "Do you want to do this?" He simply assumed Barry's agreement for radiology, the obvious next step of treatment.

It might have been obvious to the doctor, but for us, it was a step toward something that we knew nothing about. We had no diagnosis. No prognosis had yet been discussed. The terminology he used was foreign to all of us, which made it even more difficult to follow. The gaps in information made it impossible for us to know exactly the purpose of the radiation. We were astute enough to know that radiology was a cancer fighting treatment, but that's about it.

We had questions. Are these treatments intended to destroy the cancer and heal him over time? Or are they merely intended to extend his life for some undesignated period of time? And the good doctor offered no explanation, only a treatment plan.

Except that I had seen with my own eyes the X-ray and the mass that filled my brother's chest cavity, I might never have asked further questions. And had I not shared the X-ray with a trusted doctor friend, I might have found hope for a cure in this oncologist's words and initial demeanor that day. He seemed focused and determined. Good qualities for a doctor in this field of medicine, no doubt. But I needed to know more. Finding a momentary break in his speech, I stopped him. Timeout!

"Wait," I said, "what are you telling us? We've been waiting for the results of a biopsy that was done last week, but we haven't yet been given any answers. Is the tumor inoperable or what? We don't know what's happening here."

The oncologist seemed quite surprised and caught off-guard by my questions. The expression on his face and the way he suddenly went silent was a tell-tale sign. It seemed to me that he had found himself in the uncomfortable position of having to break the bad news of terminal cancer to a patient. I surmised that he wasn't accustomed to this part of the process. My eyes were locked on his and his on mine at that moment. He took a deep breath as though to gather his thoughts. Then he paused to look at each of us individually, connecting eyes with one of us, then the other, and then the last without saying a word.

As he began speaking, he chose his words carefully. He explained that the radiology treatment Barry would soon begin receiving was not to cure the disease (this is a layman's transcription of what he described to us in more complicated terms). The purpose of the treatment would be an attempt to shrink the tumor. They hoped to give Barry some relief from the pain he was currently experiencing. He explained that the tumor was so large that it was pressing against Barry's spine and was squeezing his heart.

As I pressed him for more information, he stated unequivocally that Barry's cancer was inoperable and incurable, but they were determined to do their best to give him as much relief as possible. Hearing those words knocked the breath out of all three of us. I can't say that any of us was fully surprised, but to hear those words spoken aloud was unsettling, to say the very least. We had tried to brace ourselves for the impact, but I'm here to declare that no amount of effort prepares one to hear these words. Not by a long shot!

The doctor left the room with his plan firm to return in a little while to take Barry down to the Radiology Wing. Soon after he had left the room, a female doctor walked in and stood at the left-foot corner of the bed. We learned through her broken English that she was a chemotherapy oncologist and that she, too, was assigned to Barry's case. We learned less from her than we did from the radiology oncologist. We did learn of her plan to send Barry for a brain scan. We understood that scan would reveal whether the cancer had reached Barry's brain. With that, she was out the door.

At this point, the words we were hearing sounded foreign and almost meaningless. Our hope of a cure left the room with each doctor. We seemed to be mere spectators in a large room with an echo.

The devastating news had been given, so nothing else we heard from that point forward seemed to make any real difference.

Everything was happening much too fast. We didn't have time to process one announcement until another doctor or nurse was in front of us. A half hour may have passed before a nurse arrived with a wheelchair to transport Barry to Radiology. I went with him, and Mom stayed behind in the room. Her feet and legs were swollen so badly she could barely carry herself. Besides that, she was exhausted from the sleepless night and the news of the day. I told her to sit tight, and we would be back soon.

Still dazed and confused at this point, we had no choice but to follow through with the specialists' recommendations. I told myself that we would figure out the rest as we went. We didn't tarry very long in Radiology. They didn't do a treatment that day, but this first visit was intended as a preparatory assessment. The first treatment was planned for the following day. I learned that the treatments would be daily for a little while until they could determine whether or how the cancer would respond to them.

My mind raced with questions.

How do people—patients, families—face this? I silently pondered, *How will we manage the daily transport needs? Mom has other obligations, and besides that, she isn't healthy enough to take this on alone.* I wondered, *Should I get another opinion or find a more intense treatment at MD Anderson or some other cancer treatment center?*

These and a hundred other questions passed through my thoughts over the next few minutes. I had no real answers, but I told myself that I would walk through this with him—*with them*—regardless of what was required of me. This was the least I could do.

By the time we got back to his room, it was nearing noon. Lunch arrived, but he ate very little. His preacher came by to visit and to pray with us. This was the first time I had met the man that Barry had described to me as the man who had become like a father to him over the past several months. It was evident from that first "Hello, I'm Steve Etheridge" that he and Barry had forged a genuine friendship. He had a gentle spirit, and his expressions revealed a generous heart.

I slipped out of the room to call my office while he visited. I called my dad and other family members to give them an update on all that was happening. I lingered in the hallway and a nearby waiting area so as not to be too far away in case another doctor came by.

An hour or so passed before another person arrived with a wheelchair announcing it was time to go down for a brain scan. Barry made it clear that he wanted to go alone, so I stayed behind with Mom. While he was gone, a few more friends came by to visit.

It was midafternoon when Barry returned from having the brain scan. He seemed alert but different somehow. He began to share with us what he had seen while he was gone.

"When they wheeled me into that waiting area, all I saw were faces of despair. They had this look of hopelessness," he began.

I wasn't there, so I can't attest to it, but I have to wonder if that feeling of helplessness was within his own soul in that moment. *Could the sense of hopelessness he saw in the faces of others have been a mere reflection from his own heart?* I wondered. I guess I'll never know.

He went on, "I've made a decision." He made this statement with a firm expression of resolve on his face and in his tone. When he said this so matter-of-factly, Mom and I both looked at him with questions in our eyes. What came out next was not at all what we expected to hear. "I'm not taking any treatments!"

"What? "Why?" we asked. "We don't even have the results of the CT scan."

"Well," he said, "I sat there looking at all those faces in that waiting room. They were all so sad. They looked so hopeless." He continued, "And, this is what I know: I know that God has been at work in me since early this year. I had reached the end of my rope. God knew it. So did I. He also knew *this!* He knew what was ahead of me. And he was preparing me then for the news I got today. He also knew in January and February that I was not in any condition to hear what I heard today. He knew that if I heard this news back then, I wouldn't have been able to handle it. In fact, I probably would've run the other way. But in his mercy and grace, he opened my heart and my ears to hear his voice. And he changed me! Besides all that, God gets no glory from radiation or chemotherapy."

Those words hit me hard. I had no argument for that.

He went on, "I want people to understand that it's not *because* of this illness that I've been changed. God changed me *before* I knew any of this! And I *know* he is able to heal me. But even if he doesn't heal me, *I know* where I am going!"

Again, his words left no room for argument.

"So I just want to go home. I have people I need to tell. While I have time, I have to tell my story."

He finished his speech with such conviction and determination that our only reaction was to sit there for a moment in stunned silence. Our eyes filled with tears. But our hearts overflowed with gratitude for the grace and mercy God had shown him. I had no idea what Mom was thinking, and I wondered how his daughters might respond. I could see in his eyes and hear in his voice, however, that his mind was made up. And when he set his mind like that, I knew there was no changing it. Besides that, how could I question the truth of what he had just stated? And I couldn't say that I would not have made the same decision had I been sitting there in his place.

It was late in the day, but we told his assigned nurse of his decision. We asked that he notify the doctors and anyone else who needed to know. Later in the evening, I learned that Barry's daughters and their mother planned to drive from North Carolina through the night and would arrive on Tuesday morning. I told Mom, but we didn't tell Barry. He had had quite a day already, and he needed to sleep if that was at all possible. We all needed quietness and peace as much as it was possible to have in this moment. We sent Mom home to prepare for the visitors and for his homecoming.

A little while later, the chemotherapy oncologist came by to give us the results of the CT scan. She explained that the cancer had spread to his brain. We were quite surprised at this early stage, and Barry told her that he had decided against treatment. He asked her, "How much time will I have with my right mind?"

She responded, "Days to weeks."

We all fell silent, and she left the room.

*****

As we sat alone that evening. Barry said to me, "If you or anyone wants to know what it feels like to be told that you're dying, just ask me. I'll tell you."

The sincerity in his declaration was profound. Wow! I could only imagine the depth of his thoughts and the magnitude of knowing that you're in your very last days. Although I never asked him to fully describe it, over the next weeks, I would have opportunity to explore his thoughts more deeply in daily communications.

*****

The night passed quite peacefully, and we were able to rest. At his announcement that he wanted no treatment, no further tests or medical experiments were necessary. The nurses continued to check on us and to administer pain medications. Tomorrow, we would prepare to go home.

The following morning, a team of doctors arrived together in Barry's room. We learned that Barry's case had been discussed among all the doctors (these along with several others) assigned to his case earlier that morning. His "no treatment" decision had also been announced during that early morning meeting. Rather than merely accept Barry's decision and make preparations for his release, the lead doctor decided to make a personal visit to confirm that what he had been told was true. He brought with him one other doctor along with five students who were still in training to become part of someone's treatment team.

I had met the female doctor, the one second-in-command to the lead doctor, briefly the day before. The lead doctor sat down on the bed next to Barry. With a somber tone and serious expression, he began to speak while everyone else stood silently and at attention.

"They tell me that you've decided against treatment," he said.

"Yes," was Barry's brief reply.

"Can you tell me why?" the doctor inquired.

During the next few moments, all eyes in the room were focused on the patient. His voice was strong, his conviction firm, his witness convincing. The words rolled off his tongue without any hesitation.

His speech was the way I've imagined Peter and Paul, disciples of Jesus, declaring their convictions convincingly to their audience when they were called upon to give an answer for their faith.

He began to recite a brief history of his life. He took a few minutes to share with them the poor decisions he had made over his lifetime. He told of decisions that led to much heartache, brokenness, loss of family, and even hope at times—decisions that led him even to this day and this very illness from which he now suffered. At that moment, he professed to this roomful of doctors all of which he was convinced in his own heart. He declared to them the very same words he had spoken to Mom and me the day before, avowing once again, "My God has changed my heart and saved my life! He will get no glory from chemotherapy or radiation." He told them, "I *know* that he is able to heal me if he chooses to. But even if he doesn't, I know where I'm going!"

At that, the doctor turned to me and asked, "Are you okay with his decision?"

All I could say in that moment was, "I am. How could I even begin to argue with what he has just told you?"

As I looked around the room, there was no dry eye to be found, except for Barry's. His testimony had a profound impact on every person who stood there and heard his strong and convincing testimony. Not one person uttered an argument, not even an attempt to change his mind.

The female doctor walked over and embraced me. With tears in her eyes, she said, "I had you all on my heart all night last night."

With that, I sensed just how dire was his condition and how final the prognosis. The only hope for longer life was in the hands of God Almighty. Only he could change the course.

God himself was present with us in the room that day. His Spirit spoke through Barry with purpose and conviction. Barry shared his faith with everyone who came and went from nurses and aides to counselors and hospice care planners.

This I know—not one illness nor any hopeless case is beyond God's knowledge. Not one tear or faith-filled cry for help ever escapes his attention. Even when we can't see him, he's working. Even when we don't feel him, he's still working. He will never stop working, not until he has accomplished every infinitesimal detail of his plan for the salvation of every person whom he calls his own.

Even when I had all but given up on my brother.

Even when it appeared to me that his soul was eternally lost.

Even at what appeared to be the final dangling threads of a hopelessly frayed rope, God said, "I've got this!" and "I've still got him! Nothing—not addiction, not cancer, not even Satan himself—can take my son from My hand! He's mine! I will say when it's time."

THE GIRLS ARRIVE

Shortly after the doctors left Barry's room that Tuesday morning, his daughters arrived at the hospital. He was completely unaware that they were coming or that they had been driving all night to get there. Their mom came with them.

His face lit up like Christmas morning at the sight of them walking through the door. Had it not been for the circumstances and the emotional pain too deep for words that was evident in all sets of eyes, it would have been a very happy reunion. They exchanged warm hugs and smiles.

I excused myself to give the group time and a little space to reunite for a few minutes. Besides that, I didn't know what to say or do in this awkward moment. I'm sure none of them did either.

Too many things seemed to require our attention at once. Decisions had to be made, many of which would be irreversible once we left this hospital. We had never passed this way before. Every single one of us seemed to be bobbing in an ocean uncharted. We remained afloat somehow, but with each wave that washed over us, it seemed that it might be the one to take us under.

Barry longed to sit and talk for hours with the girls, but his weakened condition and physical pain were too much for him. After a few minutes of talking, he called for his pain medication and simply asked for a quiet room.

The medical team—doctors we would never see nor hear from again—issued and signed orders over the next few hours that would carry us to the next stage of care. Orders to prepare him for release. Orders to surrender his care to a third party. *Hospice.* These home caregivers are helpful and necessary, especially when a terminally ill patient prefers to be at home with his or her family. But I've always presumed such an assignment to be a kiss of death since I have never known of a case where hospice care ends before the patient passes on. A hospice care group had to be decided upon that very day before they would allow us to leave the hospital.

Counselors and advisors began to arrive to talk with him and the rest of us as he was able to receive them. A list of hospice providers was placed in front of us. How do you choose one over the other? I had no experience with this. Mom had worked with elderly patients for several years and was familiar with the care but not the process of selection.

Once we had selected two different providers to interview, the hospital social worker scheduled them to come by and meet with us. One came, and then the other. Each one told glowing stories of their genuine care and concern for their patients. They described the specific services they would provide, each making their own unique promises as the best caregiver. I was surprised to learn that once a provider is chosen, all medical questions must go through them. No more calling a personal physician or making a trip to a hospital without consulting the hospice provider first. That made me a little nervous.

With each visitor, even these hospice representatives, Barry told his story—the story of a man brought out of darkness into the light, out of death and into life.

Light and life were what we clung to that day. It was all we had to hold on to as the angel of death lurked in the shadows and the corners of our minds. Satan himself slithered there, looking for the slightest opportunity to inflict more pain, to tell more lies. He is a ruthless thief, a destroyer of everything sacred and holy. He never gives up but is intent on inflicting as much pain as possible in his quest to destroy a soul. He cowers in every dark corner and space he can find to conceal his wicked plans. He was not finished thrusting his arrows of abuse at my brother. Lies and the fury of hell itself were still among his planned afflictions. He refused to give up, even though Barry's life was nearly over.

Satan was angry. He hated that Barry was giving God any praise or glory. He wanted revenge, and he sought every opportunity to undo what God had declared would never be undone. Barry was a child of God, and Satan spewed hatred at the very idea that he had lost this battle. He had held my brother captive for decades, but he had lost this war. Barry had broken free. Today, he continued breaking free, and he told everyone who would listen all about the freedom he had found. The battle raged on, but the war was already won!

I was delighted that Destini and Jazlyn were able to hear their daddy tell his story to others that day. They needed to see his face and hear him tell of his deliverance. I'm confident that they will never forget. At least I hope and pray they never forget. This writing will serve as a continuing reminder of that day.

I was particularly glad for Jazzy to hear him tell the story as hard as I know it must have been for her. She had very little firsthand experience or any memory of her dad's past life, except the accounts she heard told by others. She spent very little time with him over the years, not from her own choosing. She was very young when Barry and Deana divorced, and they moved far away. He missed most of her growing up years. It saddens me to think of it. But here she was at the age of sixteen, all grown up, and seeing her dad in his final days. Somehow, it doesn't seem fair. But that's how Satan works. He seeks to steal the best years of a person's life. And, this time, he did that. As angry as he is that he lost this one to Jesus Christ, I'm just as angry at how he took my brother's best years and stole precious childhood memories that could have been made. I pray this cycle stops right here! Right now!

I sat and watched as this father and daughter tried their best to make up for lost time. Neither really knew the other. It was for her physical and emotional protection that her mother had kept her at a careful distance from him most of her life. Personally, I don't blame Deana. I'd have done the same. I'm certain of it. Some might try to argue that it was cruel and heartless, but I had seen him under the influence of drugs and alcohol. It wasn't a pretty picture. Even more than that, he had put them and his own self in serious danger on more than one occasion. I mostly heard the stories and saw the aftermath, but I'd personally been spared the very worst of those times. Deana, however, walked through some of the darkest times with him when the girls were very young. Some of these experiences were so vile that no wife, and certainly no child, should ever have to witness them. So for that motherly protection of her daughters, I'm grateful to Deana for having the wisdom and tenacity to walk away. I've no doubt she struggled to make it through hard times when he had little to offer any of them.

Yet, in this moment, I sensed all hearts were breaking for wasted years, wasted life, unredeemable time, and family experiences that were forever gone. Still, they loved him. And it was obvious that he adored them. Even at the darkest, lowest points in life, the earnest yearning that poured from his lips was always for his daughters first. He deeply longed for the capability to show them just how much he genuinely loved them. The desire was there, hidden in his heart; but the self-control to overcome the substance abuse eluded him. For this theft of life's most precious and sacred moments, I was vehemently angry! All that Satan had stolen from him and from his children was unforgivable!

I'm quite certain that Deana's heart, too, was breaking at the sight. She sat quietly and listened to the man—the father of her two youngest daughters—speak with such genuine conviction and humility about his past failures and the transformation he had undergone. The thoughts that must have been going through her mind now. *Oh, to have the time and ability to unwind the clock and wash the slate clean of these horrendous memories.* How wonderful it would have been to rewrite the story. His story. Their story. To wash away the pain. The guilt. To make this family all that it was supposed to be. To erase the scars and the pain. All that might have been but would never be on this earth. She must have seen the change in him. Surely she did.

It was undeniably and unmistakably evident to any who knew what he had been in the past at the change evident now. The story was being rewritten. It was his story—God's story—the amazing story of my brother's redemption written with a firm hand in God's Book of Life that cannot be erased. Not by time. Not by the deepest red hues of sin or hurt or pain. Not by any hateful, slanderous accusations that Satan himself can spew. All because the blood of Jesus Christ has washed it all as white and pure as a newborn baby's flesh. Transformation is a beautiful thing.

Over the next few hours, a hospice provider was selected, plans were made for home health equipment, and medications were ordered in anticipation of what was coming over the next few weeks. It was as though we were preparing for a coming storm about which we knew nothing. I sent the others ahead of us to prepare the house as best as they could, and he and I would follow as soon as we had everything we needed for the final release.

STRUGGLES

We arrived at home midafternoon on Tuesday, September 25. The entire house seemed to be in an uproar, *not* what I'd hoped for. Not what Barry needed. He was accustomed to days at home alone where he could sit on the back patio in the quiet and sunshine. This had become his quiet place where he pondered life of late and the grace God had extended. Now the house was full of people—people with endless questions and expressions that matched the anxiety in their thoughts. Today, his anxiety level reached higher. An old familiar scene from past years seemed to be unfolding. I hadn't seen or heard this kind of anxiety in him since this entire saga began. I could see it now. It was written all over his face. I could hear it in the way his feet pounded as he paced the floor.

His former go-to relief had been a cigarette when nothing stronger was available. He gave these up several months earlier. So he went in search of a more quiet place away from the chaos in the house. When I found him, he was in the bedroom, lying with his eyes closed in the hospital bed that had already been delivered by the hospice provider. Mom had them set it up in a spare bedroom that was not his own. Why? I can't really say, but it was her preference. So, already, his place of familiarity and peace was being turned on its head.

The way he lay there, all alone with his eyes closed, curled into himself in the fetal position, brought tears to my eyes. Had he already given up? It certainly appeared that way. When he opened his eyes, his faraway look seemed to silently whisper, *This is my destiny. This is the place I will lie until it's over.*

Mom struggled. She is a fixer, and this matter was beyond her ability to fix. Besides that, all the changes and the flurry of visitors in her otherwise orderly home were also beyond her control. She, too, was accustomed to a quiet home where she lived with just her son. Certainly, the quietness was interrupted by bursts of anger between them at times, but it had become her place of familiarity. Outside influencers were rare or even desired. She preferred that no one know anything about the times that were bad. She alone could choose what was shared and with whom. Every secret she chose to conceal was no one's business but her own. That's how she wanted it.

She—a woman with a Martha heart—finds peace in a clean, orderly environment. She doesn't tolerate clutter well. Crowds and noise and out-of-place furniture arouses anxiety in her which she can't seem to contain. At least not for long. Now her house was turned upside down, inside out. That's how she viewed it anyway. It really wasn't so bad, but she believed it was. Other people were making decisions for her and about her living space that didn't meet her approval. She was not happy. I watched as the chaos brought out the worst in her. She needed time to acquaint herself with a new normal, but this situation did not lend itself to time. Time was the one thing we were quickly running out of and with no way to get more.

The girls struggled. They had questions, and they wanted time—more time, more days, more years—with their dad. They had missed too much of his life already. Jazlyn struggled with how to forgive those she believed had prevented her from getting to know her dad, and the little time that remained wasn't enough to make up for the loss. When she talked about it, there was a longing in her heart to know him as her dad—the loving father she saw today, not the beast of a man she had only heard about from the past. She had questions, but the answers that came failed to satisfy the longing in her heart to know her dad. The explanations and excuses were unable to reach the pain that existed deep in her heart—pain that would become even more evident as the days advanced.

Destini bore her own pain too. She had experienced much more of the effects of her dad's struggle with addiction over the years than did Jazlyn. From the time Destini was very young, she witnessed many of her dad's highest highs and lowest lows, triggered by his life-long struggles with substance abuse. She had felt the exhilaration and joy that came with his good days when she lived temporarily with my mom several years ago. She also bore the scars of anger and rejection that came when he chose the drugs over her. I recall a question she once asked my mom: "Why does Daddy have to do pills?"

Children should never ponder such questions and much less feel the need to ask them. However, the truth is that far too many children experience the harsh realities brought about by the brokenness in our world. It's not the way God designed it to be in the beginning. Children were never meant to suffer pain, neither physically nor mentally. They aren't meant to live their childhoods separated from Mom or Dad. Abuse is not a word that any child should hear, let alone experience.

Destini also knows the pain of across-the-table visitations between father and daughter that take place in a prison yard. My brother's incarceration lasted less than two years, but there's no doubt that the memory of these visits are seared into her brain. It wasn't an environment suitable for children nor was the time spent there with him of any good quality. How I wish she could have been spared that pain and the memories that remain. Nevertheless, her desire and willingness to go there proved her love and longing to know her dad and to support him the only way she knew how.

I sympathized with the girls' struggles, but empathy was not something I could truly give them. Although I had experienced my own joy as well as grief and pain in my interactions with him over the past fifty-plus years, I had never experienced the kind of struggles they were exposed to. It broke my heart to watch it unfold when they were so young, and even now. Yet today I realized that we didn't have any time to waste in regretting or wallowing in what might have been. What we had to do now with the days we had left was to redeem the time as much as possible. Each of us needed to say what needed to be said. Time spent talking, confessing, forgiving, and enjoying the company of one another would be precious and necessary for future healing to occur.

Time—with each *tick-tock* of the clock's hands, time was running out. I could feel it. I could see it. The ticks seemed to tock faster and faster with the passing of each day.

He lay down on the bed with oxygen flowing through tiny tubes into his nostrils. It was as though he anticipated the end, and all he could do was lie there and submit to the inevitable: eternal sleep.

Sleep. *Do any of us really have time to waste on sleeping when our clock is winding down,* I wondered. If it were possible, I would have forgone all sleep right up to the end.

*****

I wanted to be near him so that he didn't feel alone. I sat beside his bed. The constant reminder of "the message" loomed large in my thoughts. I wanted to talk to him about it, but I had no idea how much time we had. It was difficult to find the right time to approach the subject. In the depths of my soul, I knew the outcome was sealed. Somehow I knew that physical healing was not to be. I knew just as surely as I knew my own name. How could I tell him? How was I supposed to offer him encouragement and hope for today and then disclose the words of his eulogy? The whole matter seemed twisted and surreal.

I fell asleep with these thoughts. The mental exhaustion overcame my will to soak up any more of life in this moment. Tomorrow. We would have tomorrow. I banked on that.

Sinister Encounters

Wednesday was a blur. People were coming and going all day long. Some were family, others were friends from the community or the church. Still others were new people we had never met—his new caregivers. We saw nurses and social workers and even a chaplain. Two of these people became close confidants to Barry and good friends to our family over the next two months—Janitha, the nurse whom Barry came to love with all his heart; and Phillip, a wonderful chaplain who spent hours with him and us, just talking and praying. Their genuine care and concern for him was evident each time they stopped by to visit.

We met both of them this first week home, although several others came by as well. They walked us through the generalities and expectations of days to come, answering our questions and helping to guide us regarding pain management and who to call when there was an emergency. Much of these first few days at home is a blur to me now, although I recall bits and pieces of them. The latter days with the caregivers are more clearly stayed in my mind.

I took lots of notes and planned a schedule as to what medications were due and when. We bought a weekly pillbox so I could sort everything by day and hour. It was overwhelming. The hardest part was deciding how to control the medicine supply. Knowing his propensity to addiction and the potency of some of the medicines the hospital had supplied, I worried about how to keep these from becoming an allurement to him when the pain increased. How could I protect him from his body's own addiction propensity and still provide the pain management he needed?

One particular medication which made me particularly nervous was one I'd never heard of—Fentanyl. It was a pain patch that was intended to be placed directly onto the skin. The medication absorbs slowly into the bloodstream without the patient needing to swallow a pill. Barry was familiar with it, and he told me of someone he knew who had accidentally overdosed and died after getting into a bath of hot water while wearing it. The heat from the water caused too much medication to be released too quickly. The nurse, too, warned us of the need to avoid hot water while he was wearing the patch. She urged us that it should be removed while bathing and advised us to place it on a more muscular or fleshly part of his body and not on a bone.

There was so much to remember. I was quickly being schooled in nursing care, not a job I'd ever imagined or desired. How could I remember all of this and be able to train others who would be here when I couldn't be? I took good notes, but it still seemed inadequate.

The nurses explained that his prescriptions would be refilled in a two-week supply, not your typical thirty-day supply. *Why?* I wondered. Then it became clear to me. Many people, once placed under hospice care, don't last longer than two weeks. But from what I gathered from the vagueness of their instructions, it seemed they anticipated a much longer time for him. Certainly no one knew how long he had—only God. Still, we would need to visit the pharmacy much more frequently than normal folks do.

Barry had a small metal box with a key that I used to store the most potent of medications along with those that we would not need until the end drew closer. I read each bottle and listened as the nurse described what each one was used for. I didn't want to think about administering those. I wouldn't. I couldn't. I'd let the nurses do that. When the time came that those were needed, surely they would be here to do that. At least, I told myself that's how it would be.

Thursday, September 27, 2018

On Thursday morning, I vaguely recalled having left Barry and Deana in conversation on the back patio the night before. I rose fairly early as I was accustomed to doing to find some time and space for quiet meditation, prayer, and scripture reading. My spirit craved it. So I made a pot of coffee and looked for a secluded spot away from the sleeping bodies scattered throughout the house. With three extra people in the three-bedroom house, locating an "alone space" wasn't easy. My alone time proved to be short-lived that morning.

As soon as Barry was awake, he came looking for me all in a panic. He told me a disturbing story Deana had shared with him the night before of things that had been happening with the girls over the past few years and more recent months, events that had been kept a secret from him and all of us. The bizarre nature of the sinister encounters was quite extraordinary and disturbing, so it took time for the girls and their mother to piece it all together. "I have to call Bro. Steve," he began in breathless urgency. "He has to come over and talk with them! I don't know what else to do." He was visibly shaken.

When I had calmed him down enough to try and make sense of what he was telling me, my heart sank. I sensed the all-too-familiar chill of darkness that I'd felt so many times before. Satan is relentless. It seemed in that moment he was pulling out all the weapons in his arsenal and commanding every demon of hell to do battle for the purpose of squeezing the very last ounce of life and hope left within my brother's soul. His soul was desperately clinging to life attached to the hope of his salvation.

"Deana told me," he said, as he shook with fear, "that strange things have been happening with the girls. It's all my fault!" He recited the spine-chilling episodes she had shared with him. She told of voices coming through televisions that were not turned on, of invisible forces holding the girls down on their beds and rendering them immobile for a period of time, of dark shadows that appeared without warning and just as soon disappeared, and of ordinary household smoke alarms triggered by no apparent event or source. The smoke alarm event happened repeatedly, she had told him, and during the most recent occurrence, she and her husband removed the alarm from the room where it was installed and brought it into their own bedroom. When it continued to erupt, they removed the batteries from it and laid it on a shelf. All was well until the disarmed device, devoid of any power source, issued another shrill alarm as if to say, "You can't stop me!"

Deana was terrified. These episodes had continued until she was determined to move her daughter out of the house to a new location. Both girls had experienced their own bizarre incidents of dark, shadowy movements and sensations of being held down by forces they couldn't see. All of them were at a loss to explain the strange events that continued to occur over a long period of time.

"It's all my fault," he urged again. "Don't you remember when I promised my soul to the devil? All those years ago when I was under the influence of the drugs?" In this moment, his panicked soul was in desperation. "Don't you remember the time when the tree fell on the house in the middle of the storm, and the storm didn't occur anywhere else in the community? The wind blew only at *our house?* And the tree that fell, it fell across the girls' bedroom! The rest of the neighborhood was completely calm. The *wind*…it was only around the house where *we lived!*"

This is just what the enemy of our soul does to us. This is his tactic. He loves nothing more than to bring up the sins of our past and to beat us senseless with them. He accuses us. He uses us. He abuses and seeks to destroy our faith with every brutal memory of past failures.

He continued shaking as he stood there that morning. He was full of fear as he rehearsed scene after scene from the past, vividly recalling specific instances of demonic forces that had chased after him, intent on destroying him and his family for twenty years and more. Even Jazzy, who was too young to recall those disturbing scenes from her early childhood, had heard the stories her mother and sisters told. Deana told him of how Jazlyn began to question, "Mom, is this happening to me because of Daddy? Of the things he did when I was younger?"

Certainly, Deana had no answers to all these questions, except that she believed the current events were somehow connected to the past. I can only imagine the thoughts and fears that must have raced through her mind with each new unexplainable episode. Fearful, no doubt, for her daughters' physical safety and mental anguish, she felt compelled to share it all with Barry now. Perhaps she believed this was her one and final chance to do something to help the girls find answers. Perhaps, by chance, they could find some way to reverse the curse. Unfortunately, the timing for such discussions would never seem right given the circumstances we were facing now. I questioned the timing and the approach in my own heart but summarily concluded that I, too, would have felt compelled to do the same thing if I had been in Deana's shoes at this moment. So I chose to offer grace and prayers.

Could it be? I wondered. *Could former invitations of demonic influences, ushered in by my brother's past drug-induced state of mind, have opened a gateway into the very world where his daughters and their mother lived and worked and attended school?* I've heard of generational curses, but whether such curses follow the children and grandchildren of one who has made poor life choices, I can't say for certain. Children often lead lives that seem to follow the familiar path of their parents. They're certainly influenced by these experiences as we all are. Many sources also point to the fact that addictions of various kinds may follow family bloodlines as well. As for demonic forces and their power over individuals and families, I don't have answers. Yet I do believe they're real. As to how they move and who they choose to torment, however, is beyond my ability to comprehend. I am convinced that in the unseen spiritual realm, forces of good and evil consistently do battle. I'm also convinced that having the protection of God over body and soul is of utmost importance for humans.

Any person who would argue that the spiritual realm doesn't exist, that the only part of life's reality is that which we physically see and feel or that we aren't impacted in the physical by the spiritual should consider it again. For those who have yet to recognize the two dimensions, biblical writings and the Scriptures recount multiple examples where these powers of darkness and angels of light wield their swords and clash head-to-head as they do battle for the souls of men and women. I recall such an encounter from the book of Daniel, chapter 10.

Daniel had been fasting and mourning over the condition of the hearts of his people and over their continued exile in Babylon. The scripture says that a message was revealed to Daniel, which was "true and one of great conflict," but he understood the message and had an understanding of the vision. It caused him great distress, so much so that Daniel had been mourning and fasting for three weeks after seeing it.

One day, he was standing on the bank of the Tigris river, and he saw an angel. He was terrified. The angel spoke to him and said, "Do not be afraid, Daniel, for from the first day that you set your heart on understanding this and on humbling yourself before your God, your words were heard, and I have come in response to your words. But the prince of the kingdom of Persia was resisting me for twenty-one days; then behold, Michael, one of the chief princes, came to help me, for I had been left there with the kings of Persia. Now I have come to give you an understanding of what will happen to your people in the latter days." The angel went on to tell him, "I shall now return to fight against the prince of Persia;... there is no one who stands firmly with me against these forces except Michael your prince."

Even Jesus himself was led into the wilderness by the Spirit to be tested (Matthew 4:1–11). While he remained there for forty days, Satan spoke to him and tempted him. Whether Satan appeared to him in physical form, the scriptural account doesn't say, but one thing I do know is that one of the greatest battles for the souls of mankind took place at that time. Good versus evil. Life versus death. Eternal life versus eternal damnation hung in the balance. And Satan lost!

Have you ever stopped to consider how busy the angels are? They have assignments from God, and many of those assignments involve your protection and mine. In Psalm 91:10–12, David reminds us, "No evil will happen to you, nor will any plague come near your home. For He will give His angels charge concerning you, to guard you in all your ways. They will bear you up in their hands, that you do not strike your foot against a stone." We may not be able to see God or angels with our physical eyes since they exist in the spiritual realm. But they are just as real as the people we see and hear. Satan, demons, and forces of evil are also real. We would do well to remind ourselves of this often. In recognizing that such powers and influences exist, I also acknowledge that they're of a force too great for me to fight or even encounter in my own strength. Spiritual battles can only be fought and won with the use of spiritual weapons. The fact that we each wrestle with spiritual forces is noted in Ephesians chapter 6, beginning at verse 10.

> Finally, be strong in the Lord and in the strength of His might. Put on the whole armor of God that you may be able to stand against the schemes of the devil. For we do not wrestle against flesh and blood, but against the rulers, against the authorities, against the cosmic powers over this present darkness, against the spiritual forces of evil in the heavenly places.

This scripture goes on to list seven weapons necessary to successfully do battle in the spiritual realm. These weapons are included in what is described as the *whole armor of God*—the belt of truth, the breastplate of righteousness, the gospel of peace, the shield of faith, the helmet of salvation, the sword of the Spirit (the Word of God), and prayer. To fully explain all of these weapons and how to use them would take more time and space than this writing can supply. But for those who may be reading this and want to understand this more, I encourage you to begin by reading the New Testament scriptures. Then simply pray for wisdom and understanding and seek out a trustworthy Christian counselor who can explain it to you more fully.

*****

On this September morning, an encounter with demons was not what I had expected. I urged Barry to contact his pastor as soon as possible. We needed the best spiritual advice and guidance available. I knew enough about this sort of thing to know we should not take it lightly or pass it off as *not a thing*. We needed as many believers as possible in the house with us that day. Certainly, my brother's illness was of the utmost importance, his was short, and the girls would be returning home soon. Yet, this was a serious matter that couldn't wait. It must be dealt with as soon as possible for everyone's sake.

By midmorning, the pastor had arrived. We all sat in the living room together—Barry, Deana, Jazlyn, Destini, Mom, Brother Steve, and I. Brother Steve began by reciting what he understood the issues to be, then asked questions to understand what was happening a little better. He allowed time for each person to share their own unique experiences. Some encounters were more recent than others, but all appeared to have a common denominator—dark unseen forces had been and continued to be hard at work in the lives of this family. In truth, every person in the room, except for the pastor, had at some point been a target of these demonic influences over my brother's life. I had personally encountered them on more than one occasion.

Demons are real, but so are holy angels. Satan rules the darkness; Jesus rules the light. When we live in sin, darkness prevails, and Satan is granted control of our thoughts, actions, and outcomes. When sin is exposed to the light, darkness can't stay. In the light, Satan no longer has any authority or power to control us, our thoughts, our actions, our present, or our future.

In this room on this day, light was present, and the darkness was fully exposed! While my brother's past life and bad decisions became a gateway for evil to enter into the space where he had once lived, and even into his daughters' world, the darkness and the curse were now exposed to the light. The girls had a choice. Their mother had a choice. Each was presented with this truth and each one's choice regarding what to do with this knowledge of truth—to accept it by faith or to reject it—would determine their individual futures.

Brother Steve explained to them that day that spiritual forces of darkness are very real, and the only way to successfully overcome them is through the power of God. This power is available to individual people through faith in Jesus Christ. When Jesus died, his blood was poured out as a sacrifice for sin. When Jesus rose to life again, this sacrificial event had broken the curse of sin, and by it, Satan and death were overcome. Jesus made a way for humanity to be reconciled to their Creator.

This was the truth that demanded a choice that day. In other words, Deana and the girls had to decide whether to believe it and accept it along with divine power to overcome the darkness or they could reject it and continue their feeble attempts to fight these forces on their own. It was a battle they were ill-equipped to fight in their own human strength. I only hoped they could understand this and receive it. Regardless of their choice, the battle had to be fought and either won or lost. The outcome would depend upon the individual decisions made.

Certainly, to the doubting skeptic, all of this may seem quite unrealistic. Some might sneer and argue that it's merely irrational Christian babble at best. At worst, others might wag their heads in disbelief and brush it off as a dramatic account of a sad broken life. In fact, if I had not personally experienced a small portion of this tragedy, I, too, might question the authenticity of these stories and of powers and battles occurring in realms none can see. I, too, might pass them off as dreams borne of a fantastic mind. But I've felt the chill of the presence of evil spirits and the way they've sucked the very breath right out of my lungs.

I've experienced the hurl of angry hurtful words that cut to the very core of my soul and slammed me face down to the ground when I least expected it. I've been driven by the power of the Spirit of God to rise early in the morning and to go in an attempt to save my brother from certain death. I've walked by faith into a darkened travel trailer where my brother hid himself with clothes nailed to the windows to keep out the light. I've sat with him and cried when he was down to his last handful of pills and where he confessed that he planned to die. I've been in the same house with this same man, gentle on this day, but once controlled by evil forces, I couldn't explain. I've stood face-to-face with him on more than one occasion when what I saw in his eyes was not the fun-loving boy I grew up with. I've witnessed in him the embodiment of Satan himself who had taken control of my brother in a way that shook me to my core.

How did we get here? How was it that he came to travel this path? We grew up in the same house with the same set of parents, the same upbringing. If I had not lived it, I, too, might doubt. But based upon personal experience, I assure you that not one word of this story is imaginary or dreamed. Oh how I wish it were! A sleepless night filled with horrors of the mind would be much preferred to these real-life terrors our family has faced over the years. Thank God that such things can never follow the believer past the portal which takes one away from this life and into the next. Thank God for the "great gulf fixed" between heaven and hell (Luke 16:26).

All three—Deana, Destini, and Jazzy—prayed and verbally announced their belief in Jesus Christ that day. A sense of peace and calm swept over us all. The house was filled with quiet peace once again. Barry was beyond thrilled. He had frequently shared with me that his greatest desire was for his girls to know Jesus. Today, he was satisfied that they'd allowed the Lord to fill their hearts with his peace in the same way he himself had experienced. His earnest prayer had been answered.

Breakthrough. It was happening. I knew more than I could bring myself to tell anyone at that point. I knew why all these things were falling into place. It was part of *the message—the promise!* It was unfolding right before my eyes, and I was speechless.

What a brutally hard day, but what an incredibly wonderful day it was!

THE REVELATION

I don't recall, just now, the precise timing of the exchange of house guests; but at some point between Friday afternoon and Saturday noon, the girls and their mother left for home with the promise that the girls would return as soon as they could make proper arrangements at work and school.

Almost as soon as the other group had left, my dad arrived. I had daily kept him fully informed of all that was happening. He had waited, wanting to come and spend some time with Barry but knowing that lots of people were in a small space. I knew that he wanted desperately to be of help during this time. He came with the intention of giving me relief to go home, but more than that, to try and mend some of the broken bridges that miscommunicated longings for acceptance and forgiveness had left between the two of them.

Years of broken promises and shattered dreams too intense and personal to be named had torn father and son apart long ago. The lost years were far more than could ever be redeemed, even if Barry lived many more months or even years. It was truly heartbreaking to think of the "might-have-been" father-son experiences and memories that would never be. So many angry words, suppressed hurts, and moments of intense anguish were buried alive in the hearts of both men, neither of which could fully comprehend the magnitude or depth of pain that existed inside the other. Oh how I wanted this brokenness to be completely healed.

My spirit remained heavy and my heart torn, ripped open day by day as each new reminder of our reality bore down upon us, forcing its unwelcomed presence into our lives. All our hearts were throbbing from the raw brokenness and the deep-seated pain, which lay mostly silent there. Yet, the growing peace triggered by the truly amazing grace of God for the redeemed soul of our son and brother could not be denied.

I thought ahead to the plans that David and I had made months earlier. The mission trip to the Dominican Republic with a group from our church was preplanned and paid for and was set to begin in two weeks. I was reminded of the Proverb, "A man's heart plans his course, but the Lord determines his steps." Barry had made plans. We had made plans. Every one of us inside this house today had plans that were now interrupted by unexpected events. Our course was suddenly altered. But God's plan, his order for our steps, remained intact.

"I can't go," I told myself. "If he has only weeks to live, then I have to make every single day count for him. I want to take him places he's always wanted to go and spend as much time as possible with him to help him achieve some of his unfulfilled dreams. I must satisfy my own heart that I've done everything within my power to help him. If I fail in this, I will have a lifetime to regret it. These are days we will never get back. Other mission opportunities will surely come. My life can be placed on hold. His cannot."

These were my thoughts as I lay in bed on Friday night and Saturday morning. I was still making plans in my mind—plans that were not mine to make on his behalf. Nevertheless, I contacted a friend at home to see if she would be willing to take my place on the trip. It was short notice, for sure, but I was certain she would do it if anyone could or would. I also contacted the missions pastor to let him know of my dilemma and that I'd need to bow out of the trip. I requested permission to allow Julia to take my place. David would go ahead with them, but I'd stay behind. I had it all figured out—or so I thought.

I contacted my boss to fill him in on what was happening. So many competing thoughts. So many decisions. So much to do and so little time. I talked with Barry about my plans. I'd help him do things he wanted to do and see places he wanted to see. I thought he would be excited. Much to my surprise, he seemed quite disinterested. He encouraged me, "You just need to go home. I want to spend some time with Destini and Jazlyn. I want Mama and me to just get back to our own lives, just be normal."

How stupid of me. How silly me! Of course he wanted spend time with his daughters. What was I thinking? How selfish was I or how vain to think that a person would want to spend their last days doing things they'd never done before or going places they'd never been. Places and things mean nothing to a person who has only days or weeks yet to live. Time was all he wanted. Time to look into his daughters' eyes, to say all the things he hadn't been able to say to them with a clear mind in years! He wanted to see his granddaughters grow up and to teach them to fish, to hunt, to shoot fireworks. He wanted time to make up for all the hurts and heartaches of the past that lingered in his mind. He ached to make amends and new memories to replace the old ones that haunted him and them.

In my head, my grand plan was to travel with him to where his daughters and grandchildren lived so he could enjoy them and they him for as long as he had strength and his right mind. It seemed, though, that life was getting in the way of even this. Demands of the ongoing everyday life of his daughters didn't change merely because their father was suddenly facing a grim reality. Time or the lack thereof fought vehemently against the cancer cells, which were quickly multiplying, spreading, and invading his chest cavity and into his brain. Jazz's teachers were already threatening to fail her if she missed any more days in the classroom. *How heartless*, I thought. *Can't these people put themselves in this child's shoes?*

Destini's boss, a bit more understanding, was willing to give her time off to spend with her dad; but she had two small daughters of her own at home who were missing their mommy. Disparate lives created a chasm between what each heart desired and every reality dictated. As hard as I tried, I couldn't begin to imagine all the thoughts that ruled his mind each day and over this past month, especially over the past seven days. He needed space and time to process it all as short or as long as that time might be.

Reality won the battle. After the girls had left, I, too, elected to honor Barry's request to let him get back to as normal a life as he possibly could. So I prepared to go home the following day. Oh how

I longed to make time stand still until we could catch our breath! It remained a longing for an impossible exploit.

Still, I thought, *there's no way I can leave the country. His birthday is October 11, and I can't be out of the country. No! I have to be here. I have to celebrate his last birthday with him.* So I told myself that I'd go home, but I would come back in two weeks. *I'll take him some place special. Any place he wants to go. That will be his birthday gift from me!*

How truly ignorant I was. As I try and wrap my mind around what a person thinks about when given the news of their imminent mortality, even as I sit writing this now, such thoughts will not fully form in my mind. But I tried to imagine. I imagined spending lots of time praying and preparing myself for what I might say to Jesus when I first see him in heaven. I imagined seeing my grandparents, aunts, and uncles who will greet me upon my arrival there. I imagined meeting Peter, Moses, and Mary, the mother of Jesus. What will they look like? Will they know me? All that I've ever heard or read about heaven—the quiet streams of water with fruit trees growing alongside it; the emerald throne and golden streets that appear as glass; angels everywhere, and every saint who has ever lived will be there around God's throne—I imagine spending the first thousand years, maybe more, thanking Jesus for his amazing wonderful grace. After all, time has no meaning in heaven. Time will no longer be a thing. So many questions:

What will Jesus look like?

What will heaven feel like? Is it cool or warm or sunny?

Will I have a body? Or will I just be a spirit?

Will I run freely? Or will I simply bow at my Savior's feet?

What will all these people I see and hear today be doing the day I leave?

Who will I meet in heaven? Will I know my family there? Will we talk of all they missed here on earth? Will they tell me all I've missed so far in heaven?

How will friends and family respond to my passing? Will they miss me? Will they cry? Will some be happy that I'm gone?

Have I done *enough*?

Have I shared God's love and the truth enough?

Did I make a difference to anyone at all?

And this last question is truly the sum of it all: whether I've made a difference in the lives of others. Whether my life really counted not to people but to God himself. It won't be about all the places on earth I was able to see nor the number of thrills I experienced before my last breath. It won't be about how big or elaborate my house was or whether I even owned a house. *Barry didn't own a house.* His possessions, what few there were, he could pack neatly into a half dozen file boxes. He had lived fifty-six years, and what was there to show for it? Did it even matter whether he could fill six boxes or sixty square miles *with things?* I'm confident in saying, "It certainly did not!"

Only one thing will matter in the end: Did you say *Yes* to the Savior when he called you by name and invited you to become part of his family? Every single human has or will receive this same invitation. Each one's response to the invitation will determine their eternal destiny.

*****

There was *one more thing* I had to do before l could go home. My heart raced at the thought of it. The time had come, and I had to share *the message* with him. Not a soul in this house had any awareness of the message I'd been given six years earlier. It had been too mind-boggling, too sacred to expose to anyone until now. But I couldn't allow him to pass without knowing how his story would unfold. After all, God shares his heart and secrets with humankind, and he had chosen to share this special promise with me.

Why me? I can't say why me; all I know was that in this moment, my heart beat wildly inside my chest. The sound of it in my ears was deafening. Barry was already talking about funeral plans, and I was confident he hadn't contemplated the thought of his own sister delivering his eulogy; and not just any eulogy but *the message!*

I sat with him as he lay on his hospital bed, watching one of his usual TBN shows on Saturday night. Mom and Dad were in the living room, talking. I couldn't bear to leave him alone. I sat quietly, watched, and listened for just the right moment.

He closed his eyes and shook his head as though he was attempting to shake off something that didn't belong there. He looked at me and said, "What was that?"

I asked him to explain, and he tried to describe as best he could how it felt like something inside his head was short-circuiting.

"Surely, not this soon," I told myself.

He spoke with clarity, and his mind seemed clear. But neither of us could explain the strange sensations he continued to have for the next hour or so. We didn't talk much. We just *were*.

Not yet. The time just isn't quite right.

I went to bed without another word.

Sunday, September 30, 2018

With the house still occupied with house guests and a sense of unrest, I confirmed one last time that I had written detailed instructions concerning Barry's medications for those who would be around over the next days and weeks. Everything was color-coded, and I made sure that my younger brother and sister understood the instructions and coding. My bags were packed and in the car.

Around 9:00 a.m., I walked into the room where he lay resting. His eyes were shut, but he wasn't asleep. Hearing me enter the room, he opened his eyes and smiled. I pulled up a small stool and sat down.

"I have something I need to tell you," I started.

"Okay," he responded.

I had my notebook open, but I prefaced the message by reminding him of the events of six years earlier when I had found him near death in the trailer where he was living in Dothan, Alabama. I walked through the story to the point where the two of us had driven to Okeechobee, Florida, to Faith Farm Ministries on that fall day in 2012. He recalled the almost three months when he had lived there and had gone through their rehabilitation program. It was during that time that I struggled with unrest and worry that he wouldn't stay the course. Bad memories haunted my dreams of so many times before when he opted to leave similar programs before completing them.

I've strived to understand why a person relapses during rehab. Through Barry's jaded explanations of how daily life goes in these places, I concluded that when men or women struggling with the same or similar addictions begin sharing their stories with one another, it often ignites the taste and desire for the "highs" they've experienced in the past. When that happens, the whetted desire triggers something in their brain that is often stronger than their ability to resist. Hence, they relapse. I don't know the answer to overcoming these particular challenges, since part of the treatment involves group discussions of individual experiences and struggles. What a vicious cycle! What incredible odds against them as they continue to fight the demons that haunt their own dreams!

I told him how I had awoken in the middle of an October night after having a troubling dream—a dream so troubling and so vivid that I couldn't return to sleep. At that point, I began to read *the message*. His eyes filled with tears. They were not tears of sadness but those of *knowing, of peace, of satisfaction*. By the time I was finished, both our faces were wet with matching streams of water trickling down our cheeks. He didn't argue; he didn't question any of it. He simply said, "You have to do this! You have to tell them!"

A fresh tear swells in my eye as I write and then escapes to drip slowly down my left cheek. I recall the scene as though it were yesterday. Each time I sit down to write, it's a new battle within my mind and over my will to keep writing. I don't want to do this. I don't want to recall the anguish and the raw pain of that moment and of the chasm between life and death that divides us in this moment. Even three years post-departure, it requires such self-discipline to stay this course and to tell this story. Yet, *the message*, but more so *the promise*, continues to propel me onward. Not a single day passes that the Holy Spirit of God doesn't remind me that this task remains unfinished. The fulfillment of the promise, I'm convinced, will not be complete until I have finished writing the story and sharing the message with every person to whom it was intended.

In all honesty, I don't even know who all those people are. I have some idea, but only God knows each one. He's merely patient with me to complete my mission, the purpose and the plan for which he has placed me right here, right now.

Barry's story and God's amazing power and purpose in it, nevertheless, is enough to keep me moving forward—one written word at a time. I pray that if you are one to whom this is written, you will know and you will receive the message and the promise.

*****

I kissed him goodbye that Sunday morning at approximately 11:00 a.m. I hugged mom and dad and climbed into my Jeep. I pushed the start button, put the gear in reverse, and backed out of the driveway. At the end of the street, I paused. My usual route home required a left turn, yet I had a strong urge to turn right instead.

I was exhausted, full of questions, and in desperate need of understanding and strength. I not only needed strength for the six-hour trip home but also for the unknown days ahead. I needed something that was beyond my own physical ability to create. Knowing that services were beginning at the little church where Barry and Mom attended and that it was only ten minutes away, I decided to go there. Perhaps this overwhelming urge that compelled me to turn right was just the prompt I needed to find some answers.

The service had already begun by the time I arrived, so I slipped quietly into the last pew at the back of the building. As I'm writing this, I honestly cannot remember exactly how the sermon went that day, but I do recall that it was exactly what I needed to hear. I also recall one precious lady, whom I didn't know at the time, coming up to me as I prayed silently in my pew. She touched me on the shoulder, and without uttering a sound, I knew she was praying right along with me. I would later learn that Barry had shared his personal story with her and that they had shared many stories together about his struggles.

I don't know the level of details he shared, but I sensed there was a special connection between the two. She was a bit older than he, but she seemed to understand his pain and longed to help him find peace in the middle of it all. I found new strength that day, strength I would need in the days to come.

By 12:30 p.m., I was back in my car and en route home. I drove in silence for quite some time as I pondered the past week and wondered about days that would be coming quicker than I wanted them to. I devised plans in my mind with imperfect data. Making the most of the days and hours he had left was *key*.

The text messages began again six hours later, just as I entered my driveway at home.

Me (6:54 p.m.): I'm home! You be strong! Be courageous! I love you. See you soon. Let me know if you need me before I get back!

Barry (6:55 p.m.): K. Thanks. I love u.

I fell into the arms of my husband, desperately needing his companionship, compassion, and quiet understanding. We talked a lot about the upcoming mission trip, both agreeable that the circumstances required me to remain stateside. If possible, maybe our friend Julia could go in my place. Regardless of any monetary loss, and even if she was unable to go, it just didn't matter at this point.

What I didn't know at the time, but later discovered, was that David was freaking out about traveling without me. He had never been on a trip that required air travel when I wasn't there to direct his every step through the airports and beyond. Plus, he had only been outside the US twice—once on our honeymoon and once on another mission trip we took together to Colombia, South America, a few years earlier. I have the tendency to stretch the dear man well beyond his level of comfort far too often. Nevertheless, he was determined not to show any fear or anxiety.

Monday, October 1, 2018

Barry (7:30 a.m.): Hey, sis. I'm fine. I'm praying for u. How was church yesterday?

Ah! I knew that someone would rat me out. I hadn't told him or Mom that I had taken a detour on my way home and had gone to their church. But no secret (even if it isn't intended to be a secret) stays that way for long. I chuckled to myself.

Me:(8:01 a.m.): Thank you. I'm praying for you too! Church was good, but God is better!

Me (8:17 a.m.): I love you. You'll be secure because there is hope; you will look about you and take your rest in safety. You will lie down with no one to make you afraid. Job 11:18.

I tried every day to give him some word to hold on to, something to ignite courage and faith in his heart. And I prayed! Oh, how I prayed, "Lord, *please* don't allow his faith to fail!"

Tuesday, October 2, 2018

Me (6:08 a.m.): "The Lord will fight for you; you need only to be still" (Exodus 14:14). I'm so thankful for this promise. I pray your day is full of joy and peace. Rest in the Lord who is our hope. I love you.

I didn't hear from him on Tuesday, but I did receive a message from Deana. Destini was planning a return trip to Hartford, and she wanted to know the nearest airport and if we could have someone there to pick her up when she arrived. Since I wasn't down there, it was difficult for me to say who might be available to drive to the nearest international airport, which was in Panama City, about an hour away. I asked her to let me check on something and I'd get back to her. Pulling up my Delta account, I began to search for flights that might work best for those who could help with transportation. I found flights into a regional airport in Dothan, Alabama. The cost was higher, but this would be a much better solution for my mom or sister if we could make it work.

Deana and I communicated back and forth until we were able to arrive at a workable plan. I had accumulated quite a few sky miles over the past few years, which remained unused. This seemed like the perfect opportunity to cash these in. With that, and 40,000 sky miles later, I had Destini booked on a flight from Raleigh to Atlanta and then to Dothan on October 8. She would have ten days to spend with him, and she would be there for his birthday. The time would fly by quickly, but it would be ten priceless days of memories and mending for father and daughter.

Me (9:25 a.m.): Bubba, please help me pray for wisdom about this mission trip. David and I are scheduled to go to the Dominican Republic for a week. I tried to cancel my part of the trip, but they won't let anyone go in my place. I wanted to be there for your birthday next week, but if I go on this trip, I will miss that. I also know that you want peace and quiet, and I want you to have as much time with Destini as possible while she can be there. So, please pray.

Barry (10:39 a.m.): Thanks for helping Destini. Means a lot, Sis.

Me (10:44 a.m.): I was just happy I could do it. This is an important time for healing for you two. So very precious.

Barry (10:47 a.m.): I really feel that and really appreciate it. You've been a miracle from God. Will need u and others later. Now's the time for Mom and me and Destini. Dad's trying, but it's time he gives us a break.

Me (10:52 a.m.): I agree. God is performing miracles all over the place. I feel like this mission trip may be my first assignment to bring Him glory through your story. Kisses and hugs!

Barry (10:54 a.m.): Amen; as long as He gets the glory. But I want u to speak what u said God gave you at my funeral.

Me (11:01 a.m.): I will definitely do both those things. I love you so much, and I'm glad we had time to talk about all of this last week and even now. You wait for me, okay!

Barry (11:02 a.m.): Ok.

My last statement to him—"You wait for me, okay!"—was the same last words I had spoken to my grandmother about eight years earlier as I walked out of my dad's house the last time I saw her alive. I sensed it that day—that this was the last time. The words I spoke to her meant, "*You wait for me in heaven because I'm coming soon.*" I spoke these same words to him in the text message that night, but the meaning was different. I wanted him to wait for me to return to him before he took his final trip. I believe with all my heart that each one of these precious family members knew the precise meaning of my words, and each agreed.

I talked to him later in the day, and he had plans to go with his pastor to share his story with some guys who were struggling with their own addictions and other problems. He was eager to get out and talk about all that was happening with him. While his body grew tired and weak, his spirit seemed to strengthen. He also encouraged me to proceed with the planned trip. Following that conversation, I called my boss to get his thoughts and his blessing. I knew he would give me that without question—it's just the kind of man he was and is to this day. He said to me, "You need to do this, Diane. You made a commitment to David and to the church, and you need to fulfill it."

Believing these encouragements were the answer to my prayers, and not knowing how long this cancer battle would last, I contacted the missions pastor to let him know that I would be going with them after all. He and his wife were excited and relieved as well. With only three days left before the departure date, I began packing my bags and promptly prepared for a week away from work.

Me (9:11 p.m.): Hey Bubba. I know you've had a very busy day and you're probably sleeping. But, I was thinking about something, and I wanted to ask you before doing it. How do you feel about me putting a short message on my Facebook account letting folks know that you're sick and request prayers and words of encouragement for you and our family? If you don't want me to, I won't. Just let me know. I love you!"

Thursday, October 4, 2018

Barry (6:30 a.m.): What's up!

Me (6:31 a.m.): Hey Bro!! Just about to get a shower so I can go sit in meetings all day and talk to people about stuff that doesn't really matter! ☺ How are you this morning?

When faced with a situation like this, one's priorities certainly shift. Those urgent tasks at work, which I once believed I couldn't walk away from, seemed trivial in light of our present circumstances. A desk piled high with papers, reports, demand letters and legal questions become mere piles of meaningless words destined to become someone else's problem the day I choose—*or am chosen*—to leave them behind. On this particular day, the meetings on my calendar seemed almost a waste of precious fleeting time.

Time—there's that word again; a concept so real yet impossible to grab hold of.

Barry (6:36 a.m.): U text me yesterday about asking me a question.

Me (6:41 a.m.): Yes. What's your thought on that?

Barry (6:42 a.m.): On what?

Me (6:43 a.m.): Whether to put a message on our Facebook pages to tell your story and request prayers.

Barry (6:46 a.m.): Well, I need to talk to u about a few things first, when we can find time.

*****

Finding time. To find a thing requires that one must first seek for it. We look for time; we search for it; we long to slow it and to spend it. Sometimes we wait for it, and just when it arrives, it seems to brush right past us with hardly a sign. And then we waste so much of it. Have you ever given any thought to that? If you knew today exactly how much time was left in the total number of your days and years of life, how would you spend it? With whom would you spend it? Embrace every fleeting moment. Cherish them—every single one.

*****

Me (6:47 a.m.): Ok. Can I call you when I'm driving to work? Be about 45 to 50 minutes before I'm ready to leave.

Barry (6:48 a.m.): Yes.

I called him on my drive into work. He had nothing in particular to discuss about my sharing of his story. He just wanted to talk about all that was happening in his days and the way he was seeing others respond to the message he was personally sharing. It was heartwarming to hear the genuine humility and gratefulness in his heart. I'm learning the importance of being present. Often, the best gift we can give a person is our presence. Being present simply means listening to all that's in the other's heart, laughing with them, crying with them, encouraging them without offering unsolicited advice, and just letting them know they are loved unconditionally.

Me (8:34 p.m.): Goodnight. I love you!

STORMS + SUNSHINE = RAINBOWS

I woke up early. Much earlier than usual because I had a story to post. I titled it "A Rainbow in the Storm." Facebook readers tend to avoid long posts. That's why I decided to post two segments. His story isn't so unique. Others have similar problems—addictions and brokenness of many varieties—and all too often seclude themselves because they believe they're the only one. I wanted as many people as possible to see it, read it, and know they aren't the only one, they aren't alone, and there's a possibility for rainbows no matter how severe the storm. So I made the post *public*.

A Rainbow in the Storm—Part 1

"The rainbow shall be in the cloud, and I will look on it to remember the everlasting covenant between God and every living creature of every kind that is on the earth" (Genesis 9:16).

I *love* rainbows and white fluffy clouds. I could sit for days and gaze at them. More than the beauty, I *love* what a rainbow represents—God's forever-promise that he will never again destroy all living creatures on earth by a flood of water.

Within this promise and the sign of the rainbow, I find even deeper meaning and hope. When we consider the necessary conditions for rainbows to appear, we understand that rain or storms must also be present. But in the midst of these storms and rain, the light of the sun breaks through the clouds in an incredible display of brilliant colors—colors of hope and eternal promise.

In my next post ("A Rainbow in the Storm—Part 2"), I will share with you a personal story about a present storm and the rainbows we are finding here.

A RAINBOW IN THE STORM—PART 2

I'm sharing this story with my brother's blessing and his request for specific prayers. It's difficult to know how to begin, so I'll get right to the point ...

The storm

On Monday morning, September 24, 2018, after two weeks of testing and scans, we received the heartbreaking diagnosis that my brother, Barry Wilson, has small cell lung cancer. Over the several hours following this news, we learned that the cancer is very aggressive, very large, and has spread to his brain. It wasn't until Barry announced to his doctors his decision to decline all planned radiation and chemotherapy treatments that they gave us the hard truth—"short of a miracle," Barry's condition is terminal, regardless of any treatment.

The rainbows

It's amazing to me the sheer number of rainbows I've seen this year alone. More amazing, however, is the number of double rainbows I've seen. In this story, I can already see at least two rainbows.

Rainbow #1—For those of you who know anything about Barry's life story, you are aware that he has experienced a great deal of brokenness, pain, and suffering from addiction. For many years, he has tried to overcome and break the chains of addiction, but has failed repeatedly. His immediate family and our larger family have suffered through this pain along with him, which has left all of us tired and broken. Although we tried many times, we were at a loss to find a way to help him. For those of you who have walked a similar road with a loved one, you understand this pain and the many struggles that come with it. For those of you who haven't, I pray you never do.

But that's not the end of this story.

Six months ago—of his own accord and with no prodding from anyone else—Barry desperately sought once again to be freed from these chains of addiction. During a counseling session one day, a counselor he was working with told him, "Barry, you have a spiritual problem."

Barry told me that he rejected the notion at first, but later, he experienced something amazing. He heard the voice of God speaking into his heart that what he needed was him. The answer to all he had been seeking was the Lord. He said this moment in time changed *everything!* In complete surrender, Barry found *hope, redemption, cleansing,* and *peace.* His chains of addiction were broken in the moment—a decisive moment when he released control over his life and trusted Jesus Christ to make him brand-new to give him knew desires and a new way of living.

Barry's story is still being written, and it's an incredible story of life change and transformation from the inside-out. This is his personal statement to me:

> Sis, I'm completely blown away by God's grace and mercy! He is so *good!* If I had received this cancer diagnosis six months ago, before the Lord saved me and changed me, I'm afraid that I would have been very angry and would never have known Him. God knew that, and in His mercy, He kept me from this hour until my heart was ready. And I can honestly tell people that I didn't turn to God for fire insurance because I had no idea about this cancer at the time. I accepted

Him when He called me with an unmistakable voice that I knew was only Him. I realized that I had not gone too far and that He loves me and forgave me!

As I write this story, my own emotions are all over the board. I am eternally grateful for God's grace, mercy, and incredible power to transform lives. Yet I'm heartbroken to see my brother facing this violent storm. Tears of sadness and tears of the deepest joy converge together as they stream down my face, and I try hard to swallow this lump in my throat as I write.

Rainbow #2—God is doing even more miraculous healing work in our family. Relationships that have been broken for many years are being mended right before our eyes. That, too, is a miracle. All of it is a powerful display of brilliant light and color emerging in the darkest time my family has ever known. We have hope and we have peace in this crazy storm!

Barry and I discussed whether or not to share this whole story with the world. Oftentimes, people choose to live privately and to hide some of the ugly truth about their struggles. But, folks, I have to tell you—*the struggle is real!* Life can be very messy, and we would prefer to hide those skeletons in our closets. The truth is, however, that sometimes the story of our struggles and transformations can bring hope to others walking through the same thing or something similar.

Barry isn't on Facebook or any social platform, but he asked that I share his story all for God's praise and glory and with hope that it may help someone else find their way through a storm like this. He wants you to know that there is One who is in control of the universe. Only One who has the power to transform *any* life!

Barry, together with the rest of our family, believes that God truly has all power to do anything, even to physically heal him in spite of his diagnosis. And, just like in the rainbow, we have a promise that God is completely in control. He has the last word! God appointed the date of our birth, and he knows the date when we will breathe our last breath. Not one of us is exempt from that hour.

What makes all the difference in the end is the choice we make to receive or reject God's gift of eternal life. It's a gift because it's available to each and every one of us without cost. Barry *and I* plead with you to accept and not reject the gift.

Barry asks for your specific prayers for him for a miracle of physical healing so that he may continue to share his story of amazing life change. In his words, "God has the power to heal me. But if he chooses not to do that, the end is the same—I will be in heaven, and I'm so *excited* about that!" The smile on his face and the hope in his voice when he shares this truth is unmistakably genuine. It gives me such peace to see and hear it. To God be all the glory!

TAKING THE STORY WITH US

The morning of our departure for the Dominican Republic arrived, and we had to be at the airport by 4:30 a.m. The first Delta flight out of Jackson to Atlanta is at 6:00 a.m. The full story of our mission is not important for purposes of telling my brother's story, but I'll share a few details about where we were and what we were doing, just to help make sense and bring clarity to some of my dialogue with him during this seven-day period.

At 3:17 p.m. on that Saturday, he wrote, "Kavanaugh wins!"

Barry had been watching with great interest over the past several days the confirmation process of a new US Supreme Court Judge. He was in the camp of devoted conservative Christians and others who believed that Brett M. Kavanaugh was the right person for the job. The final confirmation occurred on this particular Saturday in October. In what was one of the narrowest margins in history, and amid angry demonstrations and protests on the streets in Washington DC, Judge Kavanaugh was confirmed as the 114th US Supreme Court Justice. It was a brutal fight to the end. The most significant allegation made against him was one of sexual assault involving a young woman, which allegedly occurred when both were teenagers. Kavanaugh denied the allegations.

God only knows the whole truth of the matter. Beaten down and bruised from the fight to uphold his honor, Mr. Kavanaugh took his place alongside the other Supreme Court justices that day. One of the others was Justice Clarence Thomas, who had also been accused of sexual harassment at one point in his past.

I'm always saddened to see the pain inflicted on families when the political limelight and angry mobs choose to expose sins of the almost forgotten past. They dig and dig until they uncover the most egregious actions they can find and then expose them for all the world to see and jeer about. I have to wonder how many of their own sins lie hidden—horrific things that, were they known, would mark the accuser of another as the most ungodly one of all.

None of these facts are of any great significance to the continuation of my brother's story, except to show the similarities and contrasts that exist in the lives of every single one of us. The fact is that we all have things in our past that we'd much rather forget than remember, things that, if it were possible, we would wipe clean from our own memory and the memory of others. It's unfortunate that we can't wipe the memory slate clean, particularly from those who wish to remind themselves *and us* of our past mistakes and sins. Too often, during the heat of an argument, one party or the other decides to make a current issue out of the other's past mistake or bad decision. In that moment, the past comes forward in the ugliest way. Barry fought this brutal battle against accusations and reminders of his sins over and over throughout his life. Sadly, they continued even to his very last days.

But on *this day*, he celebrated that Brett Kavanaugh had overcome a brutal battle, a battle that would scar him and his family for many years to come. Perhaps Barry understood the pain the man carried and somehow felt a strange connection to him in that way. It's a unique sense with which God has equipped us to empathize with the pain of others because we understand their pain in a personal way.

Barry was continuing his spiritual healing day by day as his soul and spirit drew closer and closer to God. But the scars were still there, and they will remain and outlast him. They are visible even now in the lives of his daughters, his mother, his father, and others who loved him most. *Time* will help to fade those scars, but nothing is able to fully remove them. Time to heal. Time to forget. Time to forgive.

I'm reminded of the scars that Jesus still bears in his hands and his feet. His were inflicted at the hands of evil men, and he remains fully innocent. I recognize them as beautiful sacred reminders of his love for me—for all of us. And I believe that as he continues to see them, He, too, is reminded of the *why* of his purpose for taking on a human body.

His scars; his death; his resurrection; and his ascension—all of it means *life* for anyone who puts their trust in him.

Because of our traveling, it was a few hours before I received his message about the Kavanaugh win.

Me (6:34 p.m.): Awesome! We have been climbing a mountain for an hour. I hope we will be there soon. Y'all okay?
Barry (6:52 p.m.): Y'all be safe. We're okay. Thanks.

We were in the Barahona Province in southwestern Dominican Republic. The scenery on this particular day had the look of a jungle. Our lodging for the week was behind a locked gate with a high fence all around. A giant avocado tree was in the front yard, and banana trees filled the back. Coffee plants were growing wild along the roadsides.

Barahona is one of the prominent coffee-growing regions in the Dominican Republic. I've traveled quite a bit, but I'd never been to a place quite like this one. I was intrigued, but my heart and mind were mostly someplace else.

October 7, 2018, 8:31 p.m.

Me: I hope y'all are good. Love you.
Barry: Great.
Me: The Lord is good! How was church today?
Barry: Awesome.
Me: Yay! We just got back from the local church here. Very different but good. We rode in the backend of a truck to get there. LOL.

Transportation was very limited where we were serving. Not everyone could fit inside the cab of the tiny truck that was our only mode of transportation. In fact, only three adults could squeeze inside. The rest of us piled into the bed of the truck.

I hadn't been on such a ride since Barry and I were kids. Dad often took us into the backcountry when we were young. Most often, these leisurely rides took us in search of wildlife, particularly deer; but there were times when we ventured out on a hot day to find a nice, cool swimming hole where we could play for hours in the fresh streams. We loved nothing more than an opportunity to let the wind blow in our faces as we rode unrestrained in the bed of our dad's pickup truck. Such sweet memories.

Barry: That's good… Pray; the prayer of faith will save the sick.
Me: Yes!

I sent him a photo of the front porch of the church with people standing in the doorway. As it was with Barry, thoughts of his healing were constantly on my mind. That was our deepest desire for him.

Barry: Looks different.
Me: ☺ Sure does.
Barry: What do y'all do? Do u preach or teach?
Me: We just meet and talk with people and share experiences. Tomorrow night, Tuesday and Thursday, we will be sharing scriptures and just encouraging the people. It's a young church. They just need people to show them they aren't alone… We are also helping this young missionary couple do some work on the house they've just moved into. They have two small children. Wow! What a commitment to move your family from Mississippi all the way here with no family members nearby… It's a hard life for them.
Barry: Is it hard to get around? When I'm completely healed, the Lord will place me somewhere; I know!
Me: Yes. We are in the mountains and some of the roads are bad. Some are good; most people don't have cars. We see people mostly with transportation like dirt bikes. Mud everywhere.

Me: That will be great! Such an honor to serve.

Barry: I know. I got tons of people believing for a total recovery.

Me: Your story has blown up on Facebook. People praying everywhere! It's awesome! Praise God!

Me: I hope you and Destini have a good week together!

Barry: We will.

Me: Ok. We are about to turn the lights out here. I love you. Goodnight.

Barry: Goodnight.

October 8, 2018, 11:25 a.m.

Barry: Thanks for blessing me and Destini.

Me: You're welcome!! Did she make it okay?

Barry: Yes; now.

Me: Awesome!! Y'all have a great week!

Barry: Thanks.

October 9, 2018, 4:45 p.m.

Me: Hey. Just want to check on y'all. It sounds like the weather is going to get rough there. Y'all okay?

6:13 p.m.

Barry: Hey, Sis. We're okay. Got your letter today. Thanks. Love the bracelets.

Me: Great!

I had mailed a letter to him before I left Jackson along with some rubber bracelets that had encouraging words imprinted on them. I thought he would enjoy wearing them. He loved that kind of thing.

October 10, 2018, 6:39 p.m.

Me: Have y'all had any bad weather?

Barry: Nooooooo; not bad weather. Haha!
Me: Awesome!

We had heard reports of hurricanes brewing in the area close to the Florida coastline. He made a joke of my question.

Me: Happy, Happy Birthday! Y'all do something fun! But don't go to the beach. ☺ Love you!
Barry: Thanks.

Barry turned fifty-six years young on October 11, 2018. It would be his last birthday on earth, and I was so happy that his oldest daughter was there with him to celebrate it. I was sad that I couldn't be there too. Just knowing that he was happy on that day was enough to satisfy my sad heart. And he was happy!

Me: How are y'all today? We are heading home soon. Yay!!
Barry: We good; praise God.

I never cease to be amazed at how quickly our days pass. This week passed like the speed of light. The time we spent with friends and new acquaintances that week are seared into my memory, though. The sights, the sounds, the smells, the activities, and even the thoughts that scrolled through my mind as each day passed remain permanently planted in my heart and mind. The time I was unable to spend with Barry is seared there too. As I look back now, however, I know the decision to go was the right one. He didn't want or need me hovering over him. He needed to *live*—just to feel alive one day at a time.

Me: We are in Atlanta. Almost home. I'll try to call y'all when I get there. It will be around 8:30 p.m.

October 14, 2018, 8:22 p.m.

Me: Hey! Just checking on you. We are home. I called Mama's phone last night. She said you were already in bed; so I didn't bother you. I love you.

Barry: K. I love u 2.

Me: I don't want to bug you. But let me know if you want to talk.

Barry: I will. It's been a life-changing two weeks.

Me: Oh! Yeah! None of us can even imagine. I wish I could, but I can't honestly say I completely understand. I hope you and Destini are having a good visit.

Barry: Yeah. It's a lot!

Me: Just stay focused on God's promises. Never forget in the darkness all He has shown you in the light. Satan can never steal what our Father has given you.

Barry: Amen. I need those reminders. Thanks.

Me: Yes! I'll keep reminding you.

Barry: I guess we all need reminding.

Me: Yep! I know I do! That's why I have to pray and stay in the Word every day!

Barry: Boy, u were right on time!

Me: The Spirit knows!

Barry: Does He ever! We just got back from church. It was good, but that one sentence from u was the meat and potatoes.

Me: You know what? I needed to hear that! I often feel like I only exist and make little difference in anyone's life. So I'm so glad to know that a simple sentence has made a difference for you today. Good stuff! God knows how to confirm when we need confirmation.

Barry: It changed my whole outlook on several things, and built my faith.

Me: Hey! Tried to call you. Hope you've had a good day! Call me when you feel like talking. Love you!

Me: "Beloved, we are God's children now, and what we will be has not yet appeared; but we know that when He appears we shall be like Him, because we shall see Him as He is. And everyone who thus hopes in Him purifies himself as He is pure" (1 John 3:2–3). This is pretty awesome! When we see God, we will be like Him, and that is a sight that no man has ever seen. We will be pure and beautiful because He is pure and beautiful. We will be radiant and holy, because He is. We will be pure love, because He is! Man! This list goes on and on!! Praise Jesus who died and rose to set us free!!

Barry: Amen; and we must keep our faith tank full.

Me: Amen! You feeling spunky this morning?

Barry: Not really.

Me: Bummer! Hey, was thinking about driving down this weekend to pick you up and bring you up here for a week or so. Maybe we can go hunting, and you can have your quiet space that you need for a few days, or whatever you would like to do. What do you think?

Barry: I want to get out. I can't seem to find the energy. I'll talk to you maybe later today. When u get time.

Me: I wonder if the nurse might be able to give you a Vitamin B-12 shot for energy. Do you have plenty of those Ensure drinks to help keep your energy up? Want me to call you now?

Barry: Yeah.

During our conversation, we talked a lot about how he was feeling and the daily challenges he was facing. He was experiencing a great deal of anxiety, which he attributed to relentless questions from Mom and the feeling that she was constantly watching him.

She was actually trying to help, worried that he might need something and just wouldn't ask. She didn't quite know how to *just be there* without talking, without questions, without trying to fix what couldn't be fixed. That's all he really needed or wanted.

The constant questions were wearing on his nerves. He was beyond anxious. Restless. What would tomorrow hold? Where exactly was heaven? How would he get there? Would Jesus greet him? Or would he have to go in search of him? Would it hurt? So many questions filled his mind. It all remained a mystery because no one alive could give him the answers.

*****

He was at home alone quite a bit because Mom helped care for an elderly man several days a week. He continued to participate in a prison outreach ministry with his church as well as a food distribution program in the community. He loved doing these things to be with people and share his story. He wanted to make a difference in these last days. Still, he continued to struggle with his communications with Mom, and he didn't know how to handle his thoughts and feelings about all that. It seemed to me that this was a weakness that the enemy of his soul chose to take advantage of. To inflict more pain. To grow animosity. It was a relentless battle.

I listened and offered encouragement in every way I knew how, but being so far away, it was difficult to be of any meaningful help. He struggled, too, with the decision he had made to forego medical treatment and to put all his faith in God, regardless of the outcome. Doubt tried to overtake his faith as the weeks passed.

No matter how strong our faith may be, we all have questions and doubts can arise if we forget where we came from or where we're going. Most often, doubtful days occur when the pain is particularly intense or when our prayers seem to yield anything but what we so desperately want to see.

I sensed the confusion and the fear that was creeping in on him. He wanted so badly to trust that God was going to heal him, but at the same time, I knew he was recalling *the message* I had shared with him before I left him the last time. I, too, struggled with the same thoughts. Oh how I wanted God to heal him and give him more time. I wanted him to be able to share his own story. In my mind, that would be the most impactful. But in my heart of hearts, I was convinced that this was not God's ultimate plan. And God's plan is always perfect. Barry's time was almost gone. I knew it. He knew it. I wanted to do something, *anything*, but this was too big for either of us. All of it was in God's hands—the timing, the outcome, *everything!*

October 17, 2018 7:38 p.m.

> B: I AM HEALED.
> Me: Praises to our God, who heals, and who lives!

This was the extent of our communication that day. I did and said everything I could to support him, to encourage him. And, yes, he was healed. He was healed in the deepest most incredible way. His soul was healed. His body remained wrecked with cancer, but cancer can't take a soul. It may claim a physical body, but the spiritual being inside of that body—no cancer or any other disease can destroy.

Some days, our hearts were so full that the formulation of written words just would not come. We each pondered a great deal as I know the rest of our family did. The thoughts inside my own head questioned much.

I wondered and I prayed, *God, what does this mean: "I am healed!"? I know what you've revealed to me, so help me to understand this. I want to believe that he is truly, physically healed; and while you've not given me a day and an hour, you, once again, have reminded me that his death is imminent. Please have your perfect will in this, and help me to understand what I need to know right now, and then have faith to leave the rest to you. Amen.*

October 18, 2018, 7:24 a.m.

Me: Jesus told the woman in Mark 5:34, "Daughter, your faith has healed you. Go in peace and be freed from your suffering." There's a lot packed into this verse. This woman was a daughter of God and fully loved by Him. Faith is the most powerful part. It is able to heal us of all disease and able to move a mountain out of its place. We can have ultimate peace with God, in God, and even in the world that is so full of unrest. We can have freedom from suffering because our Lord lives. He died, rose, and now lives forever to give us His freedom. Wow! That's good stuff!

Me: I was reading last night in a book titled *Whisper: How to Hear the Voice of God*. I found this powerful statement: "God is not great just because nothing is too big; God is great because nothing is too small. God doesn't just know you by name; He has a unique name for you. And He speaks a language that is unique to you." In other words, He sees us and knows us on an individual level—not as just one of a billion humans on earth who live in a tiny space of time and then vanish. We are more than just one tiny creature living in the vast universe He has made. I heard someone say one time, "If God has a refrigerator, your picture is on it!" LOL. This blows my mind! Our Father is amazing!

Barry: Good stuff, Sis. I feel like shouting because God is so great!

Me: Then go right ahead and shout! It's okay to do that anytime you feel like it! Yay! Love you!

October 19, 2018, 7:11 a.m.

Me: "And he arose and came to his father. But while he was still a long way off, his father saw him and felt compassion, and ran and embraced him and kissed him."

"But the father said to his servants, 'Bring quickly the best robe, and put it on him, and put a ring on his hand, and shoes on his feet" (Luke 15:20–22_. I'm so very grateful that even when we were a long way from our Father, He saw us coming, and He ran to meet us and hugged and kissed us; and He has put the family robe and ring on us to identify us as His children! Amazing Grace! Oh how sweet!

12:49 p.m.

Me: Hope your day is good! I love you!

I received no response to my messages that day. I tried not to press him too much when he remained silent. If too much time passed with no response, though, I called him or else I called Mom to get an update.

I worried about the mounting struggle and fear he faced. He was being as brave as he could be. This kind of bravery can only come with a heart settled safely on a firm hope. Regardless of that, I needed to keep watch and to assess the progression of his disease. It was a constant guessing game. We were headed straight into the eye of the storm. *Father, help us. We need you now!*

Prayer continued to be my constant source of peace and strength through it all.

October 20, 2018, 3:27 p.m.

Me: Love you! Hope you're having a really good day. "Now to him who is able to keep you from stumbling and to present you blameless before the presence of His glory with great joy, to the only God, our Savior, through Jesus Christ our Lord, be glory, majesty, dominion, and authority, before all time and now and forever. Amen" (Jude 1:24–25).

Barry: Thanks. It's a great day. God is opening doors everywhere for me to give my story. It's awesome. He's getting all glory, and I'm receiving peace, love, and joy.

Me: That's a perfect gift for you and perfect praise for the Father! Love it.

Barry: So humbling; and all the little things in my mind, He's taking care of those too.

Me: He just needed you to be focused so you can hear Him.

Barry: He's leaving nothing undone. It's wild!

Me: Ha-ha! We have no idea what all He has in store for us!

Barry: We know so little. He is organized and in order.

Me: You're right!

Me: Just thinking about you. Hope you're having a good day!

Barry: Having a great day. Thanks. 7 people got saved and delivered. The Lord's using me mightily.

Me: Wow! That's awesome! God is so amazing. The way He uses our stories and even our pain to help others find freedom is truly incredible! Keep telling your story! It's changing lives!

Barry: I know. The preacher said I did an awesome job. I said, "No! The Holy Spirit did!"

Me: Exactly!

Me: We are ALIVE! "But God being rich in mercy because of His great love for us has made us alive in Christ Jesus! By GRACE we are saved!" (Ephesians 2:4–5). What a gift! Praise God! Hope you have an awesome day!

No response.

Barry: I'm sorry if I hurt your feelings. Didn't mean to.

This statement was quite out-of-the-blue. I had no clue what he was even thinking about or referring to.

Me: You didn't! Why would you think you did?

Barry: Crazy thinkin', I guess!

Me: Over thinkin'. ☺ Love you!

Barry: Yes. Thank you.

Looking back, I now recognize this was a turning point in our communications. His thought processes were changing dramatically as I would soon discover in a much more tangible way. The "days to weeks" predicted by the oncologist were upon us. Barry's messages became much briefer and less frequent. I often had to guess as to their meaning. His mental capacity was quickly diminishing.

October 25, 2018, 6:32 p.m.

Me: I hope your day has been good! It's been raining here all day.
Barry: An awesome day; and rain also, but a great day.
Me: Fantastic! God is GOOD!
Barry: So good!

October 27, 2018, 8:42 p.m.

I sent him some photos of deer tracks I snapped on the way to my deer stand that afternoon. I told him, "You have to come and go hunting with us!" I meant it. I longed for him to have this one last hunting experience. All I was waiting for was for him to say the word.

October 28, 2018, 11:13 a.m.

Barry: I'm ready.
Me: Want me to come get you this week?

2:08 p.m.

Barry: What up?
Me: Not much. Just finished lunch. What y'all doin'?

October 31, 2018, 6:32 p.m.

Barry: When you get in from your next trip, let me know so we can plan a deer stalking. Can I hear a big 10-4, good buddy?
Me: Awesome! Okay!!
Barry: Do u know about when?

Me: I finish my last trip on the 16th. So I can drive down that weekend or wait until the next. Whatever works best for you!

My last three business trips for the year were scheduled back-to-back in early November. In spite of my booked calendar, though, I was mentally taking each day one at a time. If I had to drop everything and go, the calendar would have to change. I've learned this over the years. Not every plan we make will come to fruition. We sometimes have to improvise as the circumstances require it.

He seemed to be doing okay under the current circumstances, so my thought was, *Give me two more weeks, and then I'll be free to go for the rest of the year.*

November 1, 2018, 8:56 a.m.

Me: Psalm 34 is so awesome! I pray you have a magnificent glorious day praising the King of kings and trusting in His power and might. No weapon—not one—that is formed against you will prosper! That's a promise straight from heaven. "Many are the afflictions of the righteous, but the Lord delivers him out of them all" (Psalm 34:19).

5:35 p.m.

Barry: Y'all huntin'?
Me: Nah! It's been raining. I'm at work. What you up to?
Barry: I went lookin' for a bow.
Me: Cool. But you can use mine or David's.
Barry: I'm going to hunt here.
Me: Ok. Awesome. You can be practiced up!
Barry: Yeah. I'm goin' to.
Me: Did you find anything you liked?
Barry: Yeah. Can't think of the name, but its $349. They say it's the best. I've got to go back and let him set the scope.
Me: Nice. Mine is a Barnett. David's is some off-brand.
Barry: It's nice. It came from a bow shop.

Me: Crossbow?

Barry: Yeah. I'll find out.

Me: Nice. You'll have to be sure you get the tips for a crossbow. They're different from other types of bows. Also, you have to make sure you don't dry-fire it. That destroys them. You will have practice tips to use to practice with.

Barry: I know. He's going to train me.

Me: Perfect!

Had I known the full story about how it was that he had come to visit the bow shop, I would not have been so encouraging of his purchase or his hunting endeavors. I later learned that he had Mom take him to this bow shop. She described the visit as one where he was almost childlike in his behavior, as though he was a ten-year-old again and about to purchase his first BB gun, one he'd been dreaming about for months. She told me how she explained to the owner about his illness, and though both were concerned about the purchase, they opted to move forward with the transaction and fulfill his grand dream. Ignorant of these important facts, I played right into the unfolding of a potentially dangerous outcome.

In a follow-up telephone conversation that day, Barry explained to me that he was a little short on funds and that he would have to wait until his social security check arrived so he could finish paying off the bow and be able to bring it home. Ignorant as I was in this moment, I couldn't bear the thought of him missing out on a single thing. I decided to send him some money to help him finalize his purchase. I wanted to help bring about his last wishes as quickly as possible. But, for some reason, I hesitated to speak it out loud just yet. I would just sleep on it for a night and then see how I felt.

I recognized that something seemed *off* in our past few conversations, but because I wasn't present face-to-face, I couldn't quite put my finger on what it was exactly. I later learned that several other disturbing things were happening, things Mom chose to keep to herself. That's how she has dealt with him for years. Her pattern is to avoid talking about unpleasant things or things that might cause us to ask more questions, thinking they will get better eventually. She always hoped for the best and only reveals the truth when things get completely out of control.

Me: Hey; I'm going to put a check in the mail to you today to help you with your bow purchase! Love you!

Barry: U don't have to do that, Sis.

Me: I know but I want to.

Barry: I appreciate it a lot.

Me: You are WELCOME! I just want you to get a big deer!

Barry: I will. Might go up a notch on my choice.

Me: Ha-ha! I wrote you a $200 check. Hey, whichever one will make it easiest for you. Is that enough?

Barry: Cool beans.

Me: Super. Cool beans with deer sausage sounds pretty good.

Barry: For real.

My phone rang, and it was Barry. I was in a business meeting, so I couldn't answer the call immediately. Quickly, I tapped out this message to let him know I couldn't talk at that moment: "Sorry. I'm in a meeting. Do I need to excuse myself and call you now?"

Receiving no response, I called him as soon as I got a break. His conversation centered on whether I sent him the money I promised, the urgency of the hunt, and his anxiousness for getting the opportunity to try out his new bow.

I knew for sure now that something wasn't right. His communications with me reminded me of when we were teenagers. The cancer invading his brain was slowly taking control of his mind, his thoughts, and his capacity to think and reason. I struggled with what to do, whether to try and get through the next two weeks or to ditch the whole travel agenda and get myself to south Alabama. The clock was spinning; time was racing against us, and it was winning.

Barry: Why?

Apparently, he was reviewing his messages and seeing that he hadn't responded to my earlier message. He asked, "Why?" forgetting that he had called me earlier in the day, and I had returned his call.

Barry: What's up?
Me: That message was from this morning. I already called you.
Barry: Ok. Was you satisfied?
Me: Yes. I answered your question. It's all good. Let me know when you get your check.
Barry: Ok. Luv u.
Me: I love you too!

Barry: Things kinda strange around here.
Me: Why? What's up?

Me: You okay?
Barry: Fine.

TWENTY-SIX DAYS

There are seasons in life when it seems the challenges we face are insurmountable. It would be much easier to let go of life, to give up. The year 2018 was one of those seasons for me. By November, the waves of pain and suffering crashed against us so relentlessly that we gasped for breath between each wave. I can't describe what others felt, but for me, it was as though we were being violently dashed against the rocks, wave after pounding wave crushing my will to keep fighting for another breath.

As we clung to the Rock of Ages, the swirl of the current from beneath pulled at us harder still. With each new day, the struggle became more intense. I thought I was prepared. I wasn't.

It took every ounce of faith and energy I could muster just to keep putting one foot in front of the other. All I wanted to do was let go, to allow the waves to carry my weary soul out into the deep. At this moment in time, the lure of closing my own eyes and embracing the silence of death was much stronger than it should have been. Surely, there I could find rest, a reprieve from this nightmare.

But as it is with the human soul, we cling to life with all we have. We fight the death angels with vigor and determination. We *never* give up!

Tuesday morning, November 6, 2018

This November day began with my usual routine of getting out of bed at 4:30 a.m. I prepped the coffee to brew while I went to my prayer closet to seek for strength and wisdom to make it through another day. I sensed the presence of the Lord with me that morning, reassuring me that I wasn't alone. As I've read so many times in scripture, the Lord reminded me again, "I am with you. I won't leave you. Ever. No matter what you face today, I'm here!"

This source of strength is foreign to many, but my faith in God is my lifeline. It's how I find my way through the dark. It lights my path, pointing out the "next right step" at each fork in the road. He grants me wisdom to know which way to go when competing voices and responsibilities pull me in a dozen different directions. When these heartaches leave me too broken to move, too lifeless to stand, and too weak to hold on to life any longer, he catches me in his everlasting arms and breathes fresh air into my deflated lungs, reviving me sufficiently so I can get up and fight some more. I cry from the very depths of my soul, "*I will never give up!*"

*****

Our journey through life requires that we make hundreds of decisions throughout the day, often without even being conscious we're making them. It's as though we flip on an *autopilot* switch and just move through our day without ever really thinking about where we will go, how we will get there, or what we will do once we arrive. Many of us could probably navigate the majority of our daily routine in our sleep. Few of us ever give any thought to our capacity to think, to reason, or to make decisions at all. Perhaps some of you are thinking, *This is much too philosophical to waste my time thinking about.* I urge you, nonetheless, to contemplate these things for just a few minutes as you read the next few pages.

Reflecting, as I am now, on the bigger picture of what took place during Barry's last four weeks helps bring this decision-making capacity into full focus for me. I have a new appreciation for it. The incredible capacity of our ability to think, to reason, to decide what we will do today and how we will respond to each challenge exists deep inside each of us. Yet we do it without deliberation or any conscious appreciation for it whatsoever.

As I sit propped up in bed this morning with my laptop perched on a pillow in front of me, I look around the room and wonder, *How many millions of decisions have I made over the past fifty-six years, which have brought me to this day and this place?* It's overwhelming to consider the multitude of decisions made in just the past week or the past twelve months. I'm not thinking merely of the *big* decisions but all the semiautomatic choices I make every day. *What will I eat for lunch? Where will I spend my Saturday? Which route should I take to work? Should I stop at this light that just turned yellow in front of me or speed through it? Should I react to that condescending email message with what I really want to tell my coworker or do I take the high road?*

All of these and hundreds more decisions are made every single day. To think of how many I've made in the span of my lifetime is sobering, to say the least. One alternate decision made in a moment of anger, stress, pressure, loneliness, or jubilation could have taken me down a completely different path and led me to a completely different end. My life's story and yours is being written each day with every small or significant choice we make.

In the weeks and months leading up to these last days of Barry's life, he often reflected on the choices he made in the past. He frequently reflected with much regret about his choices, even prior to these last months and days. I and others have shared in his sorrow with many tears when he talked of unchangeable decisions he wished he could undo. During the year 2018, he talked a lot about his regretful past choices that had stolen his best years, and it was inspiring to hear how his reflections changed. He embraced this one most important fact: God doesn't hold his past against him.

Barry came face-to-face with the ultimate decision: to either accept God's gift of grace and forgiveness or to reject it. If he had rejected it, you wouldn't be reading this right now because I wouldn't have been able to bring myself to write his story. I can't imagine—I don't even want to imagine—how difficult a task that would have been since it's been the most gut-wrenching experience of my life to write this one; one that has a beautiful ending.

Reflecting on decisions made in the past can help us to make better ones today and tomorrow. Although we can't change the past, we can take lessons learned from the past and apply them to what we do with *today*. With that said, it's important that we resist the temptation to allow our reflections of bygone days to negatively impact the here and now. Rather than allow your reflections to signal regret, identify ways to change your course for good. Make every decision with this goal in mind.

*****

Driving down Lakeland Drive in Jackson, Mississippi, at 7:30 a.m. on a Tuesday has the potential to raise one's blood pressure to an unhealthy level to say the least. Rush hour traffic sets me on edge. A sea of red taillights signaled a momentary pause in my commute as I passed Jackson Preparatory School. With both hands on the wheel, eyes keenly on the taillights in front of me, and my right foot firmly on the brake, I continued talking with my mom on the way to work. The stress and urgency in her voice today signaled an alarm. "I just can't do this anymore!" she said to me.

As I questioned her further, she explained Barry's bizarre and irrational behavior and his ridiculous accusations against her. Paranoia was surfacing. She had trouble articulating exactly what was going on, but I knew the time had come for me to go.

I drove about one more mile down the road, made a U-turn at the Forestry Museum on Lakeland Drive, and headed back home to pack my bags. As I rerouted, I called my assistant to inform her, "The time has come. I have to go." Without any explanation necessary, she understood exactly what I was saying. Weeks ago, she had fore-warned me that this time would come because she had faced a similar situation with her father a few years earlier. I asked her to cancel all my flights and hotel reservations and to make apologies and offer explanations to whomever needed them.

I called my boss and my husband, too, to explain the situation. Giving only the necessary details, I promised more information as soon as possible. This would be an open-ended journey. I had no idea how to judge the time or when I might be able to return. Having reassurance and support from everyone I spoke to that morning, the decision I'd made was final, and a new chapter began.

Back at home, I gathered everything I thought I might need for the next few weeks. It was November, and we were headed straight into the Thanksgiving and Christmas holidays. I had given little thought to preparations for these holidays before now. I hadn't purchased a single gift, and no decorations or holiday festivities had yet been planned. In all honesty, preparations for this season were the last thing on my mind. The thought of celebrating *anything* was the furthest one from my mind. I simply trusted that it would all work out in the end.

Knowing that Barry had his heart set on a deer hunt with his new bow, I packed my own along with some warm clothes for hunting. I grabbed the notebook containing "the message," which I knew I would need before I returned home. In my conversations with Barry over the past few weeks, I also knew how much he wanted a dog to love. He loved animals, particularly my dog, Samson. He had fallen in love with Samson during the time he lived with us in 2013. He had begged Mom to let him have a dog, but she continued to resist that idea. So in a last-minute decision—which, as I reflect on it now, was a bad one—I decided to take both dogs with me, hoping that Samson might be a calming influence for Barry as we moved forward.

By 11:00 a.m., my Jeep was packed so full I could barely see anything through the rearview mirror. I grabbed the dogs, and the three of us began our six-hour journey. As I drove, I called my dad, my sister, and my younger brother to update them about everything. The trip took longer than expected. The dogs are often very nervous when we travel, and today was certainly no exception to that rule. One hour into the trip, I regretted my decision to bring them along, but I kept telling myself that they would soon calm down and that all would be fine. How wrong I was! By the time I rolled into my mom's driveway around 6:00 p.m., I was completely exhausted, the sun had set, and it was already dark.

Barry was unaware that I was coming. The look on his face when he saw me appeared to me as one of relief. Thinking back now, I'm not sure that was it at all. He gave me a quick warm hug. Then, just as quickly, he went on about his business as though I wasn't there and that nothing out of the ordinary was happening. When I saw Mom, her face told a different story. Hard lines of worry creased her brow, but she reflected an expression of silent relief. Sometimes we have to face life's challenges alone, but it sure is easier when we have others to walk alongside us. And this was one of those times. She was no longer alone, and she welcomed the company.

I let the dogs down to stretch their legs and find a fire hydrant before unloading. As I looked around, I saw that the patio furniture was stacked one piece on top of the other in a bizarre arrangement. I asked her, "What's this?"

Mom explained, "Barry did that. He stacked up the chairs and table so he could use it as his pulpit. He's been preaching." She went on to tell me how he had been teaching or preaching to an invisible audience. She didn't elaborate any further, and we promptly dropped the subject, exchanging silent glances that revealed the worry in both our hearts.

Barry was excited when he first saw Samson. He recognized him quickly and cuddled him for a few minutes, but his attention soon turned to other things. He seemed almost unaware of the dogs' presence after that. His thoughts were scattered and his mind restless, moving from one thing and then to another as I've seen children with short attention spans do. Not long after I arrived, he went to his room and was soon sound asleep, which had become his daily routine. He spent the majority of time in his room, watching his favorite religious broadcasts on TV or sorting through his personal books and papers.

Mom and I talked for a while that evening about what had been happening over the past several days and weeks since I was last there. I assured her that I was there for the duration and there was no need to worry about being alone anymore. I quickly surmised that her being so close to the situation this whole time had made it difficult for her to see the dramatic changes in him, which I quickly recognized. She knew he had become more difficult to communicate with, but she didn't understand that his anger and frustrations were emotions triggered by his deteriorating brain functions.

I had done quite a bit of research over the past few weeks and had read all the material they gave us before leaving the hospital in September. I went through that packet of information again that night. The material was written in a way that allowed for the varying experiences of individual patients. Everything I read was vague with respect to how much time we could expect at this point. Each person's journey is unique and dependent on so many factors. Enough information was provided, though, to help us know what signs to watch for and the general order of the cancer's progression. I recalled the oncologist's words again. "Days to weeks," she had said. We were exactly six weeks beyond that conversation.

Wednesday, November 7, 2018

Wednesday morning, I awoke with the sunlight streaming through the blinds in my room. The hospital bed, which had been there the last time I slept in this room, was gone. About three weeks earlier, Barry and Mom decided they didn't need it—at least not now. The home health company came by and took it all away, including the oxygen tank and several other items that they had been using when he first came home from the hospital. They wanted to live a normal life as long as possible, and I can understand that. But six weeks slip away so quickly. Time stops for no one.

I was tired and wanted to sleep longer, but the dogs were restless and wanted to go out. So I rolled out of bed and quietly carried them to the door, trying to keep from waking anyone else. It took a minute to move all the chairs Mom had placed against the door (that's how she feels secure in the house, even today).

The morning was warm but pleasant. What would this day bring? *Lord, only you know. Please give me wisdom and strength to face whatever challenges are coming*, I prayed as I breathed in fresh air and gazed at the sky overhead. Once Samson and Gracie had relieved themselves of a full night's bladder holding, we came inside, and I brewed some coffee.

Mom awoke first and met me in the kitchen. Still showing significant signs of distress, she told me she needed to go and make some arrangements for the care of the elderly man she worked for, but she would be back as soon as she had everything in order. She was the primary caregiver and confidante of the old man. At ninety-five years old, he didn't trust anyone other than her to care for his daily needs. She knew the time had come for others to tend to him while she took care of her son.

She and I vowed to face this challenge together. My sister had her hands pretty full with her girls and hair salon. Our younger brother had some work responsibilities and travel plans he was working through. My dad was not well enough himself to handle this kind of intense care. Each promised to be there to help whenever and however we needed them. It would take a village, and a village we were!

I decided to wait until after talking with the hospice nurses before contacting Barry's daughters. They talked with him frequently over the past weeks, and I was grateful for this renewed connectedness. He needed that, and so did they. I couldn't be sure whether they had recognized any of the changes Mom and I had seen in him more recently, but I didn't want to raise any unnecessary concerns to them until I had the best information possible.

At this point, too, I didn't know what the hospice nurses were seeing or thinking about his condition. The details of their visits were not shared with me, and I'm not convinced that anyone actually inquired of them much about his progression. I hoped to get some answers today.

Barry got up, smiled a sweet "Good morning" and, with a cup of coffee in hand, made his way to the back patio. This was his customary morning routine. I soon discovered that this routine was about to be severely disrupted. Morning coffee would be the *only* normal part of our days going forward.

As soon as Mom left the house, he started talking. I mean *talking a lot!* He had remained rather quiet up to this point. But, now, whoa! He unloaded. The things he said caught me completely off guard. I *knew* from his text messages and phone calls that the two of them were at odds, but I had no idea how intense their emotions had become. The accusations he made against her were beyond my wildest imagination. I didn't know whether to believe any part of what he was telling me or to chalk it up to another episode of irrational thoughts brought about by his diminished mental capacity. Nevertheless, I listened, took note, and followed up.

I suspected that the story he told me was a bit self-serving and perhaps the result of paranoia he was unable to control. I tried not to draw any quick conclusions without more information, however. Something was causing this disturbance, *but what?* It's become second nature for me in my role as an attorney and a compliance officer to take facts from all sources available, analyze them, and draw a reasonable conclusion. I've learned to question everyone, investigate everything, and arrive at a conclusion only after weighing all the facts and circumstances because, more often than not, the *real story* is rarely ever told by a single individual. The truth is found somewhere between each person's own unique perspective. I hesitate to call it self-centeredness, but I'm inclined to believe that, for most people, self-focus and self-talk leads them into a reality unique unto themselves.

After a good long talk, he wanted to take his car to a little shop nearby to have the oil changed. He asked if I could follow him there so he could drop it off. The little shop was only about a mile from the house, so he hopped into his car and took off. I got into my own and followed fairly close behind him, since I didn't know the precise location. I didn't want to get lost. As we drove, I was instantly alarmed at how he drove—all over the road, first on the right side of the road, and then to the left. It was a small two-lane road, and thankfully, it was not heavily traveled.

Alarm bells continued to ring as we drove into the parking area of the country shop. He didn't slow down much but drove to the opposite end of the man's shop. I parked and walked around. My heart was in my throat when I saw he had driven the car dangerously close to a large pit that had been purposely dug to allow the mechanic to work beneath vehicles. Barry had driven within three inches of the edge of the hole and got out of the car. One more rotation of the wheels, and he would have crossed over into the hole. I waited without saying a word while he asked the man if he had time to change the oil. We agreed to leave the car and come back in a couple hours.

Back at home, Barry was eager to show me his new crossbow. We took it outside and set up the practice target. He was so proud of his new purchase, and his smile spread all across his face. He tried but didn't have the strength to pull the string back to cock the arrow in place, so I helped him with that.

I was amazed at the accuracy of his shots. He hit close to the bull's-eye every time. We each took turns practicing our skill, and we talked about where we might find a place to hunt nearby. We planned to go to a farm where Mom's elderly friend owned some land and had given us permission. I planned to take him there as soon as he felt strong enough to go. Today, he wasn't up for that challenge, plus we had a scheduled meeting with his nurses for early afternoon. So we spent our time just talking and being.

Mom got back around lunchtime, still stressed to the max. I briefed her about our morning but didn't go into the accusations he had made. Around midafternoon, Janitha, the hospice nurse, came by. Nurse visits were scheduled only two or three times a week. They primarily took his vital signs, checked his medications, and did a basic wellness check. During today's visit, I noted that she asked him lots of questions. Things like "What's your name? What day is this? Who is this nice lady sitting beside you? Who is the US President?" He was able to answer all the questions promptly and accurately.

He loved Janitha, and they joked with one another a lot. She told me before she left that it appeared things may be changing a bit, and we would need to keep close watch on everything. After sharing some of my concerns with her, she adjusted the visit schedule to have a nurse come by daily.

After the nurse left, I decided I needed to talk to Mom a little more. She and Barry had to get to a better place in their communication and relationship or this was going to be much harder than necessary. We talked a little, particularly about the things Barry had told me. I questioned her about some of the specific accusations he had made, and she was immediately defensive. That concerned me, but I listened and took note there too. What I concluded was that the general facts were true, but each one's perspective and rationale was completely different. I did my best to ensure that each one was appeased and that we could move forward with less anxiety and friction.

Regardless of any concerns or issues that had arisen between them, I was here—for the duration—and I would monitor all interactions very closely. Again, I assured her that I wasn't going anywhere and we would face this together.

Later that Wednesday afternoon, we decided to take a little road trip to the nearest shopping center. Barry needed a phone card for his cell phone. He used a pay-by-month phone plan, which required a monthly purchase of a card that gave him Internet data and call capabilities. His prior month plan had just expired, and he wanted to call his daughters. I drove, he rode in the passenger seat beside me, and Mom was in the back. The tension in the air could have been "cut with a knife," as the old saying goes. So we drove mostly in silence as we headed to a Walmart store about eighteen miles away. This seemed to be the best option since we needed a few other things. I didn't ask where they wanted to go, and no one made any specific requests, so I just went to the only place I knew.

When we had driven *maybe* four miles, we passed a small convenience store in the middle of nowhere. It never crossed my mind to consider stopping there when he suddenly began yelling for me to stop. "There, there! Stop there!"

His tone turned to anger when I didn't instantly stop. He yelled at me, "Why didn't you stop there?"

I responded with a surprised, "Why?"

"I can get a card there!" he said with more angst.

I explained to him that we were only a few miles from Walmart, so that's where we were going. His entire personality changed instantly, and he continued to stew. He yelled at me again, "You're just a hard a———!"

He was so belligerent that it took me by surprise, and I didn't respond well. I told him to calm down or I'd put him out, to which he began demanding that I let him out. I continued to drive, and he mumbled under his breath until we reached our destination. Immediately upon arriving and parking, he jumped out of my Jeep without saying a word and disappeared into the store.

I sat there, stunned for a moment. The look in Mom's eyes was telling. *This* was the kind of anger issues she dealt with and refused to tell us about. Catching my breath, I asked if she was ready to go in. She told me she wasn't feeling well and would just sit in the car. I made a quick mental list of things she needed and went inside. It took me a few minutes to find everything, and I took my time so I could calm down more before looking for him.

Once I had everything on our list, I went to the electronics department to see if I could spot him. He was nowhere in sight. I meandered all over the store searching for him but couldn't find him anywhere. Believing he had found what he needed and returned to the vehicle, I checked out and went there myself. Much to my surprise, he wasn't there. Mom said he hadn't been back to the car. We sat there for a few more minutes, and when he didn't return, I went back inside, looking for him again.

When I walked in the door, I thought I heard my name called over the intercom. I thought, *What? Did I just hear my name?* So I strained to listen to hear above all the other noise in the store. Again, I heard what sounded like my name. I looked all around and spotted him near the service desk area. He was standing in the middle space between the checkout kiosks and the service desk. He stood there, turning around and around with searching eyes. Then he saw me and pointed in my direction with a big smile on his face. We walked, one toward the other, and met in the middle.

His tone and expression had changed again. He looked at me with a calm serious face and said, "I couldn't find you!" He went on to tell me that he had gone to the service desk and asked them to call me.

"I looked all over the store for you," I told him, "but I couldn't find you. Then I went to the car, and you weren't there. So I came back inside."

I confirmed that he had found the phone card he needed, and we began walking to the car. Once outside the store, he paused. In a childlike shaky voice, he turned and said to me, "Sissy, I was so scared! I reported myself missing because I couldn't find you. I didn't know what else to do."

I looked him in the eyes and saw fear there that matched his words. It broke me! Right then, right there, I stopped. I hugged him. We cried.

I never shared with him how scared I was in that moment, but I will never forget that day or how I felt. He responded to my embrace by hugging me back with a genuine childlike embrace, clinging as a child does to his mother. I said, "It's okay! I've found you now, and it's going to be okay! Let's go home."

*****

Back at home, everything remained relatively quiet for the rest of the evening. We never spoke again of the angry exchange. This was the first of many escalating bouts of anger and intense frustration we would experience over the next two weeks.

We ate dinner together, and as usual, he ate very little. He took his bedtime medications early, then went outside to call his daughter.

Thursday, November 8, 2018

Thursday began much like Wednesday. Barry's thoughts and speech were on point much of the time, but he went off the rails at other times. I shared Wednesday's events with Janitha. She urged us not to leave Mom alone from this point forward. Barry needed constant attention and care. The urgency of Janitha's words was all I needed to hear. Barry was still able to answer the basic questions she asked, but she was alarmed about the sudden bouts of anger and frustration followed by childlike behavior.

As our situation allowed, I took time to make calls to my office and check e-mail to address urgent things at work. I was so very grateful for my team's willingness to step up to the plate and for my boss's understanding and patience. I love how the Lord supplies for every need we have, even to supplying people and friendships through every season of our lives. Nothing happens by chance. I firmly believe that "to everything, there's a time and a season, and a time to every purpose under heaven" as Ecclesiastes 3:1 says. I believe that every person we encounter along the way is part of our story and of God's grand unfolding of his plan for us and for the greater good.

I worried about Barry's sudden urge to start smoking again. He had quit for several months, but now he seemed to be reverting to his old habit, a habit that had been woven into his daily routine for decades. *What's happening here?* I wondered. I questioned whether he might have been smoking all along and no one knew. Or had his mind reached that point where he was merely returning to the familiar from the past, his brain reconnecting with past memories like that of an Alzheimer's patient? Taking into consideration all that I had observed in the last two days, I was convinced that his brain was taking him to a familiar place. He seemed to struggle with the right and wrong of the whole matter. One minute, he felt guilty for smoking, and the next, he was searching for the package he had only moments before instructed me to throw away.

I remember many times when we were growing up, he struggled with right and wrong, often being remorseful for something he had done. It was a constant wrangling of emotions. I heard him ask one of the rotation nurses one day if she thought it was a sin for him to smoke. Those were the kinds of questions he would ask my mom when he was a boy. His nurse tried to comfort him by saying, "Well, I think God will understand."

Her response disturbed me. Who was she to tell him such a thing? It was obvious to me—and I thought it should have been to her—that this was more than just a passive harmless act or question with which he was struggling. Giving her grace in this moment, however, I accepted the fact that she was not a psychologist nor a spiritual counselor. She also had no knowledge of his past, so she couldn't understand or appreciate the spiritual significance of his question or how this act of smoking was affecting his mind, will, and emotions.

More on this later...

*****

Since I arrived Tuesday evening, an evolution of dramatic changes had unfolded. As each hour passed, it seemed as though the sand flowed ever more swiftly through the tiny hole in the hour-glass—the last hours of Barry's life. I mostly sat with him to talk. When he went silent, I lingered near to observe his actions. At one point on this particular afternoon, he sat on the sofa with his eyes closed, with his fingers fidgeting with an unlit cigarette, putting it in his mouth and taking it out again without any attempt to light it. The movements seemed almost involuntary. Habitual. As though the *familiarity of the process was strangely comforting to him.* His eyes were weak, but his body remained quite strong. He played with the dogs occasionally but mostly ignored them.

Mom and I decided to take him for a drive Thursday afternoon to get him out the house for a few hours and give ourselves a break as well. We found a little barbeque restaurant in a nearby town and stopped for a bite to eat. The place was rather quiet with only a hand-ful of other patrons. He ate and talked very little, more introverted than I'd seen him in a very long time.

We tried to act and speak as normally as possible, taking extra care with our words so as not to arouse him or cause a scene. As soon as we had finished eating, he headed outside and lit a cigarette. We kept a close eye on him from inside until we could pay and head home. Mom had the radio on a Christian station. As we rode, I could hear Barry humming a familiar tune to himself in the back seat. This gave me an idea.

After the song had finished, I turned off the radio and asked if they would like for all of us to sing. With no response, I started to sing the hymn "Amazing Grace." Soon, I heard this beautiful bari-tone voice coming from seat behind me. I turned on my phone's recorder to capture the beauty of this moment. I couldn't let the opportunity slip away. We might never again hear anything more precious for the rest of his days or ours—an unforgettable, unrepeat-able, priceless moment.

Friday, November 9, 2018

Barry was adamant that he was going hunting on Friday. I had put the crossbow out of sight, hoping he would forget about it. He didn't. Periodically, he would remember it and ask me for it. Attempts to distract the thought and get his mind on something else were mostly successful.

The defining moment when I knew for sure this weapon had to go came late on this Friday afternoon. An unfamiliar dog strayed into the backyard. Oddly, the dog seemed to agitate him, though I'm not sure why.

He said, "I'll take care of him! I'll shoot him with my bow!"

The way he said those words and the look of determination in his eyes when he said it frightened me. This sudden unprovoked response toward an innocent animal settled all remaining questions in my mind about allowing him access to this deadly weapon. I mentioned the incident to the nurse, and she agreed. So after he went to bed that night, I took the bow, the arrows, and the target—everything that I thought might trigger any remembrance of it—and I put them in the back of my Jeep, covered it all with a blanket, and locked the door. The nurse advised us to remove all weapons—guns, knives, or anything he might be able to use to harm himself or anyone else—from the house. We even hid the kitchen knives. Except for this one incident, we had not seen any violent tendencies, but given his state of mind and the fact that he was quickly losing his mental capacity, we had to take every precaution possible to keep him and the rest of us safe.

Friday, November 9, 2018, 4:40 p.m.

Barry: When?
Me: When what?

No response.
There was no context for his text message, so I left it alone.

Saturday, November 10, 2018, 9:05 a.m.

Barry: Ya!

This was the final text message I would ever receive from him.

His phone lay still and silent.
No more tapped out messages.
No more pings.
No more rings on the other end of the line.
Forever silent.

*****

As I sit here alone in this hotel room in Indianapolis and enter these last words, I can't stop the flow of tears streaming down my face. The pain of this recollection is all too real. The memories, the struggle, the laughter, and the pain of those final days are so vivid in my memory all these months later.

At the same time, too much of all that transpired in those last days is becoming cloudy in my memory. Thank God that he gave me strong prayer partners to walk with me through those dark days. Thank God, too, that he gave me wisdom and a vision of things to come, which caused me to retain all his messages to me.

These messages are a significant part of my ability to tell the story to recall dates, times, and events as we walked this journey through death's valley. They are a lifeline when I tend to forget how good God was to him and how good he is to me now. They remind me of promises fulfilled.

> The LORD is my shepherd; I shall not want. He makes me lie down in green pastures; He leads me beside the quiet waters. He restores my soul; He leads me in the paths of righteousness for His name's sake. Yea, though I walk through the valley of the shadow of death, I will fear no evil; For You are with me. (Psalm 23:1–4)

> He gives strength to the weary, And to him who lacks might, He increases power. (Isaiah 40:29)

By this date, his sense of reality was all but gone. His brain was incredibly confused, smothered as it was by the cancer cells that knit themselves tightly around it. His body was stronger than it needed to be, especially when his thoughts were totally irrational. He was quite mobile during the first couple weeks after my return. His physical strength was a liability now.

The event with the oil change led us to decide to take his car keys. We stopped short of demanding that he give them up. We just put them out of sight, hoping that he would forget them. We couldn't risk having him disappear; or worse, risk his getting into an accident. His increasing explosive reactions to physical events, together with his tendency to run away or hide from us, was disturbing, to say the least. I worried that when he ran, he might not remember how to get back to us.

These last four weeks of his life were a day-by-day downward spiral. His brief moments of lucidity followed other moments of irrational thoughts and actions. Sprinkled amid all this were tearful remembrances and eruptions of laughter, even dancing. He danced that day, right there in the middle of my mom's living room floor. We watched in amazement as he danced with so much vitality. So light on his feet, he spun round and round. We ached so deeply as we beheld this extraordinary sight. He was lost somewhere in his own mind, very much at peace, and it seemed he was oblivious to our presence. Was he dancing with the angels? Was he dancing for Jesus? I can only imagine.

Mom's and my own emotional roller-coasters matched his, loop for loop. It was a wild ride, exhilarating and frightening at the same time. It was like nothing either of us had ever before experienced.

Thinking back now, I wish we had taken the opportunity to dance right along with him. Yet the pain I recall having as we watched this bizarre sight unfold was simply more than we knew how to handle. We had never passed this way before. These uncharted waters swelled and receded in inexhaustible waves, which left us devoid of strength to stand and much less to dance.

Serene moments were much too short. We never knew how long they might last. For in the very next moment, we would find ourselves in the middle of a new scene, one triggered by an invisible spark. His frustrations led to anger, and his frustrations mostly stemmed from the fact that he couldn't remember how to do something that he knew he was supposed to be able to. It was irreversible. He was helpless. So were we.

Sunday, November 11, 2018

As the hours passed quickly by, I struggled to know what to do, what to say, or how to feel. I struggled to maintain my own sanity while watching my brother slowly slip away. My heart broke to see the pain in my mother's eyes, not knowing how to comfort her or to make this impossible situation a little easier for her to bear.

It was Sunday, and I wanted to go to church. I needed to be surrounded by people of faith. But his actions had become so unpredictable I hardly knew what to do. I couldn't go and leave him there, but if we went and I lost control of him, that could be very bad.

Tensions were high in the house. He refused to eat but took his coffee cup and went to the back patio where he always sat to think or smoke or talk on the phone. The smoking thing continued to be a significant source of anxiety for him.

In a decisive moment, I prepared to go to church, recognizing I might have to change my mind at the last minute. I watched and waited to see what kind of mood he was in and where his mind seemed to be as the clock drew nearer to 10:00 a.m. He seemed determined to go to church as well, and in a lucid moment, he made himself ready. We went with the flow of the moment. The three of us loaded into Mom's car about 10:30 and drove the short distance to the church he always attended.

Several people were already inside the small metal church building. In this small town, most churches have fewer than a hundred people on a typical Sunday morning. This one was smaller still, and that was a blessing. Once inside, a few people greeted us. I recognized some of their faces, but I couldn't recall any names. One lady walked up to him and started hugging him, crying and refusing to let go. That scene caused some others to roll their eyes. Others looked on with sad faces. I didn't know what to do or say, so I stood, quietly waiting until we could find a seat and wait for the service to begin.

Neither Mom nor I got much out of the message. Our hearts were so full and our emotions quite on edge. Barry was less than attentive. As soon as the service was over, we headed for the door, choosing not to tarry for conversation. Church members and neighbors had brought lots of food to the house on Saturday. So we had plenty (too much, actually) to eat. Rather than risk another explosive event in a public place, we opted to go home and eat leftovers. We ate quietly and waited for the nurse to come by. Philip, the assigned chaplain from the hospice group, had dropped by to check on us the day before. *What a dear man! So genuine.* So our only expected visitor for Sunday was the weekend nurse. Great. We needed rest.

While Mom and I cleared the table and worked to clean up a few other things, Barry went outdoors to his usual spot on the back patio. *This* was the one place he was most at peace. The nurse came and went with no significant concerns noted.

Periodically, I checked to be sure that he was still present and okay. Looking out the French doors leading from the dining room into the backyard, I watched with interest as he raked the few leaves that had fallen to the ground. Pin oaks are abundant there, and they drop tiny leaves all over the lawn. I was amazed at the vigor and stamina with which he raked those leaves—with determination and purpose—just as I had always seen him do, no matter what job he was busy doing. He pursued each task as though time was about to run out. He did nothing in moderation. Anything short of wide-open throttle for him was complete stillness.

Since he was occupied with raking leaves—a harmless task, I imagined—I busied myself with a book for a few minutes. Only moments later, I looked up and was startled to find that he had raked the leaves into a pile and set fire to them. Knowing that his mind was not fully functional, I did the first thing that came to mind. My motherly instinct came alive, and I marched right out the door and told him to put out the fire. In hindsight, I realize that I might have overreacted a bit. But fearful that the fire could get out of control—

because in my mind, he was like a child—I gave a command that I soon regretted.

He lost it! I never imagined that he would react the way he did at this simple statement. A bystander would have thought I had taken away his favorite toy or told him to stop playing his favorite game. He threw a temper tantrum, similar to those I've seen little kids throw when they want to get their own way. He started kicking the fire with his feet, screaming and telling me how horrible I was for telling him what to do. Burning leaves scattered in all directions.

As disturbing a scene as it was, I was satisfied just knowing the fire was out. For sure, his reaction unnerved me again, but I believed the tantrum would be short-lived and he'd soon calm down. I walked quietly back into the house and left him to his fuming.

Just to be certain that all was well, I went to check up on him a few minutes later. He had disappeared from sight! I looked and called for him, but he was nowhere, and I had no idea in what direction he had gone. It made me downright mad that he was acting so childishly. Mostly, I was scared, but I let myself believe that I was just angry at his reaction. So I did what any mother would do—let the runaway child stay hidden around the corner until he got tired of the game and came out of hiding. Nevertheless, I went to find Mom to tell her what had happened. She was in a back bedroom, having been on a phone call while all this was taking place.

"He's run away again," I told her. We each thought—and hoped—he would come back soon. At the very least, he would surely call her phone if he was lost again. He still seemed to understand how to use his phone and who to call if he was in trouble, although I was no longer assured of his capacity to reason in this way.

Several more minutes passed with no sign of him anywhere. It was dusky dark by now, and I started to panic. We called my sister, and she decided to drive around town to look for him. I thought of contacting the local police department, but we didn't want to invoke a worse reaction from him by having an officer show up. That might spark an episode that none of us was prepared to handle at this point. From his past interactions with cops, we knew we couldn't risk an adverse situation that might land us all in jail or in court. I didn't want him locked up—neither in a hospital, a mental ward, nor a jail cell. He was a very sick man, and we just had to find him.

A few minutes later, Beth drove up, and he was with her. *What a relief!* He was all smiles and seemed genuinely happy to see all of us. He had long forgotten all about the fire and the tantrum. We never mentioned it again. He told us a vivid story about meeting some people in a sandwich shop just down the street. He told how some people he knew bought him food and talked to him. We didn't know how much of his story was true reality nor did we know exactly where he had been or what he had been up to for the past hour and a half.

Later on, we were able to verify that the son of a local pastor had seen him wandering through the sandwich shop. The young man recognized him, and he bought him a sandwich. His recollection of his encounters was confusing and scattered. He was half in and half out of reality. I was just relieved to know that he was safe at home and nothing bad had happened.

I'll always remember the events of that night because of a photo my sister captured of him as he told us of his adventure. In an effort to get his mind on something positive and off the confusion he was experiencing in trying to explain to us where he had been and whom he had met while he was out, she looked at him and said, "You know what? You look really good in that shirt tonight. I need a picture of you!"

The biggest brightest smile spread across his face in that moment. He turned his face upward toward her, extended his chest, and said, "Well, git 'er done, then!"

And she did!

Barry Lee Wilson, November 11, 2018

This photo was taken three weeks before his promotion to heaven. This was one of the last and quite possibly the best photo we have of him. It makes me smile to see his smile.

Each day of the next three weeks seemed to run endlessly one into the other. Every second was so surreal. I found myself researching and reading everything I could find to try and help us understand what to expect day by day. I asked many questions, but the nurses were vague in their responses. Their prognosis seemed to change every other day. Of course, none of us—not even hospice nurses who are all too familiar with the dying process—knew the day or the hour he would let go of this life and take hold of the next. He was strong, and we didn't know how long his strength would last.

The nurses knew the signs and generally the phases of progression as did the medical and psychology writers I found in my Google searches. All that I read and everyone I asked reaffirmed that each person's journey between life and death—from the natural to the supernatural—is their own. No two are exactly alike. There are general commonalities that each person experiences, but the timing and severity of each phase of the process is largely dependent upon the individual's unique physical and mental strengths.

I'm convinced, too, that the journey is more painful or peaceful, depending on the extent of the individual's faith in God. Where there's hope of life beyond this one, it can be easier to let go of the pain that ties our spirit to this earthly body in order to take hold of one that will be pain free and full of life. But where there's fear of what lies beyond this earth and our humanity, it can be much more difficult for our spirit to let go of this body of flesh, regardless of the pain.

PREPARING TO LET GO

Firsthand experiences generally provide lasting impressions and some that a person rarely ever forgets. Barry's dying process was, by far, the most impactful unforgettable experience I've ever had and one that I'm not eager to repeat. With that said, however, as difficult as it was to experience the letting go, I would do it all over again in a heartbeat because I loved my brother that much.

Jazlyn and Destini, along with Destini's husband and children, arrived a few days after I had settled in. It had been several months since Barry had seen his granddaughters, and Destini wanted them to have one last visit with him. With things in a state of confusion and Barry's mind and emotions unpredictable, I worried that maybe having them see him in this condition wasn't the best idea. Nevertheless, I understood their need for this moment and for closure.

Having two small children in the house was very much out of the ordinary, and the noise and commotion this ignited, together with my dogs' incessant barking at strangers, quickly became a big problem. Children make some dogs nervous. Strangers, in general, cause Samson to overreact. Oh, how I regretted, again, my rushed decision to bring him along.

Believing it best for everyone, I rented a hotel room for Stephen and the children. They were free to go there to rest, play, and sleep between visits with Barry. Destini and Jazlyn would need to decide for themselves if they wanted to stay at the house or the hotel.

*****

It was essential that we monitor his medications closely. Although I had prepared a written schedule for us all to follow, I found no volunteers willing to take on the full-time administration of this task. He wasn't cognitively able to do it on his own nor was I comfortable with that idea. Seeing no one willing to step into this role, as is my nature, I took on the responsibility. I soon found the task to be an hour-by-hour round-the-clock challenge. I wasn't a nurse and had no clue what I was doing. I knew just enough to be very afraid of the process.

Fears of overdosing, drug reactions, and interactions were constantly on my mind. Giving too much of one and not enough of another could lead to big problems. If all this wasn't challenging enough, the medications were constantly being changed to keep pace with the rapidly progressing disease. I wondered at what other families and patients in this condition did. I'd never worked with hospice caregivers, so I had no idea what their responsibilities were. Obviously, they don't give round-the-clock care. At least, in our case, they didn't.

The nurses measured his vitals daily, listened to the events we described to them, and asked him and us lots of questions. Each day, they repeated questions to him like, "Who's the President of the US? What day is it? Do you know the person who is sitting beside you? What's their name?"

I'll never forget the day when it became apparent to me that these nurses and the doctors directing them had not been read into all of Barry's medical records. The day his primary nurse looked at me and said, "The doctor and I believe that the cancer has reached Barry's brain," I was in complete shock.

I said, "Of course, it's reached his brain. It's been there since the day you were brought in to care for him two months ago."

She had a look of bewilderment on her face as if to say, "What are you talking about?"

I wanted to scream, more for relief from the stresses I encountered than at the nurse. I couldn't understand. Were these people that incompetent? Or was I just missing something?

We had an intense but serious conversation at that point. I shared with her the precise prognosis as the oncologist had recited it to me two months earlier. It was clear that she had no idea what was in his medical records. In this instant, a light came on for her. Then it was her turn. She explained to me that end-of-life caregivers are not given the full set of medical records for the patients they care for.

I was completely blown away by this disclosure. How could these nurses sufficiently care for a patient whom they don't have all the facts nor fully understand the stage at which the patient is in the dying process? How can doctors who work remotely and never personally see these patients appropriately direct the nurses in this care? They are missing so many important pieces to the puzzle.

Suddenly, I felt more fear and tension rising within me than I'd ever known. That flight or fight response was triggered once more. I wanted to run, to make someone else responsible for this monumental task. But who? Who could I point to and believe they would do this for him?

I couldn't run. I had to stay. I wanted to stay, but I wasn't qualified to stay or to provide the help that was needed. What on earth was I going to do now? To whom could I turn for help and guidance?

*****

Philippians 4:6 says, "Do not be anxious about anything, but in every situation, by prayer and petition, with thanksgiving, present your requests to God."

In his writings, Paul talks a lot about the challenges we face in this life. I can't even begin to imagine facing the kinds of trials Paul faced. And, still, he had faith that God was with him through every single trial. He wanted his readers to understand this and to take hold of the richness of God's love for us and the power of our faith in him. The Lord comes through for us every single time we call out his name.

Jesus, too, reminded his disciples that their journey would not be easy. He said, "I have told you these things, so that in Me you may have peace. In this world you will have trouble. But take heart! I have overcome the world" (John 16:33). In this we can be encouraged because we can embrace the fact that the trials and afflictions we face are not extraordinary. Everyone—even the children of God—has to endure them. But where we are different is in knowing and believing that God has overcome the world, so we will too.

Surely we will face real challenges that threaten to undo us. Surely we will fear at times. Surely we will want to give up. But we must remember the truth of God's Word, his promises to us. It is essential for our survival that we read and study the Scriptures. Memorize the verses that have encouraged you in difficult times so that you can recall them when *the craziness of life* knocks the wind right out of you.

*****

Thinking now of Dr. D, my colleague with whom I had shared Barry's X-rays the day I first learned that he was sick, I dialed his number, hoping he would answer. I knew he had walked with others through a similar dying process in recent years and I knew he would be real with me. Just hearing a familiar friendly voice when he said "Hello" gave me a strange sense of comfort and security.

I shared all the crazy details of the past week. I'm sure he recognized my fears and anxious questions. He told me everything I needed to know, what to expect, and how to respond to the myriad of changes that were unfolding. He held nothing back but gave me the hard truth, which was exactly what I needed at this moment.

I get it that doctors and nurses encounter every kind of person and emotion that exists, especially those medical professionals who deal so often with terminally ill patients and their families. And perhaps not everyone is equipped to handle the raw truth about death and the dying process. But there comes a time when the person closest to the patient, the one who is charged with the daily care, needs more information. Denial of the inevitable only increases the anxiety that unknown facts provoke.

Certainly, there are times when the passionate thing to do is to continue to offer hope, even when no hope exists—short of the miracle hand of God, but I can say from experience that every person who faces a challenge of this magnitude needs someone—someone to lean on, someone they trust, someone who will tell them the whole truth.

I'm always amazed at how God crosses the paths of humans, placing specific people along life's way to encounter one another at strategic times. By our very nature, he created us as relational beings. He knows that we face challenges that are too much for us to face on our own without a friend or a family member or an acquaintance. He sends a human guide for us when that's what the situation requires. Sometimes I believe he actually sends angels, who may appear to us in human form. I remember reading a scripture that says we should not forget to entertain strangers because some people have shown hospitality to angels without even realizing it.

Regardless of whom God sends or whether he comes himself in some manner, he knows our fears; he knows exactly what we need; and if we trust him, he will supply the resources to meet whatever those needs are.

Dr. D. was not an angel, but he was a caring compassionate friend who crossed my life path at a moment when I needed it most desperately. I'll be eternally grateful to this precious man for his genuine concern and advice during these last weeks. I'm grateful to God for supplying this flesh-and-blood adviser when that's what I needed most.

*****

Barry's physical mobility quickly began to diminish as his brain function and mental capacity continued to deteriorate. I wasn't surprised that it happened because Dr. D. told me it would, but the speed at which it was happening was incredible to me. I'd never seen this kind of regression before. Hour by hour, day by day, he became less cognizant and less articulate. Dr. D. warned me, too, that his youthful vitality would work against him now, and it would create some challenges for us as we walked through this with him.

We were experiencing exactly that. He did and said things that, had he been fully aware of what was happening, he would not have done. It was tough to balance all of this and remain in control of our own emotions. Some days were tougher than others.

I frequently slept at night in a recliner during that second week while Barry slept on another opposite me. He spoke very little now, but his strength and mobility remained. Because he was still able to move freely, I felt more comfortable being near him around the clock to monitor his movements. I recall times when he would awaken suddenly and literally jump out of the recliner and run down the hallway. When he reached his bedroom door at the end of the hallway, he would pause and turn as though he didn't know where he was or where he was supposed to be going. I'd ask him, "Where are you going, Bubba?"

Most of the time, he was looking for the bathroom and couldn't remember where it was, although he had walked right past it. I quickly learned the pattern and was able to direct him where to turn without asking him.

These midnight episodes reminded me of times when, as a kid, he would sleepwalk. He actually ran in his sleep. The way he jumped out of the recliner now was similar to the way he used to jump out of bed in the middle of his dreams, waking everyone in the house with the sound of his running. I longed to rewind the clock to those younger years, to restart this process and find ways to avoid this nightmare.

SMOKING, SECRETS, AND SAMSON

Barry's urge to smoke became a daily battle for him. In a previous chapter, I noted that I would return to this subject. His urge to smoke seemed to come more from a learned habit than from a nicotine addiction. He had smoked for forty years, and the repetitive motions of holding the cigarette between his fingers or drawing one to his lips was actually more normal to him than not doing it. For him, it was like breathing in and out. It had become an involuntary action. Nevertheless, I believe that if he had his full mental capacity, he would have rejected the entire notion. As it was, however, it became a serious ordeal that had to be dealt with.

From the time I first arrived, this battle between his mind and his will was evident. His act of purchasing a pack of cigarettes, smoking only one or two—and then handing them to me with instructions, "Get rid of these. I don't want them anymore. I know I'm not supposed to do this."—was a frequent occurrence. I wanted to help him overcome the battle, so I did as he asked the first few times. But the repetitiveness and frequency of it agitated me until I realized what was really taking place. Each time he handed them off to me, only an hour or two would pass before he came back, asking, "Where'd you put my cigarettes and lighter?" I reminded him each time of his instructions to get rid of them. At that, he became agitated and demanded that I take him to the store to buy more.

After only a few of these episodes, I learned to simply put the package out of sight, hoping he would soon forget about them. Besides that, he only had a few dollars left in his wallet from his monthly social security stipend. We had to be careful how he spent what little was left as we didn't know how long we might be walking through these dark days and what the cost of care and supplies might include.

When Destini and Stephen arrived, the smoking debacle only became worse. As it is with bad habits, the temptation to partake in the activity is stronger when seeing someone else engage in that same behavior. He saw the two of them smoking, and it triggered an irresistible urge for him to do the same.

One day, as I sat watching this process repeated, it occurred to me that if he didn't win this battle over his mind and his will, his last days would pass in a state of mental anguish that was completely unnecessary. I wondered, too, whether it might prolong his passing because he was not in a state of peace but one of confusion and conflict. I pondered what to do about it, and I asked Destini and Stephen to avoid smoking in front of him. Whether they honored that request initially, I can't really say. But his anxiety and paranoia continued to escalate.

The day after Destini arrived, I learned that Barry had been texting her and insinuating his distrust of Mom and me. Mom and I had no idea about these exchanges as they were occurring because he said nothing to us. She said nothing either until a couple days after her arrival. It all came out in a very unexpected, unnecessary, and ugly way. She admitted to me one afternoon that she had contacted Barry's nurse at his request, but prior to that, she had not said anything about his anxiety or his accusations. I'm not sure why she chose to tell me then that she had called the nurse, unless perhaps the nurse urged her to.

When I prodded for more information about why she had called the nurse and hadn't informed me of it, I was shocked and angered. The more we talked, the more hurt and angry I became. I discovered that Barry had told her things in his paranoid state that were simply untrue. I was completely blown away by the accusations, which she now laughed about and assured me that she didn't believe. But the fact remained that she failed to say anything to us, and she went behind our backs and contacted the nurse. Having experienced the things we did over the past week, I understood his paranoia. Her secret-keeping was the thing I couldn't get past in that moment.

I'm convinced now that if she had been there to experience all we had, her perspective would have been vastly different. The continued loss of mental capacity was working to increase his anxiety and paranoia. No one ever told us to expect this. It was yet another thing that someone could have *and should have* shared with us before we had to discover it on our own. Had we anticipated and been watching for it, it would have saved us all a great deal of unnecessary pain and emotional distress at a time when we needed to be united, not divided.

As it turned out, though, the entire debacle was near to becoming my mental breakdown. In fact, I did just that. I broke! I was there doing things I never imagined myself doing. I did them the best way I knew how, but we were fighting a battle we were destined to lose. My already overloaded heart and emotional well-being reached its limit that day.

In this afternoon exchange, she also revealed that he asked her to tell the nurse to get the dogs out of the house or he was leaving. This was the final straw. The dogs, particularly Samson, was on my last nerve, and now I was learning that he was on everyone's last nerve. I was sorry again for bringing him. Here I was in a situation I didn't ask to be dropped into the middle of. I had put my entire life on hold. I had taken leave from my job, left my husband and my home to come and care for him, and *this* was the thanks I got for it!

Yes, I had a pity party for myself right then and there. But it was more than that. I had a complete emotional breakdown. For sure, the stress of the situation, the relentless series of daily battles, and the sleepless nights had zapped my energy and diminished my own sense of rationalization. I had reached my breaking point without realizing how far I'd come. Everyone has one, I guess. I'm not proud of it, but at this stage, I was too weak to fight anymore. I lost my temper, and with that, I lost all control of my emotions. I was done.

"Fine!" I told her. "You can have it. If this is what you want and what he wants, *you can have it* because I'm *out of here!*" I immediately went to the bedroom and began packing my bags. The rush of emotions was overwhelming. Part of me kept saying, "You can't go anywhere," while the other part of me argued, "You can't do this anymore!"

This breakdown continued as I carried my bags out of the house. Once outside in the open air and away from where Barry could hear me, I really lost it. I cried uncontrollably. I screamed to the top of my lungs. Neighbors lived close by, and I'm sure some of them heard me. But, in that moment, I didn't care who heard me. I needed release. So I screamed through the sobs, "Oh, *God, please, please* help me! *I cannot do this!*"

*****

This event reminds me of a story in the Bible where Jesus's disciples were in their boat during a storm, but he was not with them. They struggled to keep the boat afloat, rowing against the wind with all their might. They were tired and exhausted from the continuous waves that came. And they were terrified when they saw Jesus walking on the water toward them. They thought he was a ghost. Jesus saw their fear, and he spoke to them, "It's me." He said, "Don't be afraid."

Then Peter said to him, "Lord, if it's You, let me come to You walking on the water."

And Jesus told him, "Come on."

Peter, as was his nature toward boldness, got right out of the boat and began to walk on the water toward Jesus. He was just fine until he took his eyes off the Lord and focused on the wind and the waves around him. In the middle of the vast sea with waves all around him in the darkness, fear consumed him, and he began to sink. In that moment, he cried out, "Lord, save me!"

I had been bold and courageous up to this point, determined to face the challenge, committed to the purpose for which I'd been sent. But, now, the black waves of death and hopelessness were rising up all around me. I was afraid. The fear was paralyzing. I lost sight of the Lord for a moment. As I sank in that moment, craving the silence of unconsciousness, I remembered why I was here in the first place.

Still, I was too weak to continue fighting on my own. So I cried out like Peter, "Jesus, save me!"

*****

My heart and soul were torn inside me. I needed help. I needed the dogs with their incessant barking to be gone. I called my husband. "Please," I begged him, "drop whatever you're doing and come to meet me." He could hear the urgency in my words through the crying and promptly agreed to my request.

Mom and Jazlyn were not at the house during this exchange. I'm so glad she wasn't there to witness all that occurred during that half hour. She was already in such a state of distress she didn't need anything else to push her right over the edge.

I gave Destini quick directions about Barry's medications and walked away. With the two dogs loaded into my Jeep, I left the house. As I drove, I cried. I couldn't seem to stop. This flood of tears had the power of releasing all that had been building up for days. My phone rang, but I didn't answer. It was Janitha, Barry's nurse, and I didn't want to talk to her. I didn't want to talk to anyone. I was so hurt and so angry.

After I was able to collect myself enough to speak, I called Janitha. She did her best to calm me down. She laughed a little at the issue concerning the dogs and Barry's paranoia and Destini's call to her. I'm not sure how she knew to call me. I suspected that she received another call from Destini. She tried to help me understand that this, too, was part of the process. *Ya think? It would've been nice if someone had warned me—all of us, actually—that this was coming!* was my thought, although I didn't say it out loud.

She urged me not to leave, saying, "Barry and your mom need you right now."

I knew that, but in my current emotional state, I was no good to anybody. I knew that I would go back. I would keep my promise to my brother and my mother. But, for now, I just needed to drive. She was consoling and agreed that I needed a little break anyway. Before we hung up, I assured her I would be back as soon as I had taken care of this little problem with the dogs. Then I drove. This act of running, of putting space between myself and the situation, gave my heart a minute to recalibrate.

By the time David and my paths crossed that evening, I had driven about four hours. We met in Demopolis, Alabama, a tiny little town in the middle of nowhere. I drive through there every time I go to visit my mom, but I'd never stopped for anything more than a soda or a potty break. It was getting late by then, close to 9:00 p.m. We searched for a hotel with a vacancy and found *only one*. It was less than desirable, so I urged David to take the dogs and go on back home. I preferred the drive back to Hartford over staying in this place that appeared dirty and unsafe.

At his insistence that I was in no condition to drive any more that night, I had to agree with him. I was physically exhausted and emotionally drained. The tears I'd cried had washed away all the color from my face and left my eyes swollen. So we checked in at the flea bag hotel. He held me close, and we slept. It had been days since I had slept more than four hours in one undisturbed cycle. So this sleep was deep.

*****

My heart is in anguish within me; The terrors of death have fallen upon me... And I say, "Oh, that I had wings like a dove! I would fly away and be at rest. (Psalm 55:4, 6)

Have you ever longed to run? To run away and hide yourself from everything that steals your peace? The psalmist's cries in Psalm 55 filled my aching soul that night. So I ran. Oh, if I had only had wings! Running from a problem rarely takes it away. But running to the Lord for rest and time to catch your breath can prepare you to face impossible situations. The Lord promises us rest if we run to him.

Those who live in the shelter of the Most High will find rest in the shadow of the Almighty.

This I declare about the Lord: He alone is my refuge, my place of safety... He will cover you with His feathers, He will shelter you with His wings. His faithful promises are your armor and protection. (Psalm 91:1, 4)

*****

Early the following morning, we grabbed a quick breakfast sandwich. I kissed David and the dogs goodbye. Then I retraced my path from the night before. During my southbound journey, I had quiet time to think and ponder all the events of the day before and the days before that. No more barking dogs, no one to disturb my thoughts. Peace settled over me. In my heart, I knew Barry's journey was almost over. My heart hurt in the deepest places. I understood, but then I didn't understand. What is the real meaning of life anyway? I prayed a lot. I prayed for strength to face whatever the next wave would bring, for wisdom to know how to handle each one, and for a kind and humble heart to deal compassionately with each person. We needed each other now. I wasn't alone in this, although I frequently felt as though I were.

As I drove along in silence, I sensed the Lord's presence right there in the vehicle with me. He leads us quietly, not with an audible voice but with a silent voice. That voice speaks so much louder than any other I've ever known. In that moment, I sensed him giving me directions for the next right step. That step involved a discussion I must have with Destini. I gained a new confidence and strength that I can't explain.

I knew the girls needed to be with their daddy in these last days, and we each would need the other to survive. But I also knew that new ground rules had to be established. If we were going to do this thing, we all had to be on the same page. I would promptly address this as soon as I arrived back at the house.

I rolled up to the house around 10:30 and found Destini and Stephen standing outside, smoking. Barry wasn't with them. I found him in his room, sleeping. I was thankful for that because he didn't need to be present while I had this difficult conversation.

Have you ever needed to have a difficult conversation with someone, and the time just never seemed right? So much anxiety and fear can weigh you down and prevent you from doing what you know you have to do or say. Delivering a hard truth can be a daunting task, and it's not for the faint of heart. Nevertheless, approached in the right manner and with the right heart, it can be done in a way that produces unity, and if not altogether unity, at least a level of respect that allows for peace.

I asked the girls, Stephen, and Mom to join me in the dining room. We sat around the table, and I calmly and quietly began by expressing to the girls my genuine and sincere love for them and their dad. Next, I gave them the terms of my willingness to stay and continue walking this out with them. It would require a few specific ground rules.

First, Stephen had to take the children and go home. Destini and Jazlyn could stay as long as they desired. Next, we had to agree that no one would call any nurse or anyone else without first consulting me. Finally, they had to agree to a "no smoking" policy in front of Barry, and furthermore, that they would not give nor purchase cigarettes for him.

I explained the strong sense I felt that his battle with smoking was one of greater significance than a mere physical bad habit. I was convinced that it had spiritual significance for him. I truly believed that his obvious struggle with *smoking* versus *not smoking* was one last torment of the soul used by Satan himself to rob my brother of peace in his last hours.

The enemy of our souls is relentless, and he stops at nothing—absolutely *nothing*—to steal, kill, and destroy every sense of peace and tranquility available to the souls of men to their dying day. I'm disgusted and angry as I realize more and more the ruthless tactics he uses. I want to kick him in the teeth and tell him just where to go!

I was determined that day to take my stand in the gap for my brother. I resolved in my own soul to not stand silently by and watch Satan steal Barry's final hours of peace. I refused to sit idly by and allow him to steal what little was left of our family unity that day. I recognized that not everyone in the room completely understood what I was telling them, but I was bold and courageous nonetheless. Truth cannot be timid. I was convinced that Barry's suffering would continue longer than necessary and grow worse before his passing unless he was at complete peace within his own heart. That meant winning this battle over smoking.

I still believe that to this very day.

They each agreed to my terms, and so we settled on the plan. Barry had been telling all of us how he wanted to give his car to Destini. In his final days of lucidity, he had signed over the title to her. So we decided that Stephen would take the baby girls in Barry's car and go home. This would be one less thing for Barry to see and become anxious about. Destini and Jazlyn could focus on their dad and finish saying the things they needed to say.

Barry was almost immobile by this point, and he rarely went outdoors. We determined that if he remembered the car and questioned where it was, we would do our best in that moment to explain. One baby step at a time. There was no need to try and solve every potential problem before it became one.

He never asked. So we never had to explain.

*****

Janitha came by later that day. We had another roundtable discussion where she reiterated to the girls the importance of allowing me to be the primary decision-maker. We talked a lot about cancer's advancing stages. She couldn't give us a specific or even a general block of time to anticipate. Rather, she explained that the time he had left would be up to him. Only he could determine how long he would cling to life. She promised to be there for us whenever we needed her.

Stephen left that day. He made it home with the girls without any car problems. The oldest child was having some significant stomach or intestinal issues that remained undiagnosed, complaining of pain almost constantly. Destini struggled to know whether to stay with us, not knowing how long her dad would last, or to go home to be with her baby girl. Her heart was understandably torn. My heart broke for her. She finally made the most difficult decision to go home. And, looking back, it was the right one. She and Jazzy left the following day.

THE FEVER

B y now, Barry was almost nonverbal, and as he grew physically
weaker, his mobility was quickly failing. We asked hospice to
have the hospital bed brought out. We prepared for the next
phase of care. The final phase. People came and went as he continued to fade away. The house was solemn and quiet, except for the
continual hum of the washing machine and dryer, which my mom
kept running for the better part of every day. We cooked very little since friends, neighbors, and church members kept the kitchen
stocked with casseroles and prepared vegetables and meats. We had
little appetite for anything but coffee most days. I watched the clock
constantly to be sure his medications were properly administered.

Larry came to stay. Dad came too. Beth came over every day
while the girls were at school. We looked into one another's eyes, but
the myriad of thoughts and fears inside each of us remained ours to
ponder alone. It's difficult to speak some things aloud. Somewhere
deep inside, I suppose, we believe that if the inevitable is left unspoken, somehow, it won't come to pass.

I noticed as the nurses came by and made their daily wellness
calls that they paid particular attention to Barry's body temperature.
I saw concern in their eyes when his temperature was the slightest bit
elevated, but I didn't fully understand why. One day, I asked Janitha
about it. She explained that a time would soon come when his fever
would begin to rise and not go down. "Do your best," she told me,
"to bring it down with Ibuprofen or Tylenol. But you need to know
that there will come a day when his fever will rise higher and higher,
and no amount of medication you give him will bring it down."

The look in her eyes when she said it was serious and somber
as if to say, "You do know what I'm saying, right?" I felt my own

heartrate increase. I didn't really understand it, but I was curious. So I researched it. I quickly found articles discussing the fact that this is another phase in the dying process. Wow! How is it that no one ever made mention of this before? I imagined that such an unusual event would be quite memorable. Even in all my conversations with doctors, nurses, and other people I knew who had cared for their dying loved ones, not a single one had brought this up. I tucked away the nugget of information to be kept as a clue for judging the phase of progression.

Dad and Larry were great helpers for us during the day, especially at the point where Barry still sensed a need for his bowels to move or his bladder was too full. He couldn't walk on his own now and he couldn't verbalize exactly what he was feeling. But just as a parent learns the signs that their toddler needs to make a trip to the potty chair, we quickly learned that his fidgeting, broken phrases, and attempts to get out of bed meant we needed to get him to the bathroom as quickly as possible.

With Dad and Larry's help, we strived to help him retain his manly dignity by keeping the womenfolk at bay. It was a great help from a physical standpoint as well. Although the cancer had reduced his body weight tremendously, it took the strength of two men to get him out of the bed and to the bathroom timely. This phase only lasted about three days. Then he became completely nonverbal and unaware of his bodily functions. I suppose it was a blessing in disguise, but his bowels promptly stopped acting when he reached this stage of complete immobility. We worked to help give him relief by using suppositories but to no avail.

I dare say that this story has reached a point of sharing too much personal information. I share it only for the sake of those reading this who are looking for a candid and unbiased account of what this process looks like from a layman's point of view. Maybe you're in the throes of this right now. Maybe you or your loved one has been diagnosed with a catastrophic illness. Perhaps you've just gone through it and are looking for something to hope in, to hold on to. I share it because from my own perspective in walking through this, I would have found it tremendously helpful to know what to expect from day to day as I committed myself to walking my brother through to the other side.

This is real. Surely, it's a struggle. It's *hard.* But make no mistake, there's a rainbow in the storm if you will open your eyes to see it. I would do this all over again for any person whom my soul loves so deeply. And I believe you would too. Don't give up. Spring flowers follow the rains. There's brilliant light on the other side of the darkness. There's hope when it seems that all hope is lost.

It's been almost three years now as I sit, writing, but the memory of each day, each hour, and the activities and emotions between the painful hours remain vivid. This journey through the valley of death is the worst kind of curse. Death is a curse brought about by the human condition of sinfulness that reigns in our mortal bodies. Yet it's a most generous blessing when it brings you to the gateway into heaven for your loved one. When you *know* that you *know* that you *know* your loved one loves Jesus with all their heart, and you know that they're about to be delivered into the hands of a loving heavenly Father who will take them from your hands and keep them safe and secure until you reunite with them on the other side, then out of the darkest night comes the light of heaven. The journey isn't easy by any standard of measurement, but it's one that you will cherish forever.

Cherish seems a strange way to describe it, but what I mean is that satisfaction and peace that comes from knowing you did everything possible to assist your loved one right up to their very last breath. So near to heaven. So close to the face and breath of God, the one and only Creator and Giver of Life. You're in the very presence of angels who linger close as they watch and wait for instructions to transport this saint's soul to its promised eternal home. Pain will be in the past for them. Their tears will evaporate into the blissful atmosphere of heaven. Yours may remain for a time, but as you embrace the hope of eternity, you will be able to move forward in faith and confidence that they're waiting on the other side to welcome you home soon.

After a couple more days, Daddy went home. His health wasn't good, and the emotional impact and pain of all that was happening was just more than his tired heart could take. Larry stayed. Beth was there every day. Thanksgiving Day came and went. We spent the day mostly in silence, incapable of engaging in any jolly conversation. We ate the meal prepared and left for us by friends and neighbors. Sad and somber faces greeted one another, and the lumps in our throats seemed as large as the dollops of cornbread dressing found on our plates. Each swallow of food required extra effort.

The things we found to be thankful for were untraditional. We gave thanks for the food that our friends brought for us, for sure. And we thanked God for giving us strength and wisdom to care for Barry. We were thankful for nurses and medications that took the pain away. We were truly grateful that our brother (and son) had made peace with his Creator. Strangely, we gave thanks that he would soon be safely home. Mostly, we gave thanks for the hope of life beyond the grave, not just for Barry but for us all.

*****

I tried my best to FaceTime with Destini and Jazlyn as often as everyone was comfortable doing so. That's the best I knew how to do to help them stay connected to their dad. Sometimes he seemed to hear them; at other times, not so much.

A few friends dropped by, but we opted to put a sign on the front and back doors thanking friends for dropping by and allowing them to sign a paper to let us know they had been there. We were so exhausted from the process that receiving visitors was simply not appropriate. We didn't want to expose the scene from within to the world outside. Only a few visitors were invited in.

Brother Steve, his beloved pastor, was always welcome. He was usually able to elicit a smile from Barry, even in his weakened state. Janitha, his nurse, brought a smile to his face too. He had grown to love and trust her, and it was easy to see the joy she brought him just by being there. During those last few days, though, even these two became ineffective at arousing any emotion from him. These two had been his constant companions and sounding boards over the course of these final two months. Philip (the chaplain), too, was also a dear friend to him. We welcomed him each time he came by to pray or to encourage us. These three had become dear friends to all of us. They became one with us and gave of themselves so selflessly during the most difficult times of our lives. We will forever be indebted to each of them.

Each day became a methodical practice of nursing visits, administering medications, and feeding him Jell-O, vanilla milkshakes, and ice. These three small bits of nourishment kept him hydrated and gave us a sense of small accomplishment. Up until two days before his passing, he continued to try and sit up. We watched as he reached for invisible things or perhaps people or angels that we could not see. With no legible verbal cues, we could only use our imaginations as to what he reached for. He tried to communicate, but the sounds made no sense. He seemed at peace. Sometimes he could open his eyes a little. Occasionally, a smile spread across his face.

One day, as Mom and I were trying to bathe him and change the sheets on his bed, I told him to wrap his arms around me so I could pull him up. He was very obedient, and he did his best to hold to me. When we had finished the task, I laid him back against the bed. Before he released me, he planted a big kiss on my right cheek. I looked into his eyes, and he smiled the most generous smile. *Such a sweet memory.* By this, I knew that he loved and appreciated all we were doing for him.

The hours ticked by rapidly, both day and night. Mom, Larry, and I took turns keeping vigil over him at night. Conversation was minimal, and we kept the room quiet, except for soft music or one of his favorite TV stations, which we set to low volume. It was late November, so we put a small Christmas tree in his room with lights to try and cheer the space a bit. One of us was always awake while the others slept.

When I slept, I kept a baby monitor on in the other room so I could hear him. Someone was always at his side, but I never wanted to be unaware. Everything was silent now, except for the sound of his breath. Even as I tried to rest in the other room, I was constantly aware of his breathing. So labored. I found myself calculating the seconds between each one.

Then came the night of November 30, 2018. A night that no matter how long I live, I will never, ever forget. My husband had arrived that Friday evening, and I was very happy to see him. Larry and David slept in other rooms, but Mom and I were both with Barry in his room. She insisted on sitting up in the recliner at the foot of his bed. I lay on a bed beside Barry's. Occasionally, I'd rise up to look over and see how Mom was doing. She refused each offer to switch places. I drifted in and out of sleep.

Around 1:00 a.m., a sound I hadn't heard before awakened me. His breathing was rapid and quite shallow. I sat up on the side of the bed and touched his hand. I could tell from only a touch that he had a high fever. Mom was sleeping well, so I didn't wake her. I slipped the thermometer under his arm, and it registered 104 degrees Fahrenheit. I caught my breath and blinked away tears that welled up in my eyes, just as they are doing now as I write. I checked it again under the opposite arm. This reading was 104.5 degrees Fahrenheit. "*Oh, no!*" I whispered under my breath. *Is this what Janitha warned me about?* My movement around his bed caused Mom to awaken.

"What's wrong?" she asked.

"His fever is high," I told her. "Do you remember they told us it will begin to go up at some point and we won't be able to bring it down?"

She remembered. We quickly removed the covers from off his body. I went to the bathroom and soaked washcloths in cold water. We did our best to cool him down by bathing him with the cool wet cloths. We put crushed ice to his lips and gave him Ibuprofen. We did everything we knew to do. I continued to check his temperature about every half hour, anxiously hoping for a different result each time as it continued to climb—105 degrees; 105.5 degrees; 106 degrees. The sounds coming from his throat were clearly what I suspected. I'd never heard this sound before, but it was unmistakable.

I sent a text message to his nurse but received no response. It was the weekend, after all, and she wasn't actually supposed to be on duty. So I chose not to call her in the middle of the night. We were doing everything we had been told to do when this happened, so there wasn't really anything she could do more than what we were

let go of this life with all its struggle and took hold of the next with fullness of joy.

What an honor to walk him right up to the edge of this world and release him right into the arms of Jesus. I know in my soul that Jesus embraced him fully and firmly, taking hold of his other hand as I released the one I was holding. He received him with all the love a heart can hold into glory and life eternal. It is at this very place, I am convinced, that he and Jesus will be waiting to welcome me, too, on that day when I draw my last breath on this side of heaven.

> When the perishable puts on imperishable, and the mortal puts on immortality, then shall come to pass the saying that is written, "Death is swallowed up in victory. O death, where is your victory? O death, where is your sting." (Corinthians 15:54–56)

> Jesus said to her, "I am the resurrection and the life. Whoever believes in me, though he die, yet shall he live, and everyone who lives and believes in me shall never die." (John 11:25–26)

> My sheep hear my voice, and I know them, and they follow me. I give them eternal life, and they will never perish, and no one will snatch them out of my hand. My Father, who has given them to me, is greater than all, and no one is able to snatch them out of the Father's hand. (John 10:27–29

The "Message" Delivered

It was time. I held in my hands the message, transcribed from those words I heard in my dream on that October morning in 2012. I clutched the notebook to my chest. Tears fell like rain again as I held the words close to my heart. The mixture of joy and sorrow impossible to explain filled my soul.

As my mind drifted back to 2012, I recalled the memories. Each detail that unfolded over the months and years since, as though flipping the pages of a book, was painfully surreal. The broken promises, the angry words, the frightfully tense moments when it seemed his soul hung in the balance between heaven and hell rushed in. All the bad choices, which had shattered my hopes of his ever coming to true faith, wiped clean from the slate of God's record book right there. I traced in my mind the way Satan chased after him, relentless in his pursuit to steal, kill, and destroy what was left of him—right up to the very last days.

But God! On this day, my heart leapt in jubilation as I was reminded once again of the incredible indescribable ways God divinely intervenes in the lives of men. His divine presence is weaved into the complexities of our daily lives in ways we never imagine. His love is so amazing, his grace never failing. His goodness drips from the sun. His angels sent to minister and protect. The host of heaven is all around us. Can we pause long enough to recognize him?

Sadly, many never give any thought to his existence, much less his divine hand at work. As I thought of all the minute details and narrow escapes from harm and death that my brother encountered in the space of these last six years, it was too much for me to process. When I considered how God watched over him for a lifetime, I melted in gratitude. So I wept.

"You keep track of all my sorrows; You have collected all my tears in Your bottle. You have recorded each one in Your book" (Psalm 56:8).

I thought of how Barry's life had been entwined with that of dozens of others. His path divinely crossed theirs on his journey to faith, some pointing him toward death and destruction, others pointing him to Jesus Christ. How many angels had been sent by the Savior for his protection? How many faithful men and women had been sent to pull his wandering desperate soul from the fire over and over again, a mission they never fully understood?

God, you are amazing! The way in which you've unfolded the truth of this message and brought it to fruition, down to the most intricate detail, is proof enough to me that you are here and you are faithful to fulfill every promise you make.

All of this was more than my own mind could fathom. It was more than I could explain to anyone. It would take more than a rational mind to comprehend it. It would take faith of a kind that only God himself is able to produce in a human heart.

But, God, it's not up to me to make anyone understand this message. It's from you, and you alone will have to make them understand.

But that's just it. The truth and the unfolding of this message is exactly that—an offering of faith and hope and reconciliation; reconciliation that's possible only by the intervening power and might of our Creator. And so I will leave it at that. I will trust that the Lord can and will take the message he ordained and deliver it however he wants it delivered.

*****

I worried for my parents. Parents are not supposed to bury their children. It's supposed to be the other way around. Together, our family chose to proceed with the funeral service as soon as possible. All immediate family members were present, and everything that needed to be said and done had been. Barry had chosen his burial plot near the house, and Dad purchased it a few weeks earlier. The arrangements had been made for a cremation, too, although in those last hours before setting everything in motion, we simply couldn't bring ourselves to reduce his body to mere ashes. With a few last-minute changes to the arrangements, we had only to choose his burial clothes, a casket, and flowers. We each published the funeral arrangements on our Facebook pages on Sunday, and we notified a few friends and family members by phone.

On Monday, December 3, 2018, a few family members and friends gathered quietly in the funeral parlor about an hour before time for the service. Besides our immediate family, a few friends and local church members came. Barry's daughters, granddaughters, stepdaughters, and even his ex-wife were there. My mother's two sisters and a brother came too. My own children were there. Philip and Janitha were among the friends who came. These two had become quick friends and confidants to Barry and all of us during his last two months. I'm sure Barry would have smiled at the sight.

Much to our sad surprise, only one lonely flower arrangement stood in memorial next to his casket. My Aunt Charlotte sent a token of memory with a brief sympathy note. Besides that, the only flowers were those purchased as part of the funeral package. This spoke volumes to my heart as to the degree of brokenness in our extended family. How did we get here? How and when did we lose touch with family and friends to the point that their communications and sympathies were so distant?

Our family was once very close when my grandparents were alive. But now, my heart broke at the sight—for my parents, for Barry, for all the family. I've chosen to let it go and to ponder the reasons in my heart alone with a goal in mind toward doing all within my power to reconcile what's broken. What's done cannot be undone, but we can choose to forgive and seek reconciliation.

I was saddened, too, that so many of these family members wouldn't be here to hear the message, a message that I believe was and is intended for all of them to hear. "Perhaps," I told myself, "if we had given them more time, more advanced notice, others would have come." And, then again, maybe not. Only God knows.

Perhaps that's the reason for this writing. God's power to bring to pass his promises is not limited. I know this because my eyes have seen it. I saw it happen in Barry's life. And I've seen it in my own life too. I know I will see it again.

As the service began, the pastor's wife and daughter sang two songs. Barry had written a note with this request, and he shared it with me in advance. He had also given instructions to Pastor Steve that I must share a message. When he still had his right mind, he made all these requests. I sat with my family as the women sang. My heart beat wildly inside my chest. The experience was surreal. It seemed as if I was watching a scene in a movie. It felt, somehow, like I'd already been here before. It was strange yet oddly familiar at the same time. I quietly prayed that God would give me strength to do what I promised him and Barry that I would. I was resolute in my approach. No amount of fear or doubt would keep me on this wooden pew. The songs ended, and I rose to my feet, somehow carried by forces of sheer will and determination as I took each step to that stage.

I began to speak.

"Barry Lee Wilson was born on October 11, 1962. I, Patricia Diane Wilson, was born on September 5, 1963. Barry and I were born to the same set of parents. We grew up in the same house, ate the same meals, were taught the same things, and experienced many of the same things for the first seventeen to eighteen years of our lives. We fought like typical siblings, but we stood up for one another against the cruel words and actions of some of our peers. I've known Barry for more than half a century. That sounds like a really long time, and in one way, it is. But as I stand here now, sharing my heart with you, the fifty-five years I've known my brother seems far too brief. My heart longs for more.

"Barry and I chose completely different paths in life—different careers, different friends, and different passions. But for all the differences, one thing never changed: he was my brother, and I loved him in spite of all our differences. I would have done anything within my power to help him. There have been many times throughout our lives that I tried to help him with his struggles with addiction. But all my efforts, and the many efforts of our family who loved him dearly, never seemed to be enough to free him from the chains of addiction that held tight to him.

"One other thing never changed—the prayers of our precious mama. I believe God has a special star for her crown because she never gave up on her son, never failing to believe God's promise that if she raised her son to know him, when he was old, he would return to the Lord. Though there were times when her heart was shattered, she never stopped believing and she *never* stopped praying.

"Folks, the scriptures teach us that the prayers of a righteous man avails much. In other words, such prayers accomplish *great things*. Why? Because our prayers move the heart of God. In fact, the Scriptures also teach us that God leans down his ear to hear us. He wants to hear your prayers. He desires to hear your prayers for help and healing and forgiveness. When he hears you, he is quick to respond to those prayers. But it's important to keep in mind that it is the prayer of the righteous and the prayer of those who in their brokenness cry out to him for help that he hears. He is not here to satisfy our selfish prayers for things that aren't for our good.

"My purpose in standing here today is to share with you a message I received about six years ago. The Lord awakened me early—at 3:25 a.m.—on the morning of October 17, 2012. Barry had just turned fifty a few days before that. At the time, he was living at a place called Faith Farm Ministries in Okeechobee, Florida. I had driven him there in September of that same year in yet another desperate attempt to help him find freedom from his drug addiction. I had great hope of his recovery at that time. Although he didn't ultimately achieve freedom then, I know that his going there was another one of God's acts of grace and rescue for Barry. It was another act by his Creator to preserve his life until he would finally be made free. That ultimate freedom actually came in April of this year—2018!

"What I'm about to share with you I discussed with Barry soon after his cancer diagnosis this past September. I had not shared this message with anyone up to that point. He and I cried together when I shared it with him. He told me then, 'Sis, you have to share this at my funeral!'

"As difficult as it is for me to stand here today, I promised the Lord in 2012 and I promised Barry two months ago that I would share this message when the time came. I had no way of knowing who would be sitting here today to hear this when I wrote this message in my notebook all those years ago. But on that October morning in 2012, the voice of the Lord was crystal clear to me—so clear and so real that I got out of bed and wrote it all down.

"I was reminded of this message the day Barry faxed me his radiology report this past August. That very night, I sensed the Spirit of the Lord, again, speaking to my heart to remind me of this eulogy, titled 'The Prodigal Son.' When I recalled it, my mind began to whirl because I had no clue what I had done with this notebook. But just like God knows everything, he knew exactly where the notebook lay. I prayed and asked him to show me where it was. He took me right to the shelf in my library where it had lain unopened and unread for years. I placed it there when I had given up on him.

"So I ask you to please give me your undivided attention as I read to you this message verbatim from my notes. I pray you have an open heart to receive it.

"The Lord said to me that night in my dream, 'I am with you. Draw your strength from Me. Be strong. Be courageous. Tell them all that I command you to say to them. Remember My promises. Your entire family will be healed through this process.

"'Barry's voice in the end will declare My glory more than his life brought shame in his disobedience. You, daughter, must be that voice which will declare My glory. You, daughter, must tell them: the time is short. Christ's return is imminent. You came here today to pay your last respects to my brother—your son, your brother, your father, your nephew, your cousin, maybe even an old friend.'

"What you came for is slight and so small in comparison to God's purpose in bringing you here. You must each hear me now. You must each examine yourself this day and decide whether you will give forgiveness and receive forgiveness. Will you be reconciled?

"Barry lies before us now—actually, the broken shell of his body lies before us. His spirit—the part of him that God Almighty breathed life into a little more than fifty years ago, is actually present with our Creator now. That Creator, the Righteous Judge and Compassionate Father, has sent me to tell you all this.

"Barry's life is a picture of us all—every person in this room—as we stand in the sight of God. Without him, we are broken, lost and hopeless. Without him, we are doomed for destruction. No, I am not here to paint you a glamorous picture of my brother, who he was, all that he accomplished, the principles he stood for. I can't in all good conscience do that, and I don't believe he would even want me to do that. But what I can do is to declare to you the saving, transforming, unimaginable power of my God. For I have seen it! While brief, I got a glimpse of Barry's life in the end, which is a picture of one who was (who is) redeemed, forgiven, full of hope and life and peace.

"This is a picture of what God wants to do for each person under the sound of my voice today. Do not weep for Barry, for I am persuaded that he stands before God today clothed in white and kneeling before him in adoration and praise. Weep, however, for yourselves if you don't know the Savior. Weep for your children. Weep for your neighbor to whom you haven't spoken in so long. Weep for those yet to be born into this broken world. I pray that your hearts are broken today—not for me, for Barry, or for any member of my family, but I pray your hearts are broken for this world and the sin sickness that is consuming it.

"God commands us to 'Love one another,' to 'forgive that you may be forgiven,' to 'ask of him and receive,' to 'seek and find,' to 'knock and have doors opened to you.' He declares that if his people who are called by his name will humble themselves and pray, and if they will seek his face, then he will hear from heaven, and he will forgive our sin and heal our land.

"So the life that you saw lived out before you—a life of tragedy and failure for so many years—you must understand that this is a picture of how God views this broken world in which we live. But the life of my brother and the picture I paint for you now—the beautiful transformation of a broken vessel reconstructed by the Master Potter's hand in his last days—is a picture of the grace and mercy of our Lord."

"First Kings 8:56 says that 'there has not failed one word of all His (God's) good promises.' The Lord made me a promise in 2012, and in his own perfect timing and in his own perfect way, not one promise he made me will fail. Although I have had questions over the past six years—and I must admit a few doubts as my physical eyes witnessed Barry walk away from the Lord again and again—God *is* faithful, and he *did not* fail! It is only because of God's faithfulness in bringing Barry to repentance and new life in April of this year that I can even stand here and give you this message.

"The best news is that you didn't have to hear about Barry's life change through me. Those of you who have been around him over the past four to six months have seen with your own eyes the transformation. And for that, I and our family are truly grateful, and we stand in full hope and faith that we will see him again very soon. I hope and pray that every one of you sitting here today will be with us for that grand family reunion!

"I was there in the hospital room with Barry in September when he was diagnosed with terminal lung cancer, and I witnessed him share his story with a room full of doctors. The lead doctor asked him, 'Can you tell me why you have elected not to receive treatment?' Barry was quick to respond by telling his story. He held nothing back. Not a dry eye remained as Barry explained to these doctors how God had redeemed his life six months earlier.

"He said to them, 'I *know* God has the power to heal me. But *even if he doesn't, I know* that I will be in heaven with him.' And with that word from Barry's own lips, I am convinced of where he is this very day."

I took my seat beside my husband and listened to the message brought by Pastor Steve. I honestly have no idea what he said that day. I only knew that my mission for that day was finished. We buried his body in the cemetery near the house. Mama visits the site frequently to keep the stone clean and to bring bright flowers. It's her way of remembering only the good and honoring that memory.

Remember My Promises

D eath can seem so final. The days represented by the dash between the date of one's birth and the date of his death may span decades, or it may be as brief as a few minutes or days. Regardless of how long or how brief our days are on the earth, every life matters. Physical death is not the end. We may no longer visibly see some we have loved so deeply in this world, but we can hold on to the truth of God's promises that we will see them again one day if they (and we) have trusted in him as our Savior. An incredible reunion awaits us.

God made me a promise when he gave me *the message* in 2012. Barry's eulogy was not the end of the message, not by a long shot. It was only the beginning. The message I received that night included a promise that will outlive me. Not a single day passes that I don't remember God's promise to me. He said,

> "Your entire family will be healed through this process."

It is this promise that fuels my prayers for my family and myself day after day. I will never let go of it. It may take months or years to see it all come to pass, but I know it will. In fact, my lifetime will be too brief for me to see the fulfillment of it all. But that doesn't change a thing. I know beyond all doubt that God fulfills every promise he makes, and he does at just the right time.

Healing doesn't always happen instantly. It's a process that can take years to complete, particularly when the healing we need takes place inside our hearts. As I've struggled through this process of writ-

ABOUT THE AUTHOR

Diane Boyette is a graduate of Belmont University, Nashville, Tennessee, holding a bachelor of business administration degree. She is also a graduate of the University of Mississippi School of Law, Oxford, Mississippi, from which she attained her Juris Doctor in 2004. Diane currently practices law as in-house counsel, serving as vice president and chief compliance officer of Southern Farm Bureau Life Insurance Company in Jackson, Mississippi.

Beyond her professional career, Diane seeks to fulfill her genuine passion for orphans and impoverished communities by serving on missions teams—international and domestic—as well as staying involved with her local church to engage in a variety of outreach opportunities.

Diane lives with her husband, David, in Brandon, Mississippi.

CPSIA information can be obtained
at www.ICGtesting.com
Printed in the USA
BVHW080835110123
655989BV00002B/102